D0861024

TABLE OF CONTENTS

Written by Michael Lummis

PRIMA GAMES® — WE ARE STRATEGY

FREE eGUIDE!

Enter this code at primagames.com/code to unlock your FREE eGuide:

VDFE-BESA-YEGX-URUP

CHECK OUT OUR eGUIDE STORE AT PRIMAGAMES.COM

All your strategy saved in your own personal digital library!

Mobile Friendly: Access your eGuide on any web-enabled device.

Searchable & Sortable: Quickly find the strategies you need.

Added Value: Strategy where, when, and how you want it.

BECOME A FAN OF PRIMA GAMES!

Subscribe to our Twitch channel twitch.tv/primagames and join our weekly stream every Tuesday from 1-4pm EST!

PRIMA GAMES

www.primagames.com

A SHADOW OVER DUNWALL

Fifteen years have passed since Corvo Attano attempted to save Princess Emily Kaldwin and restore her family to the throne. The Rat Plague has ebbed, and peace reigned for a short time. However, a new threat is looming. Emily has been crowned the Empress and ruled well for these years, but she is not without her detractors. In fact, her rule and her life are being threatened. Murders sweep the nation, Bloodflies are breeding in record numbers, and the Empress's enemies are closing in.

To survive this, you have to choose to play as Corvo Attano again or Emily Kaldwin herself. Both characters have the potential to become powerful assassins or crafty infiltrators. As before, you can bring chaos and destruction to the land as you punish everyone who gets in your way. Or, you can use a gentle hand to turn things right without killing your opponents. These choices determine your fate, your legacy, and the health of the land.

This guide can help you. We'll explain the abilities you learn, the weapons you can use, and how to get the most out of each. Our walkthroughs give you two possible methods for completing the story. One of them will be an entirely bloodless run, avoiding combat, murder, and retribution. The other indulges itself in carnage, brutality, and heavy fighting. Try either one (or both) as you make your way through *Dishonored 2*. If you want, you can mix it all up and use a combination of stealth, assassinations, and combat to play the way that you like. Our advice will still help you to find avenues to explore, special items, and key points of attack!

Either way, your enemies won't be able to stand against you. Every dirty trick and sneaky tactic is yours to wield. We'll point them all out and let you decide what to do with them.

STORY CONTROLS GAMEPLAY WEAPONS, GADGETS & BONECHARMS THE SUPERNATURAL ARTS ENEMIES OF THE CROWN WALKTHROUGH COLLECTIBLES TROPHIES & ACHIEVEMENTS

A TIME OF SCHEMING, A TIME OF MURDER

Dunwall has been at peace for about 15 years. When we were last here, the nation was under assault from multiple forces. The Empress (Jessamine Kaldwin) was assassinated, and her daughter Emily was kidnapped. You played as Corvo Attano, the bodyguard of the deceased Empress, and now serve the same role for her daughter.

As you were driven into hiding, framed for the death of the Empress, your duty was to find and eliminate the people responsible for the murder, and you did this quite successfully. Almost everyone involved was brought to justice in one way or another, and Emily Kaldwin was returned to Dunwall and placed on the throne.

Though the Rat Plague of 15 years ago is no longer devouring the country, there are horrible problems with disease. Bloodflies have been infesting Karnaca, causing many areas in the slums to be closed off. This infestation is growing worse quickly and could become a serious threat if left unchecked.

A spate of political murders has also gotten people's attention. Many of Emily's detractors have met unpleasant ends, and people are wondering if this indicates she is taking out her rivals by any means. Corvo and Emily know this isn't the case, so they're worried about the real motivations behind the killings. Papers have dubbed this person the Crown Killer, and tongues are wagging about the brutality and horror of the scenes the murderer leaves behind. They're even saying that he (or she) is a cannibal.

INTRO

STORY

CONTROLS

GAMEPLAY

WEAPONS, GADGETS, & BONECHARMS

THE SUPERNATURAL ARTS

ENEMIES OF THE CROWN

WALKTHROUGH

COLLECTIBLES

TROPHIES & ACHIEVEM

An even stranger problem is that of the Outsider. Some people worship this dark figure, who seems to grant mystical powers to rare individuals. You know the Outsider is real, because his assistance allowed Corvo to defeat the enemies of the throne during the time of the Rat Plague. Still, it seems dangerous to trust this figure. His motivations are unclear, and morality seems to have little to do with them. What other people have the Outsider's powers, and what are they doing with those gifts?

The Overseers are a religious faction that acts as a force against the Outsider and his believers. They've been cracking down on such people, seizing anyone who is suspected of Outsider worship. They gather magical relics like Runes and Bonecharms and hoard them so that they don't pollute the world. Don't mistake the Overseers as a benevolent group; they are fanatics, and will turn their pistols and blades on almost anyone who arouses their suspicion. Their leader down in Karnaca is Vice Overseer Byrne.

Some of this game takes place in Dunwall. However, much of the story is focused on Karnaca, the largest city on the island of Serkonos. This is far in the south, at the edge of the empire. It's a meeting ground for many types of people. Corvo was born there, though he hasn't been back in a long time. Serkonos is led by Duke Luca Abele, and is protected by the Grand Serkonan Guard. Though the Duke and his friends have grown wealthy from the legendary silver mines of Serkonos, a great corruption has festered there.

Somewhere within Karnaca, a conspiracy has formed between prominent figures of society. They're moving with magic, clockwork inventions, and financial backing. You need to learn who they are, why they're coming after you, and how to defeat them all.

LEARNING THE CONTROLS

Dishonored 2 has a similar style of control to the first game, so you can skip this chapter if you already feel comfortable with the controls. Otherwise, this is where we'll quickly get you acquainted with the game's basic commands and options.

Commands

Like most games, there are quite a few controls that let you get your character around the world. Corvo and Emily have various movement options, attacks, and special abilities. Let's talk about how you use them!

MOVEMENT

Your controller's left stick or your WASD keys control standard movement. This takes you forward or back, left or right. This is all normal, so you shouldn't have any trouble getting used to the system.

CAMERA CONTROL

Your right stick or mouse controls the camera. Look around frequently so that you see patrols behind you, figure out good angles of attack, and so forth. If you get close to a corner, you can pan your camera to look into hallways without exposing yourself.

SPRINTING

If you aren't worried about making more noise and need speed instead, go ahead and sprint. This gets your character around much faster. Enemies hear your actions and notice you at a much greater range, so that is only a good idea if you're already in a fight or are in a zone that is safe (because you've cleared out the enemies or are not suspected by anyone, like in a civilian area).

Note that crouching while sprinting puts your character into a slide. This gets you under low-hanging obstacles.

You don't need any special abilities to slide, but taking Focused Slide lets you slow time while sliding as long as you have a ranged weapon equipped. You get enough time to aim and shoot at nearby enemies, gaining a major advantage over them.

SNEAKING

Though walking doesn't make too much noise, it still allows enemies to hear you once you get close to them. Sneaking makes your movement so quiet that even people inches away from you won't detect your character unless you are spotted visually. As such, you can sneak behind people and get all the way up to them without causing any trouble. This is essential for choking people out or assassinating them.

Even when you aren't going after targets directly, sneaking is wonderful for allowing you to get through areas without having to fight. There are multiple times when you need to grab an item out of a room or pass through a hallway, and it's not worth starting a fight. See where the patrollers are heading, sneak behind them when they aren't looking, and you're good to go.

The more interested you are in low-Chaos styles of play, the more important it is to master sneaking!

Another tool to help with sneaking is leaning. Hold down the Lean button, and you can shift left, right, or up to help you see around corners or over ledges and windows. Enemies won't spot you as quickly when you're doing this. Note that they still *can* spot you, so don't just stick yourself out there and relax.

JUMPING

There aren't a lot of tricky jumps or things of that sort in *Dishonored 2*, but your character is athletic and can jump across gaps without any difficulty. Combine this with Blink/ Far Reach, and you can jump over huge chasms, cross from rooftop to rooftop, and so forth.

TAKEDOWNS

If you are close to a target and they aren't in combat mode, you're able to either choke them unconscious or quickly assassinate them. There is even a short grace period once a target realizes you're there when it's still possible to take them down instantly. If someone hears or sees you, quickly tap the correct button and hopefully secure your instant victory. If you drop onto a target from above or run and slide into them, you can initiate a takedown immediately. Takedowns can also be initiated through windows or from ledges against targets that get close enough to you.

This is one of the most vital techniques for getting through the game in low-Chaos mode. You need to knock people unconscious, hide them so that other patrollers won't see anything, and then repeat the tactic against other foes in the area. By doing this, you can clear out groups and free the level for exploration without having to kill anyone or face your own death. Notice that you can transition instantly from a choke into carrying an unconscious person if you hold down the carry button as you complete your choke.

It's also possible to choke people during combat if you're really quick. Parry their attacks to stun them briefly, and use the time when they're disabled to grab the victim and begin your choke. While holding these victims, you are partially protected from enemy attacks because of your meatshield. During this time, you can move slowly. Make sure that your victim is between you and other enemies. Also, try to back away from unaware targets so that they don't see you choking their buddy! If enemies are approaching, you can throw the body shield forward and defend yourself. While getting back up, the victim is vulnerable to assassination. Grab and throw people over ledges or into breakable objects for really spectacular kills.

High-Chaos killers still use this technique as well, though in a different way. If you fall into this category, a takedown is a fast kill that either starts a fight with additional enemies or leaves you undetected so that you can repeat the maneuver and continue scoring instant kills without needing to draw your Sword.

In general, most high-Chaos players assassinate eve ryone they come across until they're detected. At that point, they draw their blade and use a mix of swordplay, equipment, and special abilities to kill anyone who comes calling. It's not subtle, but it's quite fun.

Finally, note that it's possible to do a takedown during combat if you get special opportunities. Parries leave enemies vulnerable for about a second, so you can parry and then assassinate or choke out a target. If you get behind a foe, there is also a brief period of vulnerability to takedowns. A fast Blink, 180 turn, and takedown does the trick; this isn't an easy technique to master, but it works.

SWORD STRIKES

At close range, your character is a capable killer. By carefully blocking attacks and then counterattacking afterward, you can avoid heavy damage and eliminate target after target. Practice mixing in attacks with your other equipment to kill additional enemies or to throw off the defenses of your current target.

Swordplay is extremely important in high-Chaos playthroughs. It is almost irrelevant in low-Chaos play because it's deadly, loud, and dangerous.

BLOCKING

Blocking takes up your character's time and attention but deflects melee attacks made in a wide arc in front of you. With certain abilities purchased, you can even deflect ranged attacks. In this game, you often get destroyed if you go wildly aggressive during battle. It's smarter and safer to take a little bit longer, block, play defensively, and kill everyone in the room without taking a hit.

The most important blocking technique to learn is a parry. When you hold down the Block button, it defends you constantly but won't trigger a parry. Hitting Block right before an enemy attack lands triggers a parry. This badly throws off your enemy and leaves them vulnerable to an instant kill or a takedown. The timing window for a parry is reasonably generous, so it's not too hard to master and turns brutal fights into fun frenzies of murder.

CLIMBING

Blink and Far Reach handle much of your vertical movement, but your characters can climb over ledges, jump high to catch railings, and so forth. Climbing is automatic as long as you get close enough to a ledge that your character can grab it. The Agility ability helps you to jump higher, making it easier to reach difficult places without using any magic.

SWIMMING

When you're underwater, a breath bar appears on your HUD (it's an aquamarine color, quite appropriately). If you let this run out, your character begins to drown. Make sure not to stay submerged for very long so that this doesn't happen.

There aren't many swimming sections in the game, so you usually end up submerged because you're exploring and looking for extra treasure. Come to the surface frequently to replenish your air, and then continue on your treasure hunt.

USING SPECIAL ABILITIES

Unless you're playing through the game without using special abilities, these are likely to be a cornerstone of your playstyle. Both Corvo and Emily have a number of powers that are incredibly useful for moving around, avoiding detection, surviving battle, or for raw lethality.

You only want to have a small set of active abilities. That way, you aren't using them all over the place and running out of Mana constantly. Find a balance of active and passive abilities to invest in so that your character has a strong baseline of survivability and a distinct playstyle.

We explain all the abilities at length in their own chapter.

USING YOUR EQUIPMENT

Your equipment adds ranged attacks, traps, and explosives to your lineup. These have myriad uses. You can eliminate patrollers quietly when they don't know you're there. Throw these into your melee routine to kill enemies quickly even when you're heavily outnumbered.

There are both lethal and non-lethal options for your equipment, so collect and upgrade the items you need the most for your style of play. Low-Chaos players should improve their Crossbow and get plenty of Sleep Darts (they're a godsend when you want to deal with out-of-the-way patrollers). High-Chaos players get major benefits from the Pistol and Grenades.

DRINKING ELIXIRS

There are Health and Mana Elixirs in this game. These allow you to restore yourself if you take too much damage or exhaust yourself by relying on your abilities. In larger battles or more difficult situations, use these freely and don't worry about conserving anything. But in all other cases, save up these critical items. If you have all ten Elixirs of a given type and find another one while exploring, drink one of your Elixirs to make room. This lets you top off your Health or Mana more often.

DRINKING ELIXIRS

Another way to conserve is to look for food to restore your Health between smaller fights. Similarly, let your Mana regenerate as much as possible in between uses of your abilities so that you don't bottom out and require your Mana Elixirs as often.

LOOKING THROUGH YOUR SPYGLASS *The Menu*

Quite early in the game, you get a Spyglass that lets you look at things from quite a distance. This allows you to listen in on conversations at range as well (because Corvo and Emily have awesome equipment). Use this to watch enemies from farther away, when they don't have any real chance of spotting you.

After loading the game, you are put into the Main menu. From here, you can access the Tutorial, which is short and effective for getting you used to the controls. After playing that, set up the Options to your preferences and then go into the main campaign.

Each time you start a new campaign, you're asked to select a difficulty level. We strongly suggest that you avoid the Easy setting. The game is much more complex and enjoyable if you try some of the harder settings, and even a newcomer will find that Medium is doable without investing much practice time. The higher modes are even better!

Options

The Options page lets you mess around with the controls, visuals, audio, and gameplay settings for *Dishonored 2*. We always recommend that you go through these carefully to make sure you get the best configuration for your playstyle.

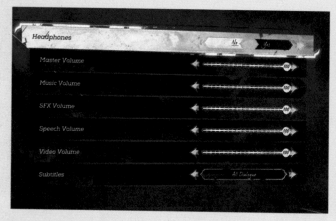

This is most important for sensitivity. Gamepad and mouse sensitivity make a massive difference in your ability to move around easily and aim. The more you fine-tune these levels, the better you can become. Make sure you can aim with precision and still turn 180 degrees without taking much time. The middle ground between fast turning and precision aiming is usually the best way to go. The game benefits a bit more from movement than from high-end sniping, so you can afford to have a little more sensitivity than you would for a pure shooting game.

This game is fairly dark in color, so turn up your gamma setting if you're having trouble seeing things clearly.

Gameplay settings are primarily a matter of comfort. You can turn on or off a number of HUD options if you prefer more information or a cleaner setup. If you get headaches from motion in games, make sure to keep the Head Bob setting all the way down. This really helps.

Your HUD

The HUD gives you a constant and impressive amount of information about your character, equipment, and abilities.

In the upper-left corner, you see bars for your Health (in red) and Mana (in dark blue). Health controls whether you live or die, so you can't afford to let that bottom out. Eat food or drink Health Elixirs to restore it beyond a fairly minimal base level. Mana lets you use your special abilities. After using one, notice that the bar falls but retains a transparent portion for a short time. This is the level of Mana regeneration you'll receive as long as you don't use another ability before the regeneration is complete. That's why you want to stagger your ability use!

In the center of those bars, you see an icon that reveals the current weapon or ability you have readied. This quickly reminds you whether you're set to shoot, Blink, etc.

In the lower-left corner, you see the equipment and abilities that are accessed by your D-Pad. This image hides itself after a moment, so tap the D-Pad if you want to see the loadout you have prepared. You can have four weapons/abilities hotslotted this way. Tap the various directions on the D-Pad to change between these weapons/abilities. If you want to switch to different ones, bring up the Radial menu and change your loadout. This pauses the game, so it's doable at any time without risking your character.

The Radial menu is also where you select your Health and Mana Elixirs, when you need to use either of those.

The lower-right corner tells you if the game is saving.

There is a reticle in the center of the screen. This shows where your character is looking, and it helps you aim your ranged weapons. For extra lethality, keep the reticle on enemies' heads before you fire to ensure you take them out with as little ammunition as possible.

Enemies give you some information through the HUD as well. People who are starting to detect your character get a charging lightning bolt symbol. If it fills up most of the way, they'll get suspicious and come to investigate the area where they saw you or last heard something strange. If they see or hear anything too weird, the bolt turns red. That means the target is fully alerted. They'll draw their weapons, grab buddies if they can, and you lose your Ghost status if you hadn't already.

Objectives also appear on your HUD. These waypoints track missions you're working on. If you take out the Heart (a piece of equipment) and highlight one of the collectible objects it detects, you can also lock that on to your HUD until it's collected.

BECOME A MASTER OF STEALTH AND COMBAT

With knowledge of the basic controls in hand, you're ready to learn about actual fighting, stealth work, and tactics. This chapter goes into the details for this game's mechanics, giving you a strong edge against the challenges ahead.

Fighting and Killing

Unless you completely master stealth, it's likely that you will engage in a number of battles throughout your journey. Either by choice or by necessity, combat can be an excellent way to deal with your opponents.

Having great reflexes and practicing with your weapons makes a huge difference, but there are also a few tactics that let you start beating enemies even sooner. We'll go over these now so that you can take on greater difficulties that much sooner.

THINNING ENEMY NUMBERS

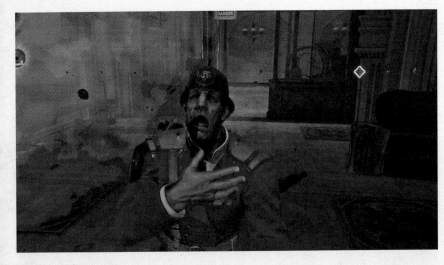

It's easy to end up in a larger battle than you expect. You see a patroller wandering around and think, "Hey, let's kill that guy." It's a perfectly fair idea, but you might not know about the two men in a side room who are within earshot. And then there is another patroller who might wander into the same room as you start to fight those three attackers. Things can get out of hand without much warning.

Even as a combative player, you need to think a bit like a stealther before you engage in a fight. Stay quiet when you're outside of combat, and look around before you attack anyone. If you see enemies who are absolutely isolated, take them out immediately. If you use stealth assassinations, you can kill these enemies and still get the jump on other targets before the loud, chaotic battles begin. It's easy to kill one or two people at once, so keep your options open by engaging in these stealth kills.

The best way to do this is to wait for patrollers to come as far out as their paths take them. Ambush such enemies from behind when they're heading back to the uncleared area, kill them silently, and drag their bodies back into a place that you've already secured. This takes more time, so you won't always want to choose this tactic. However, it's vital if you're having trouble dealing with enemies in a given area.

We usually use this as a fallback tactic if an outright assault isn't working. "Oh, I can't beat all six of those guys at once. Reload and try this a more subtle way."

On your next playthrough, you might very well be able to kill untold numbers simultaneously, but that's a lot to ask at first.

Taking Shadow Kill is a strong option for players who like to invest some time in setting up their fights. Shadow Kill automatically destroys the bodies of enemies you kill with assassinations. You save so much time with it, and it just feels cool.

If you have Shadow Kill, you don't need to waste time on bodies and can easily eliminate patrollers without anyone being the wiser. This leads to small fights when you just go against the core enemies in a room who are watching each other's backs.

Even with those groups, you can rush forward and kill the first member before they draw their weapon. Anyone else can ready their defenses, but they'll be at a major disadvantage because you've killed yet one more member of their group.

THROWN OBJECTS

Many smaller objects, like bottles, can be thrown. If you hit an unaware target in the head, they'll collapse. With the Strength ability, you can even take people down by hitting them in the head during a fight.

If you find bottles with flammable liquids inside of them, you can throw them into Bloodfly nests (or people) to set things on fire. Watch out when you try this during a Merciful playthrough, because fire sometimes catches onto people that you weren't trying to hurt.

COMBINED ARMS

We briefly mentioned earlier that it's important to use more than your Sword in battle. Corvo and Emily have multiple weapons at their disposal, and these aren't meant to be used exclusively. You don't have enough Bullets to spam Pistol shots all day and all night. You never have enough Bolts either. Instead of using one by itself, you're best off if you combine all your weapons.

Here's an example. Imagine a room with three enemies close together. You can't take them out quietly (or don't want to), so it's going to be a fight. Charging into the group lets you automatically kill one foe with your Sword because they're not ready to block. You kill this unaware target, and the other two draw blades. You shoot the first one who approaches with your Pistol. If you're lucky, you score an instant kill, but even if they survive, you can attack while they're staggered and finish them off. Block to stop the next attacker from injuring you, and then save your ammo, because a solo survivor has almost no hope against you in melee.

In this way, you take down three enemies with only one Bullet spent. But if you tried pure melee, you'd have to hold off two attackers at once, which is substantially trickier.

For larger battles, you add more pieces to the equation. Placing a Stun Mine or a Spring Razor gives you a chance to lure enemies into even more trouble. Attack with surprise, shoot someone else in the face, back around a corner where you have your trap set, lure the enemies into that, and then resume your attack.

The key here is to practice moving fluidly between different types of actions. This balances your resources (ammunition, Mana, Health, Elixirs). By relying on all of them, you are much more likely to stay alive and find items you need to top yourself off.

Players who only fight with their blades won't use as much Mana or ammunition, so some of the Elixirs and ammo they find are totally wasted. The same is true for ability users who forget to enjoy their Pistols and Crossbows. If you're a high-Chaos player, you might as well use every tool at your disposal, because you're already loud and proud. Have fun with it!

The final tier of arms combination is when you get abilities that buy you even more time to do your grim work. Bend Time, Devouring Swarm, and Doppelganger are all examples of abilities that give you tons of extra time to attack, switch between targets, and alternate your weapon use. Once you've learned one of these abilities, you can take on huge groups of targets.

FLEE AND RECOVER

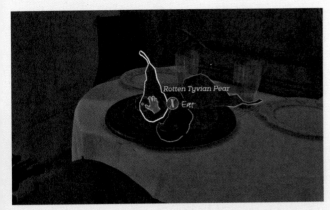

Sometimes, when you're learning your limits, you're going to have trouble. If a fight starts going poorly, you don't have to stick around and take the loss. That's not the way assassins work. Run! Get out of the area by sprinting around a corner (to break line of sight with your targets). They'll pursue, but if they can't see you, they can't shoot at you. This buys you a little bit of time to get farther away.

Eventually, pursuers hit their limits and turn around. They'll return to their initial areas to resume their duties. You get another bite at the apple and can go after them with surprise on your side yet again. Though slow, this technique allows you to thin even a group of closely clustered targets. Take out one or two in the first battle, run away, and then return for the others later on.

NEVER GET SURROUNDED

You're not supposed to be here!

Your characters are amazing, but they can't take many hits if you get careless. Enemies who get onto your flanks or rear are going to rip your people apart, even on lower difficulty levels. Though it sounds simplistic, the answer is to avoid getting into that position in the first place.

To do that, eliminate enemies in a specific order. If there is one guy off to the left and two enemies ahead, kill the singleton first. That way, you can turn and face both of the other attackers together. If you killed one of the pair instead, you'd get jumped by the survivor and by the flanker, ensuring that you end up in a tougher position.

If there are enemies on three or more sides, you can't really guarantee a safe position for your character once battle starts. So here is another trick. Start the fight on your terms with a free kill or two, and then back into a hallway or room. Use a narrow corridor or a doorway as a chokepoint that forces that group to squeeze in after you from a single angle. Now you aren't flanked anymore, and you might get to pick off someone as the group tries to approach.

In short, watch out starting fights in wide-open areas unless you know no one is going to attack you from a bad angle. If that happens, back off until all your enemies are pursuing you from a single direction.

FIGHTING WITHOUT KILLING

Just because you get into a fight doesn't mean that you have to kill your enemies. Non-lethal players that aren't perfect at stealth or don't want to be stealthy can use various techniques to survive combat and win without slaughter.

Use Sleep Darts to knock out targets ahead of time. Headshots automatically take down your targets, and Sleep Darts can be upgraded to even work well during combat! Stun Mines make great traps, but they too can be deployed during a fight; block to avoid damage while the mines charge, and watch them knock out your opponents.

Parry enemies in melee to knock them off balance, and then grab them for a fast choke. If you're only facing one final target this is highly effective; this requires good timing, but it's an amazing technique that makes non-lethal play even more reliable.

Our stealth walkthrough goes over these techniques frequently, despite our efforts to give good suggestions on Ghost gameplay.

Stealth and Subtlety

For players who don't want to rip their way through the game, many options still exist. Sneaking, ability use, and careful observation allow you to complete every objective in the game without resorting to murder and swordplay.

This makes it way (WAY) easier to avoid the high-Chaos ending, and it is required for players who want a non-lethal run through the game.

SNEAK CONSTANTLY

You simply can't get far as a stealth player without getting comfortable sneaking. Don't run unless you are certain no one can see you. Don't even walk normally unless you're almost that certain. Sneak everywhere. Patience is one of the greatest assets for a stealth player. Relax and settle into this slower, methodical style of play. It feels weird to some players at first, but realize that the glory doesn't come from downing your foes. Instead, it comes from reaching the end of a level and realizing no one even knew you were there.

You should even be careful around civilians. Though these characters (like beggars, shopkeepers, etc.) aren't out to get you, they'll still report to the guards if they see anything scary or dangerous. That includes hostile actions, certainly, but that's not all. If you spend too long walking around areas that aren't neutral territory, some civilians will freak out just because of your presence. Treat most civilians as a minor threat if you're not in a safe, neutral place. Knock out the civilians and leave them somewhere quiet so that they can't report on your actions.

OBSERVE, OBSERVE, OBSERVE

Brutes can run into a room and hope for the best, but that's not for you. You are going to think and plan every action before you take a single step. From a distance or from hiding, watch every single patroller and enemy before approaching anyone. Figure out who is in each room, how they move, and where you can hide to avoid being seen.

If you need to pass through an area, figure out a time to slip through when no one is watching. Looting or knocking out a target takes more time and preparation. When that is the case, your goal is to sneak up and choke out everyone who might spot you. Find each person in isolation, knock them out, and then hide them somewhere nobody patrols.

Blink or Far Reach behind people to get the drop on them. Use Sleep Darts on enemies too far away to reach conveniently. And always leave your unconscious victims somewhere safe unless you don't care about killing people. Dropping unconscious bodies near Bloodflies or Rats still counts as murder if the creatures decide to kill them. Similarly, people you drop from too high will die and count against you.

When you're having trouble finding a vulnerable target, create one for yourself. Hit an object with your Sword to lure people over toward a dark area where they can be ambushed. If you need someone to get farther away, shoot a Crossbow Bolt over there. The noise isn't enough to trigger an alert (like a Bullet would). Instead, it's just enough for someone to go and check it out.

Sneaking into someone's line of sight for a few seconds can do this as well. It's risky, but if you hide again before the person's attention fills all the way up you won't get busted. Instead, they'll come over to see what is going on. Use that time to sneak through their area, or to get behind them and ambush the person in question.

STAY OFF THE EXPECTED PATH

Most enemies patrol and watch major entrances and avenues through the area. They don't spend much of their time looking at rooftops, abandoned buildings, and other non-traditional routes. Because of this, you can sneak easily and somewhat quickly by getting above your enemies or around them.

Always explore to find these optional pathways. To save time, save your game and explore without worrying about lethality, being spotted, etc. Just run around and look for anything useful. After finding a few interesting possibilities, load your game again and reach those spots quietly. Doing this can actually be faster than exploring quietly in the first place, and it's kind of relaxing to spend a minute or two wandering around without being quiet and cautious.

The rooftops and upper reaches of most areas are perfect for safe traversal. Use Blink/Far Reach/Agility jumps to get as high as you can. From there, you can observe people more easily and often get around the level without being spotted. Sniping from above, launching drop attacks (lethal or non-lethal ones), and regular exploration are all much easier when you're high above the city streets.

Be careful when returning to patrolled territory. In addition, you should put extra time into watching for targets if they've already spotted you once before. Alerted enemies return to their normal areas after a while, but they'll still be more watchful and poke around to see if they can find you. Dark Vision really helps in finding out where enemies have gone in these circumstances.

BODY STORAGE

Blink/Far Reach unconscious people onto rooftops and other locations that are impossible for enemies to reach. This is usually easier and safer than putting them in Dumpsters unless targets are right next to a Dumpster when you choke them.

The Benefits of Exploration

There isn't XP or a leveling system in *Dishonored 2*. You improve in power because you get better at the game, find more equipment, and use all your assets to their fullest potential.

If you explore well, you can pull in several times more money than a casual player. This, combined with a higher number of collectibles, leads to you having a much deadlier character. You also get to find more Documents, Audiographs, and people to listen to. Exploring reveals way more of the story than you'd get by racing down the streets, shooting at everyone in sight. Thus, you get to learn way more about the world while collecting everyone's treasures.

Let's delve into the ways you can find more items.

HAVE A HEART

Very early in the game you receive the Heart. This item lets you track Bonecharms and Runes on your HUD, making them fairly easy to find as long as you're willing to put in the time to get them. Our Walkthrough explains how to get these items, with extra focus on the trickier ones that aren't easy to just walk up to and steal.

Still, even when you know where you're going, it's nice to have the Heart as one of your four hotslotted items. Slap that into place, make sure the Runes and Bonecharms are in the direction you think they are, and then set off. It's a huge time-saver.

For more information about people, use the Heart while aiming at a person. This reveals things about the target's inner life and history. It's great for background on the characters in this world. If you're roleplaying a character that only kills the worst members of society, your Heart really helps in finding the secret good guys and bad guys who aren't always that obvious.

DARK VISION

If you're a treasure hunter, then Dark Vision is a wonderful purchase. Greater Dark Vision reveals items inside drawers, safes, through walls, etc. Even items that are supposed to be hidden (likes behind bookcases and such) are clearly visible. This lets you pick up hundreds of coins in every mission that would probably be missed otherwise.

Players who want lots of expensive upgrades should really consider Dark Vision as one of their Rune investments.

PICKPOCKETING

Not all money is hidden, though. Some of it is carried around by people. You might forget about these coins, because 10 here and 10 there don't seem like too much. But try not to think that way; pickpocketing adds up way faster than you think until you try it. Wealthier Guards and civilians with better houses sometimes have pretty decent money. Ten here, 10 there sometimes becomes 25-30 a pop later in the game, and it doesn't really take any time to do this. Crouch and look for a purse on every civilian you pass. They won't notice.

And enemies you down—what's the harm in looting them! It's almost instant, and you might also get extra ammunition while you're at it.

STEALING

All the black markets have money too. Tons of people go there to buy from them, so you can steal valuable items AND get a fair amount of raw cash while you're at it. Each time you find a black market, think about how to get around to the rear of the building. That's always the key to robbing them.

If you knock out a black market merchant or scare them, they'll lock up the store. However, you can return in five minutes and everything will be open again. Just don't kill the merchants, and you can continue to buy from them.

THINGS TO BUY

THE KEY TO THE CITY WATCH ARMORY

The shopkeeper's young son snatched the key to an abandoned City Watch armory, near the gate to Dunwall Tower. This checkpoint was used to stock military equipment, which might prove useful.

All this money is useful, but for what?

When you go to a black market, you should stock up on ammunition for all your weapons. If you're badly lacking on Elixirs, buy them there too. They are expensive, so don't rely on purchasing them too often (it's better to explore, search, and steal Elixirs from other people). But if you bottom out on something, go ahead and spend the cash.

Upgrades for your weapons and equipment are also black market purchases. You can carry more ammo, fire with more accuracy, equip more Bonecharms, etc. The list of upgrades is huge, and it gets bigger throughout the game as you discover special Blueprints with otherwise locked upgrades for you. Read the Equipment chapter to see everything available.

Most black markets also contain a single special item. You might get a map to a cache of treasure, or find a key to a special location. These pay off every single time, so buy them when you see them. You get both money and materials from these locations, so you're probably doubling or tripling your investment.

COLLECTING AND CRAFTING BONECHARMS

Bonecharms grant your character minor bonuses. You benefit from these whenever you equip a Bonecharm. These items can include up to four positive effects, and a single negative effect if they've been corrupted. Corrupted Bonecharms are either found with a negative trait, or can be accidentally created that way if you use Bonecharm Crafting as one of your abilities.

The more traits a Bonecharm gets, the higher the chance it will end up with a negative one as well. This is usually well worth the tradeoff even when it happens, because four good traits can heavily outweigh a single negative one unless you get really unlucky. Bonecharm Crafting improves as you take more bonuses for it, so corruption becomes less and less of an issue.

Because the Bonecharm Crafting system is so strong, we recommend that every character look into this. You can sacrifice the Bonecharms you find, learn their traits for future crafting, and get Raw Whalebone in the process. This Raw Whalebone is then used when you make your own Bonecharms.

You're allowed to stack the same positive effect up to four times on your character. Thus, for instance, an effect that gives you health whenever you do X can be applied up to four times (either on the same item or spread over multiple Bonecharms).

This is why crafting is so useful; you can heap on all your favorite bonuses and push them to the maximum. For example, on our stealth playthroughs, we get maximum speed for our crouched movement (Swift Shadow), have a major chance to recover Sleep Darts after they're used (Lucky Needle), move faster when carrying a body (Undertaker), and choke people faster (Strong Arms).

There are many ideal combinations. You learn traits each time you break a regular Bonecharm. Whenever you find a Bonecharm with something you really enjoy, break it immediately and craft a new Bonecharm with three or four copies of that trait.

ACQUIRING RUNES

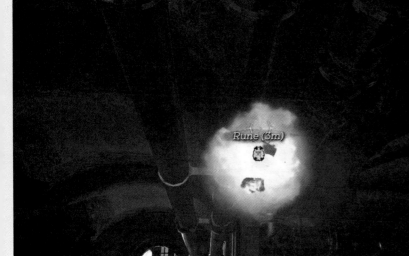

Runes let you master your abilities. At first, you won't have many to spread around, but there are quite a few of them in the game. Some appear on their own. Others are stacked onto Outsider Shrines. Both groups appear when you use your Heart to track them, so you won't miss many Runes if you're careful. Some black markets have a spare Rune to sell also. They're a bit pricey, but are always worth the cash.

PAINTINGS

Speaking of cash, there are collectible Paintings in just about every part of the game. They're worth a couple hundred coins each, so they really help to pad your bank account. Look for portraits; they're the type of Painting you can normally steal. Other things on the walls are just cheap prints or are too big to carry off.

BLUEPRINTS

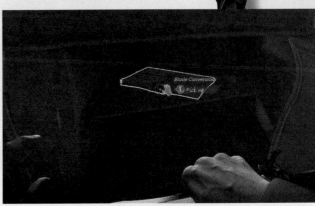

Blueprints are found on desks and worktables most of the time, as you'd expect. They are blue in color and can be seen easily once you get close to them. But they don't show up with your Heart and are sometimes in fairly out-of-the-way buildings. This makes them very missable.

SPECIAL ACTIONS

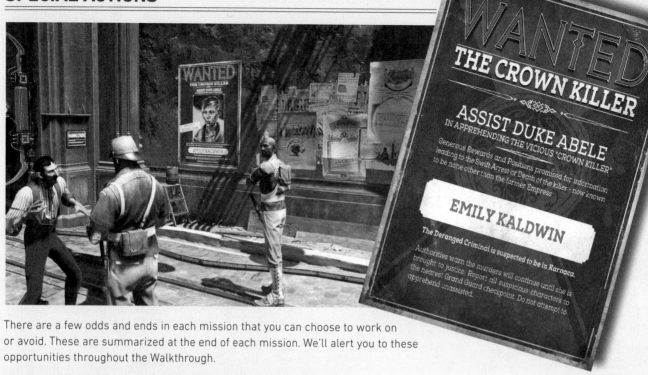

There are a few odds and ends in each mission that you can choose to work on or avoid. These are summarized at the end of each mission. We'll alert you to these opportunities throughout the Walkthrough.

END-OF-MISSION REPORTS

Once you finish your work and leave an area, the game provides an after-mission report listing the number of collectible items of every type available in that mission. You can always save your game, end a mission, and reload if you find out an item got lost in the shuffle. However, we include a quicklist of all the collectibles and their locations at the end of this guide. That should help even more!

The Chaos System and Special Playstyles

The Chaos system is a reflection of your character's morality and choices. If you kill more people, leave bodies around, and are discovered often, you will accrue a high amount of Chaos. This increases the number of enemies in a map and changes the tone of the conversations you have and overhear. People are more frightened and aggressive if you cut a swath of bloody vengeance across the Empire.

Spare your enemies, find non-lethal solutions, and use stealth frequently to stay on the low-Chaos side of the game. Your save file lets you know where you stand, so it's always clear if you're sticking to the less vicious side of the game.

This too is shown in the after-mission report. A small graphic details your quality of stealth and your use of violence. Truly excellent play in these areas is rewarded with special terms: Ghost and Merciful. These are tied up in Trophies, and they're also a badge of honor because they can be hard to maintain.

BECOMING A GHOST

Ghost play is reserved for people who have not been discovered at all. It means that you hid your bodies perfectly, avoided detection, and still completed your goals. You can still kill people and keep your Ghost rating, so this is not always tied in with Merciful status.

In fact, it's much easier to do a Ghost run if you focus on limited killing. Shadow Kill is a vital tool for this, allowing you to assassinate targets and have their bodies disappear.

If you're doing a full Ghost run through the campaign, remember to keep a save file for every single mission. Don't overwrite these files. This way, you can back up and try a mission again if you reach the end and realize you broke your Ghost rating at some point. It's usually clear when this happens (you get attacked, the Guards bark out that they've seen someone, etc.). But you don't want to risk someone in another room discovering your activities and ruining your perfect work.

A TRUE LEADER CAN BE MERCIFUL

Merciful play is easier than Ghost, but it still demands attention to detail. You cannot kill any person during your play. Bloodflies, Fish, Rats, Clockwork Soldiers, and Bloodbriars are still free game, because none of them are people. Save Bullets and Bolts for these enemies, and use abilities, non-lethal takedowns, and Sleep Darts to get through the rest of your work.

When faced with an important target, always look for a special solution. Each major NPC has a kill scenario as well as a way to defeat them without violence. Spend the extra time to go through these cool alternatives.

You don't have to be a pure stealth player to pull off Merciful. If you upgrade your Sleep Darts, you can use them in combat. With skilled parrying, you can also parry and then choke out targets without harming them. These techniques make it much easier to get a Merciful rating without having to avoid every single encounter in the game (unless you want to get Ghost and Merciful at the same time).

We still suggest that you keep a save file at the beginning of every single mission until you've beaten the game. Better safe than sorry! You lose Merciful easily if anything goes wrong. If you knock someone out and they die for any reason, you're responsible. This can happen offscreen if you leave someone where they can fall, be killed by an accident, or be eaten by animals. Look for flat rooftops whenever possible; they're the safest places to leave unconscious victims.

PLAYING WITHOUT ABILITIES

Some players like to go through the entire game without buying any abilities. Tell the Outsider to shove it! You can save the Empire on your own.

Unless you're really crazy, don't combine this tactic with Merciful or Ghost. This is already a challenging playstyle. Stock up on equipment at every black market, and then rely on your weapons and tools to defeat every challenge. This is most easily done when you practice your swordplay heavily and mix in Pistol and Crossbow shots. A combined approach of assassinations further improves the situation. Without abilities, you probably can't assassinate everyone before getting spotted, but you can thin the ranks and then fight off the remainder of the troops in each area.

Upgrading Equipment

A considerable amount of your money gets invested into your equipment. When you reach each black market, look at the upgrades you have available. Some of these are there by default, and others are unlocked as you get more and more Blueprints.

We heavily suggest that you focus on getting more Bonecharm slots for every character you play. That's a powerful upgrade once you get far enough into the game to have a selection of Bonecharms. With a full set, you start to feel extremely powerful. Bonecharm Crafting further enhances that because you get to target the bonuses you're receiving, making your specific build that much nastier.

It's easy to tap out of money when you upgrade all your favorite things. Search mission areas carefully to get as much money as possible, and look at the Walkthrough suggestions to get more. For example, all black markets can be robbed. If you upgrade first, you can then rob the stores to get valuable items free of charge and then steal some additional goodies as well. This won't count against your Chaos unless you kill the storekeepers in the process.

Prioritize your best weapons and most valuable equipment instead of upgrading everything at once. Make sure the first upgrades go to any weapons you keep equipped in the lower-left corner of your screen. They're obviously the tools you're using the most!

If you find the Master Blueprints for your weapons and armor, you're allowed to craft unique upgrades for them. These are really cool additions to the later game and should be sought out exhaustively. The Equipment chapter lists all upgrades in the game, and what they do for your character.

Understanding Security Systems

There are quite a few types of environmental hazards in the game. These can be avoided if you're staying out of trouble, but they can also be exploited if you're not afraid of some Chaos.

ELECTRICAL CABINETS

These large, gray machines don't look like much until you break them open. Once hit, they fall apart and start spraying electrical discharges all over the place. These do lethal damage at close range (to you or to any enemies there). Hit the cabinets at range when your targets are close to them.

HOT STEAM

There are pipes all over Dunwall and Karnaca; it's the age of steam for them, after all. You sometimes notice soldering marks on these networks. Those are weak points that had to be repaired, and it's your clue that a potential trap is present. Shooting or striking such spots releases a gout of steam that blinds everyone who walks into it.

Use this as a way to escape from targets, leave them exposed to assassinations, etc. The steam doesn't do any direct damage, so have a plan in place to maximize the time it gives you to reposition and mess with your victims.

WHALE OIL TANKS

You find these large canisters all over the world. They power Walls of Light, Security Lights, Clockwork Soldiers, and other devices. If you remove a Whale Oil Tank, it turns off whatever the tank was attached to. Do this to remove security systems from areas you're about to infiltrate.

That's not the only aspect of Whale Oil Tanks you need to know about. They're also explosive! If you steal a tank and throw it into your enemies, you can cause massive damage. Find a group of targets and bomb them with Whale Oil Tanks to clear the area.

BREAKABLE JOINTS

Red canisters act as joints for belts, chains, and other items in the game. You see them from time to time, and it's easy to walk past them. Instead, figure out what these canisters are for. Sometimes destroying them causes wood piles to drop on people, or causes a new area to open up.

ALARMS

If activated, Alarms summon Guards from all over an area. These devices can be rewired ahead of time if you get to their security panels. Doing this turns the Alarm into a trap that kills the first person who tries to operate it. Afterward, the Alarm breaks, so it's a win-win for you.

Don't let anyone get over to unaltered Alarms unless you want a very large fight on your hands.

TRIPWIRES

Tripwires and small Bolt-throwers are set up in multiple spots. These are homemade traps used by paranoid civilians and criminals, so you see them most often when you're going into privately owned residences or districts. Dark Vision with Premonition makes these super easy to spot and disable. Remember to collect the free Bolts from the throwers as payment for your time.

WALLS OF LIGHT

Walls of Light block essential chokepoints. They vaporize anyone who tries to go through them without being synched with the system. Use a Rewire Tool on the security panel for these traps to synch yourself. That lets you through them safely and quietly.

Alternatively, you can turn off the power. Find a Whale Oil Tank connected with wires to the Wall of Light, and remove the tank. That turns everything off, though Guards may become suspicious and investigate the problem.

If a Windmill is powering the Wall of Light, you can turn off or damage the Windmill to stop the security system. You can also use Windblast on the Windmill to supercharge the Wall of Light. Doing so causes the device to explode the next time it goes off, for major damage to an area. The Guards are still attuned and won't trigger it, but a thrown body or stone will do the trick.

WATCHTOWERS

Watchtowers keep light on important areas. Some of them have weapon systems as well. Take away their power source if you can, or rewire them if you want to turn the system against the Guards.

A more advanced type of machine for this function is the Arc Pylon. Jindosh invented these to blast energy at any hostile targets that are within range of the devices. They're smaller and have less range than Watchtowers, but they do damage faster, can't really be dodges, and are very dangerous. Use Blink or Far Reach to stay out of their range, and disable their Whale Oil Tanks as soon as possible to bring them down.

The In-Game Menus

When you go into the menu in-game, you see a number of useful pages. Your Mission page lets you switch which objectives currently have waypoints. Turn off mission objectives you don't want to accomplish (such as assassinations when you're playing a Merciful character).

That same page has a Mission Clues tab. It's quite nice for recording things your character has read or overheard that directly pertain to your current mission area. Always check this out to get an idea what your options are.

The Powers page lets you invest Runes into your special abilities. Every time you get a few Runes together, head over here and see what you want to purchase.

Go to the Bonecharms page to equip and craft Bonecharms, or sacrifice Bonecharms to learn their abilities and craft even better versions.

Lore and Maps lets you go back over all the evidence you've uncovered during your missions.

WEAPONS, GADGETS, AND BONECHARMS

You're going to love this chapter! Here we go over all weapons, traps, tools, and charms you find in *Dishonored 2*. We talk about the general use of these items, and how you can use them to overcome a variety of challenges!

Weapons

SWORD

Corvo and Emily both carry Swords and are highly adept in their use. These intuitive weapons are used at close range to dispatch enemies, whether they're aware or oblivious to your presence. Unaware enemies can be killed instantly via assassination. This can be accomplished by jumping down at them, attacking from behind, or making an attack from the front if they don't have their weapons out to defend themselves.

In our Gameplay chapter, you learned about combat, which included attacking, parrying, counterattacking, and blocking. Your Sword is required for all these techniques. When using it, stay close to your victims and dispatch them one at a time.

Sword-fighting is reliable against individuals and small groups. Against larger groups or distant, ranged enemies, it suffers a little. To survive these situations, invest in abilities like Reflexes and Blood Thirst so that your swordplay is both deadlier and more defensive.

After upgrading your Sword, you can craft a Masterwork version of it. Corvo and Emily get the same option here.

CHARACTER	SWORD NAME	EFFECTS
Either	Monkey Wrench	Deals way more damage against Clockwork Soldiers
Either	Occult Kiss	Deals more damage against magic-using enemies

PISTOL

Pistols are short- or medium-range weapons that deal moderate damage. They badly wound most targets if you strike them in the chest or limbs. Score a headshot and you're likely to get an instant kill. When you wound a target, they are briefly stunned. When in this state, you can assassinate or grab your victim to begin a choke or use them as a human shield while you decide what to do.

The Pistol is best used during battle to weaken or eliminate enemies while you're in between Sword swings. This makes it much easier to prevent your hero from being overwhelmed. Once you're good at aiming, it's fairly easy to take down someone with a Sword strike, fire a Pistol shot into another, and then finish a third victim all in the span of mere seconds. Even without additional abilities to help you, this can turn the tide of many battles throughout the game.

At really close range, the Pistol has a small amount of damage spread. This means that you can briefly stun a cluster of enemies if they're right on top of you.

Be cautious about using the Pistol to start your encounters. This weapon makes a huge amount of noise, and you're often better off killing enemies with your Sword or Crossbow if they're unaware of your presence. Save your Bullets for fights that are already joined against multiple targets who clearly know where you are.

CHARACTER	PISTOL NAME	EFFECTS
Corvo	The Determined Traveler	Perfect accuracy when used with the Spyglass
Corvo	The Crimson Painter	Shorter range, but higher damage, and a shotgun-like spread
Emily	The Insistent Gentleman	Fires at an amazing rate
Emily	The Red Siblings	Accurate and fires in bursts

If you get all the Pistol upgrades [Accuracy 1 and 2, Reload 1 and 2, and Magazine +1 (3)] you get to craft a Masterwork Pistol. Each character has two choices for the type of Pistol they receive.

EXPLOSIVE BULLET

Explosive Bullets are meant to be saved and savored! These expensive items have an area of effect that damages everyone close to the place of impact and throws them around as well. This kills weaker targets immediately, and badly wounds just about anything else in your way. Never use these in smaller or easier battles. Save Explosive Bullets for risky fights. The more targets you can group together, the more effective this ammunition becomes.

To aid effectiveness, lure groups of enemies toward narrow hallways and corners. They naturally group together in these smaller spaces, allowing your explosives to do their work!

CROSSBOW

The Crossbow offers a different ranged weapon compared to the Pistol. Instead of a loud weapon for use in the middle of battle, you get an ideal assassination tool. Though still functional if you need extra damage during a fight, this weapon kills targets at long range without making much noise. Use it to eliminate ranged enemies before a fight starts so that they don't give you trouble after someone raises an alert.

Headshots with Crossbow Bolts bring down almost any target. Because you're going against unaware opponents with most of your regular Bolts, take your time and aim carefully. Never waste a Bolt on a body shot because you might not kill the target. They'll make plenty of noise, call buddies, and then you've wasted your chance to thin the ranks before getting into a large melee battle.

Special Bolts are used to expand the versatility of your Crossbow. Once you get far enough into the game to gather these, you can use this weapon in even more exciting ways.

Merciful players sometimes forget to use their Bolts. Try to remind yourself to spend these whenever you fight targets that don't count toward Chaos or general slaughter. For example, any player can kill wolfhounds without negative consequences. Use Bolts for this to remain quiet and stealthy. Also, you can shoot Crossbow Bolts into walls and other objects to draw people's attention without immediately triggering an alert. Set up ambushes with this method.

If you get enough Blueprints to upgrade your Crossbow far enough, you can create a Masterwork version of it. Upgrade your Accuracy, Extended Range, and Reload Speed to enable this. You can then choose from two Masterwork versions of the weapon.

CHARACTER	CROSSBOW NAME	EFFECTS
Corvo	The Dealer	Can lock on to three characters and fire simultaneously
Corvo	Coffin Nails	Very fast firing
Emily	Long Distance Lover	High damage, and perfect accuracy when used with the Spyglass
Emily	Piercing Insult	Best possible damage, can pierce through targets

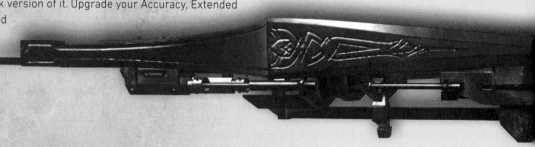

SLEEP DART

Sleep Darts give you the rare ability to bring down targets at range without ending their lives. For non-lethal players, this is a massive boon, because everything else in your arsenal requires more setup time or a lethal conclusion.

Watch enemy patrollers to find out when they're out of the way. That's the best time to put them to sleep. They won't be discovered, so you don't need to move their bodies. If there aren't any secluded locations on their patrol, hit the target when they're close to your hiding spot. Dart out, grab the sleeping guard, and get them someplace they won't be found.

Normally, these darts take a few seconds to knock someone out. Headshots negate this problem and take out the target almost instantly. With a vital upgrade, Sleep Darts can be improved to work instantaneously, even during combat. This doesn't help Ghost players, but it's perfect for stealth users who sometimes get discovered yet don't want to kill anyone. Pop someone with a combat Sleep Dart and be done with it!

Major stealth players in general should also look for Bonecharms that give a chance to recover Sleep Darts. Break these charms and remake them with Bonecharm Crafting. A charm with four sets of this ability gives you a very good chance to recover your Sleep Darts, allowing you to use them almost with impunity.

INCENDIARY BOLT

Incendiary Bolts do initial damage like a normal Crossbow Bolt, but then also deal damage over time to anything they hit. This supplementary damage is useful for helping to kill off heavier targets. However, Incendiary Bolts cause a huge amount of noise because the victim screams like murder. Use these during combat, or when a large fight is unavoidable.

HOWLING BOLT

A gang of criminals in Karnaca developed the Howling Bolts. These special weapons blind and deafen a target for several seconds. The blindness fades first, and then the deafness goes about a second later.

Use these shots to disengage from combat with really dangerous targets you don't want to fight directly. Slam a Howling Bolt into them and get out of their line of sight before they recover. You get a second chance to assassinate these victims, or you can leave the area altogether.

These weapons don't have any effect on mechanical targets. Save them for Elite Guards, Veterans, and other tricky foes.

STINGING BOLT

Enemies struck with a Stinging Bolt flee from the intense pain this item causes. This buys you time to finish a fight, escape, or get into more trouble. People who've been affected by a Stinging Bolt forget what they were doing. If you shoot a single target and move away before they recover, they'll go back to their post and continue doing whatever they were doing.

If a single target is in your way and you don't have a better solution, use a Stinging Bolt and get them out of your hair for a short time.

Gadgets and Consumables

HEALTH ELIXIR

Health Elixirs are bright red in color and restore quite a solid amount of Health. Their effect is instant, and you can save your life by drinking these when a battle turns against you.

Enter your Ability menu and look for your Elixirs to the upper left of the Radial section. That's where you see how many Health Elixirs you have to spare.

MANA ELIXIR

Mana Elixirs restore lost Mana instantly. They're hard to find, and heavy casters will rarely have more than they can spare. Mitigate the shortage by casting slowly and giving your character time to regenerate after each spell. Low-cost abilities like Blink, Far Reach, and Dark Vision can be used indefinitely as long as you do this.

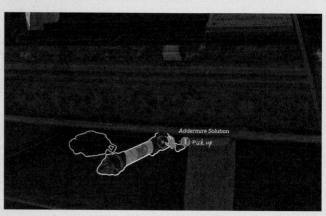

THE HEART

Equip the Heart to make Runes, Outsider Shrines, and Bonecharms appear on your HUD. You get to see their location, distance, and the type of item in question. This is invaluable for hunting rare collectibles.

If you highlight one of these items with the Heart out, you can pin the item's location as a waypoint, making it even easier to track down the item you want.

Listen to the sound of the Heart as you approach a rare target. The Heart beats louder and louder to let you know how close you are. Once you've picked up the item, the Heart stops making noise so that you can focus on a new goal.

Using the Heart while targeting an area gives you more information about the background of that locale. Do the same thing while targeting a person to hear about that target's thoughts and deeds.

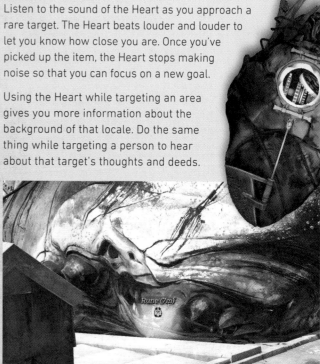

TIMEPIECE

This item is only used during a single mission, over halfway through the game. Equip and use it to shift between two time periods. This does not cost you any Mana, so it can be used constantly. The only restriction is that you can't switch timelines if there is an object blocking you in the other timeline.

A lens is attached to the Timepiece. Unfold this to see the effects your actions have on the other timeline without having to go there. This is a fast way to see what is blocking your transition, and if there are any enemies ahead of you in the other time.

IMPACT GRENADE

This is a standard thrown weapon. It explodes after four seconds of being lit, or instantly if it makes contact with a living target. You can cook your Grenades by holding down the Item button. This lets you burn down some of the fuse before throwing if you need the Grenade to explode soon after landing.

Don't ever hold a cooked Grenade for too long. The effects are about as grim as you might guess.

Impact Grenades are wonderful when you have enemies coming toward an enclosed area. You can bounce one off a wall and into a group of enemies without exposing yourself. Very powerful.

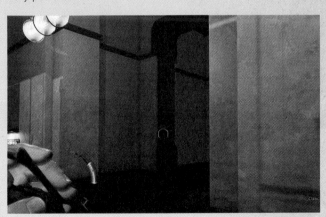

STICKY GRENADE

Sticky Grenades attach to walls, living targets, ceilings, floors, etc. They explode in four seconds and do a huge amount of damage to anything close by. When you're chased by enemies, leave a Sticky Grenade on the wall as you sprint away. The fools who run after you are likely to get a painful surprise as they approach.

SPRING RAZOR

Spring Razors are useful traps because they don't have a timer or detonator. Instead, they go off whenever an enemy gets too close. Set up lethal areas ahead of time in a place you've already cleared. Then, use noise to lure an enemy closer. Or shoot at a group from range, and run away through your trapped location. If you put the Spring Razor at a corner, people are almost certain to run over it as they chase you.

Watch out, though. Spring Razors won't trigger on you, but they blow up whenever anyone else gets too close. That can kill civilians just as easily as it kills Guards. Use these in areas where there aren't any friendlies around.

STUN MINE

Stun Mines take several seconds to activate, but when they blow up they'll disrupt everyone within a moderate area of effect. Use this to safely take down targets without killing them. If you're comfy with murder, you can always slice them up later.

Stun Mines are perhaps the best weapon in the entire game against Clockwork Soldiers. Two of these, placed near each other, will kill a Clockwork Soldier outright. Even a single one is quite disabling for the powerful machines.

Place these in an area where you know the Clockwork Soldiers will follow, and then lure them over the mines.

SPYGLASS

The Spyglass lets you zoom in on distant targets. You can hear their conversations much more easily, and see what they're doing. This helps with aiming ranged weapons, figuring out patroller routes, and with general scouting.

Using precision weapons (like the Crossbow) is really fun when you have the Spyglass out. Headshots, even at very long range, are much easier to pull off. Use the Spyglass outside of combat to ensure you don't miss when going after tricky shots.

REWIRE TOOLS

Rewire Tools allow you to change the properties of various mechanisms. These turn off security, allow you to use Walls of Light safely, reprogram Clockwork Soldiers, etc. Though expensive to purchase, these items are very powerful. Search carefully around people's apartments to stock up on Rewire Tools; there are often enough of them in missions that you don't need to buy them from the black market!

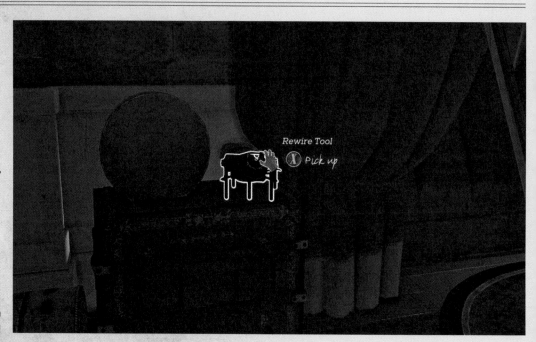

Upgrades

Purchase these improvements to your gear are at the black market. Some of them have no requirements (save for money to get the work done). Others require special Blueprints you find as you proceed through the game. These Blueprints are called out in the Walkthrough and again in our Collectibles section at the end of the guide.

CROSSBOW UPGRADES

UPGRADE NAME	REQUIREMENTS	EFFECT
Accuracy	None	Improves accuracy
Ancient Howl	Master Ammo Blueprint from The Royal Conservatory	Howling Bolts disable magic users
Bolt Capacity +5 (+10)	None	Adds +5 to your Bolt capacity, and then +10 when you purchase the second upgrade
Coffin Nails	Master Blueprint Crossbow from the Royal Conservatory	Fires Bolts very quickly
Combustion Bolts	Must have unlocked Incendiary Bolts	Incendiary Bolts gain a larger area of effect
Deep Howl	Master Ammo Blueprint from the Royal Conservatory	Howling Bolts frighten Wolfhounds
Extended Bolt Range	None	You can hit targets from much farther away, and the Bolts fly faster
Hardened Bolts	Hardened Bolts Blueprint from Edge of the World	Bolts inflict greater damage
Howling Bolts	Howling Bolts Blueprint from Clockwork Mansion Streets	You can purchase Howling Bolts
Incendiary Bolts	Incendiary Bolts Blueprint from Edge of the World	You can purchase Incendiary Bolts
Instant Sleep	None	You can purchase Sleep Darts
Long Distance Lover	Master Crossbow Blueprint from the Royal Conservatory	Your Crossbow becomes a very good sniping weapon
Piercing Insult	Master Crossbow Blueprint from the Royal Conservatory	Bolts are higher damage and pierce targets
Reload Faster	None	Decreases reload time
Stinging Dart	Stinging Dart Blueprint from the Good Doctor	You can purchase Stinging Darts
The Dealer	Master Crossbow Blueprint from the Royal Conservatory	Aim-lock up to three targets and fire simultaneously

GEAR UPGRADES

UPGRADE NAME	REQUIREMENTS	EFFECT
Bonecharm Slots +2 (+3)	None	Adds two more Bonecharm slots (then plus three for the second upgrade)
Collector's Carapace	Master Armor Blueprint from the Duke's Palace	Reduces damage taken
Moth Dust Wrappings	Master Armor Blueprint from the Duke's Palace	You are less visible in poorly lit areas
Refined Lens Optics	None	Adds a second level of zoom to your Spyglass
Silent Running	Silent Running Blueprint	Make less noise when running
Silent Sprinting	Must have purchased Silent Running	Make almost no noise when sprinting

GUN UPGRADES

UPGRADE NAME	REQUIREMENTS	EFFECT
Accuracy 1 and 2	None	Improves Pistol accuracy and reduces dispersion
Armored Bullets	Armored Bullets Blueprint from Clockwork Mansion	Bullets ricochet off of unbreakable surfaces
Bullet Storage +5 (+10)	None	Adds five Bullets to your storage (+10 for the second upgrade)
Explosive Bullets	Explosive Bullets Blueprint	Allows you to purchase Explosive Bullets
Explosive Clusters	Must have already purchased Explosive Bullets	Explosive Bullets fragment and explode individually
Magazine 1, 2, and 3	None	Adds a Bullet to your magazine for each upgrade
Magnetized Bullets	Magnetized Bullets Blueprint from Clockwork Mansion Streets	Stuns Clockwork Soldiers briefly
Reload Speed 1 and 2	None	Reduces Pistol reload times
The Determined Traveler	Master Pistol Blueprint from Crack in the Slab	Makes the Pistol extremely accurate with the Spyglass
The Crimson Painter	Master Pistol Blueprint from Crack in the Slab	Makes the Pistol more like a shotgun
The Insistent Gentleman	Master Pistol Blueprint from Crack in the Slab	The Pistol fires at a wonderful rate
The Red Siblings	Master Pistol Blueprint from Crack in the Slab	Bullets are fired in bursts of three

GRENADE UPGRADES

UPGRADE NAME	REQUIREMENTS	EFFECT
Impact Grenade	Impact Grenade Blueprint from the Royal Conservatory	You can purchase Impact Grenades
Discreet Inquiry	Master Grenade Blueprint from Death to the Empress	Reduces Grenade noise
Sticky Grenade	Sticky Grenade Blueprint from the Dust District	You can purchase Sticky Grenades
Storage	None	Increases Grenade storage by two
The Expansive Lady	Master Grenade Blueprint from Death to the Empress	Expands Grenade blast radius

SPRING RAZOR UPGRADES

UPGRADE NAME	REQUIREMENTS	EFFECT
Double Slice	Spring Razor Double Slice Blueprint	Each Spring Razor works twice
Max Radius	None	Increases the damage radius of Spring Razors
Storage +2	None	Improves Spring Razor storage by 2

STUN MINE UPGRADES

UPGRADE NAME	REQUIREMENTS	EFFECT
Chain Lightning	Chain Lightning Blueprint From Clockwork Mansion	Hits enemies near the primary target when the Stun Mine goes off
Charge 1 and 2	None	Allows Stun Mines to function twice (and then three times if both upgrades are purchased)

SWORD UPGRADES

UPGRADE NAME	REQUIREMENTS	EFFECT
Crossing	None	Makes it easier to win when Swords get locked
Monkey Wrench	Master Sword Blueprint in Death to the Empress	Deals more damage against Clockwork Soldiers
Occult Kiss	Master Sword Blueprint in Death to the Empress	Deals more damage against magic-using enemies

Bonecharms

There are almost 100 Bonecharms in the game, not including those you craft on your own. This leaves a huge number of effects to improve Emily's and Corvo's stats. You get to equip several of these as soon as you get a collection together, and additional upgrades to your gear let you put on more and more of them.

Use Bonecharms to focus your build around your primary activities. Don't add effects for Health and combat if you're a stealth player; get Bonecharms that help with your Mana supply, movement, and ability to remain undiscovered. Similarly, combative players should focus on their Health, ability to kill quickly, and anything that improves their deadlier abilities.

Some Bonecharms have only a single effect, but others can have multiple effects (some of them negative). Look carefully at each as you decide what you need the most and what you're willing to sacrifice. Some negative effects might be irrelevant to your character, so these corrupted Bonecharms can still be incredibly powerful. For example, Shivering Silhouette lets you avoid ranged damage more often, but you are spotted more easily. This is absolute garbage for a stealth player. However, it's perfect for a combative player who doesn't care about being seen. If you like wading into battle, there is no tradeoff here to worry about.

Later in the game, you get enough Raw Whalebone and Runes to master Bonecharm Crafting and use it heavily. Crafting multiple Bonecharms with your favorite bonuses is incredibly powerful and allows you to make your character focus almost entirely on your preferred style of gameplay.

REGULAR BONECHARMS

BONECHARM NAME	EFFECT OF CHARM
Accommodating Host	Animal Possessions last longer
Acrobat	Increases your climbing speed
Agile Recovery	You recover from falls a bit faster
Agile Will	Possession lasts slightly longer
Albinos	Rat swarms include more White Rats
Aquatic Nature	Increases your swim speed
Assassin's Fortune	Bolt packs have a chance of restoring one extra Bolt
Bird of Prey	Restores some Health when you do a Drop Assassination
Bitter Blood	Bloodflies attack you only if you get really close to their nests
Blade Ballet	Spring Razors have a slight chance to destroy a victim's body
Blast Resistant	You receive less damage from explosions
Blood Sacrifice	Killing Bloodflies and Rats restores your Health
Carrion Killer	You gain Adrenaline from killing Rats and Bloodflies
Combustion	Your Grenades deal more damage
Deep Grave	Causes Gravehounds to sometimes die automatically when summoned
Duelist's Skill	Increases the damage of your Bullets
Electrical Burst	Increases the area of effect for your Stun Mines
Enduring Allies	Doppelgangers last longer
Exacting Aim	Increases the damage of your Bolts
Falling Star	Drop assassinations restore some Mana
Fencer	You win locked-Sword contests more often
Firestarter	Incendiary Bolts have a larger radius
Ground Glider	You slide faster
Gutter Feast	Consume White Rats to restore Mana
Healthy Appetite	Food restores more Health
Hot Cocktail	Exploding bottles deal slightly more damage
Leviathan's Mind	Regenerates Mana when you're underwater
Liquid Sustenance	Drinking from fountains restores a bit of Health
Lucky Needle	Raises your chance to recover Sleep and Confusion Darts
Relocation Sickness	Witches sometimes stumble after magical relocation
Resilient Allies	Doppelgangers have more health
Resounding Shriek	Howling Blasts are louder and have a larger radius
Restorative Glimmer	Health regenerates when using Dark Vision
Robust	Elixirs restore slightly more Health
Savage Scream	Nestkeeper's screams have a chance to kill all surrounding Bloodflies
Shadow Embrace	Shadow Walk lasts slightly longer

BONECHARM NAME	EFFECT OF CHARM
Spirit Water	Drinking from fountains restores a bit of Mana
Spirited	Elixirs restore slightly more Mana
Spiritual Fortune	Drinking and using Mana Elixirs sometimes restores you to full Mana
Spiritual Pool	Mana regenerates faster
Spiritual Sacrifice	Killing Bloodflies and Rats restores your Mana
Strong Arms	Enemies are choked faster
Strong Lungs	You can hold your breath longer underwater
Submerged Rage	You gain Adrenaline while underwater
Swift Shadow	Increases movement speed in stealth mode
Swift Stalker	Increases movement speed when your weapons are sheathed
Synergetic Swarm	Rat swarms last slightly longer
Tricky Timing	Enemy Grenades take longer to explode
Undertaker	You move a bit faster when carrying a body
Unfortunate Craftsmanship	Enemy Grenades sometimes malfunction
Unnerving Target	Enemies sometimes drop Grenades and debris at their feet; oops!
Unsteady Hand	Enemies have a greater chance to miss with their projectiles
Vengeance	You generate Adrenaline when you take melee damage from an enemy
Void Rapture	Sometimes enemies fall unconscious when Mesmerize ends
Whirlwind	Raises your Sword's attack speed

CORRUPTED BONECHARMS

BONECHARM NAME	EFFECT OF CHARM
Armored Bones	You take far less damage, but movement speed is reduced
Bright Moon	Doppelgangers deal more damage but last half as long
Clumsy Assassin	You gain invisibility briefly after knocking out or assassinating an enemy, but enemies can see and hear when you lean
High Pressure	Grenades, oil tanks, and bottles deal more damage but have a smaller blast radius
Lightweight	You take less damage from falling, but you lose half of your Health regeneration rate
Power Slash	Your Sword blows deal greater damage, but your Sword attacks are slower
Risky Parry	Your parries always throw enemies off balance, but you take more damage while parrying
Shivering Silhouette	Enemies miss more often at range, but you are more visible to enemies
Splintering Bolts	Bolts inflict far more damage, but they always break on impact
Stolen Breath	Pulling enemies with Far Reach is now quiet, but it consumes more Mana for all uses
Vengeance Trade	You accumulate Adrenaline faster
Void Winds	Windblast is more powerful, but costs more Mana
Witch's Skin	Taking damage drains your Mana before your Health
Zephyr	Raises your walking and running speed, but you take more damage

BLACK BONECHARMS

BONECHARM NAME	EFFECT OF CHARM
Bloodfly Alchemy	An enemy's first ranged attack turns into Bloodflies
Cornered Animal	You deal much more attack damage when your Health is low
Dark Extraction	Shadow Walk assassinations restore some of your Health
Expansive Spirit	Increases your maximum Mana
Fading Light	Far Reach and Blink cost zero Mana if used right after an assassination
Familiar Scent	Wolfhounds cannot smell your character
Fickle Beasts	White Wolfhounds fight on your side
Fleet Fighter	Your movement doesn't slow down when your weapons are unsheathed
Hardiness	Adds to your maximum Health
Invisible Thread	You are invisible during Far Reach movement
Iron Roots	You are much less likely to be knocked down
Leech Cuts	You gain Health when hitting people with your Sword or finishing assassinations
Leviathan's Breath	Running out of breath lowers your Mana before it starts lowering your Health
Lucky Jam	Enemy Pistols have a higher chance of misfiring
Mind Runner	You can sprint while inside human hosts during Possession
Separation Trauma	Enemies are rendered unconscious when you end Possession
Shadow Repose	You regain Health automatically during Shadow Walk
Solid Landing	A shockwave damages enemies and objects when you land after falling from a great height
Twin Leech	You regain Health while your Doppelganger is active
Undying Swarm	Rat swarms repopulate over time
Void Armor	Most of the damage you take is subtracted from Mana

THE SUPERNATURAL ARTS

This chapters goes into the details of your characters' supernatural abilities. We'll discuss them with an eye toward both stealthy and combative methods of gameplay.

HOW ABILITIES WORK

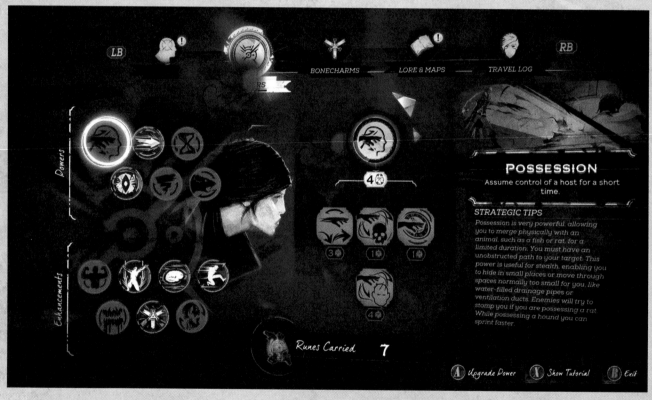

Abilities are purchased with Runes. You collect these on their own or from Outsider Shrines as you explore the game world. There are quite a few of these items, but you can't unlock everything in *Dishonored 2* in a single playthrough. Instead, you have to make tricky choices about what you need the most. This crafts a build that enhances a given style of play.

If you're a stealth person, for instance, don't waste Runes on aggressive combat abilities like Blood Thirst. Instead, focus on abilities that allow you to safely and easily avoid your enemies without getting their attention.

Shared abilities are common to Corvo and Emily. They function the same way and provide the same bonuses. Unique abilities for each character make their styles of survival inherently a bit different. Both can be stealthy or combative, but they do it in novel ways.

INTRO

STORY

CONTROLS

GAMEPLAY

WEAPONS, GADGETS, & BONECHARMS

THE SUPERNATURAL ARTS

ACHIEVEMEI

BLOOD THIRST

Build up Adrenaline in combat then trigger brutal melee fatalities.

STRATEGIC TIPS

With this enhancement, your actions in combat allow you to build up Adrenaline Assassination, attacking with a sword, parrying and drop assassination all increase Adrenaline. Once you've built up your Adrenaline, you can initiate a powerful sword attack that will kill an enemy with one blow.

Runes Carried	7
Cost	2

Once you have Runes, go into the Powers menu and look at everything your character can learn. Each has a cost between one and six Runes, so you often have to save up for the more powerful choices. Use these Runes to unlock the abilities you like the most, and always save the game before you do this. After trying out an ability, you might find it isn't much to your liking. When that happens, back up and use a previous save to try another purchase.

All abilities have secondary aspects that cost additional Runes. These secondary bonuses make the ability stronger and more versatile. It's usually best to have only a few abilities unlocked with as many bonuses as you can get. Trying to grab all the abilities at once leaves you underpowered.

SHARED ABILITIES

Dark Vision

Dark Vision is a massive aid to stealth characters. You can see through walls, detect guards, and plan your routes through an area without getting into trouble. This helps a little bit for combative players who want to set up ambushes, but it's far less impressive for them in comparison.

If you let your Mana regenerate properly, you don't end up losing Mana to cast Dark Vision. It's like Far Reach/Blink in that the cost is fully returned unless you cast another ability before you finish your regeneration period.

Note that Dark Vision updates every second or so, in a pulse. Give yourself time to see items that appear instead of sprinting through an area hoping to notice anything that you pass. It's better to move at a moderate speed and look around carefully.

GREATER DARK VISION

COST 3

This secondary bonus reveals objects and security systems when you're using Dark Vision. It's a substantial improvement, especially when you're searching levels thoroughly to find every little nook and cranny. Seeing security systems through walls helps a bit, but most of them are not subtle or hidden anyway.

Turn on Dark Vision after you've cleared an area to help discover valuable items that are hidden behind or inside objects. Your searches become both faster and more lucrative with Dark Vision on.

PREMONITION

COST 2

Enemy patrol routes show up when you're using Dark Vision. Once you know where people are and where they travel, this becomes unneeded. But when you're first learning a level, this makes Dark Vision especially valuable. Find a safe spot where you can't be detected, and use your Dark Vision in bursts to see a wide area of patrols and figure out the best ambush points.

Note that this makes Dark Vision a more visually confusing ability because you get tons of information on your screen. That makes it somewhat frustrating at times, so be careful about grabbing Premonition without saving ahead of time and testing it out for yourself.

Strength

Throw objects farther, with the potential to knock out targets even during combat if thrown objects hit them on the head. This niche ability doesn't usually fit into a major stealth or combat build. Stealth players don't want the risk of getting into combat at all, so half of the ability is worthless to them. Plus, throwing objects farther doesn't let you create particularly better ambushes. You normally want to distract targets and lure them into areas you control (not have them wander too far away and become another variable to worry about when they return).

Strength provides combative players with another tool, but there are far more potent abilities to use during combat. The only big perk for this is that it doesn't require any Mana, Bullets, or Bolts.

GREATER STRENGTH

COST 2

Destroy wooden barricades with basic Sword attacks. Again, this is a niche function that is fun but doesn't need to be part of your core build.

Vitality

This ability increases your base amount of Health. It's useful for combative players, who frequently take damage and have to survive long enough to drink an Elixir, flee, or finish their battle. Stealth players don't need this as much, because their actions are either successful or fail utterly, making extra Health somewhat moot. It's only good for them if they are mostly stealthy but don't care about Ghost and sometimes still get into fights.

GREATER VITALITY

COST 2

Health regenerates faster, and you regain more of your total Health without needing to resort to an Elixir. This is a modest bonus to add onto your Vitality, and should be taken later on if you're a combative player who has already finished with the major elements of your build.

Reflexes

Deflect incoming projectiles when you use your Sword to block. Ignore this if you're a stealth player, but take this every single time if you're a combative player. It's an inexpensive purchase that can save you from massive damage time and time again. You don't need to get all the associated secondary bonuses, but take this and use it whenever a distant enemy starts to bear down on you with a ranged weapon.

FOCUSED SLIDE

COST 2

No one can argue that this isn't a cool bonus to add onto your Reflexes. Time slows when you engage a slide while one of your precise ranged weapons is equipped. This gives you time to charge a group of enemies, slide into them, and take out a target easily before continuing the fight. It feels powerful, looks amazing, and has a high fun factor. This isn't particularly required for a good combative build, but you might want to take it anyway because it makes the game feel more epic.

SUPERIOR DEFLECT

COST 2

Bullets and Bolts can be parried into the nearest enemy target. Consider this heavily in the mid or late game when you start to face more and more groups of enemies with multiple shooters. This bonus is a good add-on to Reflexes because you're already going to make last-minute blocks to try and save yourself from ranged attacks. Instead of trying intentionally to hold back and

score kills with your deflections, think of this more as a bonus that sometimes happens as a result of your proper defensive play. In other words, don't hold back and wait for ranged enemies to attack you, hoping to get a deflection kill. Fight normally, block when the ranged attacks come, and be happy when the timing works out for a deflective parry. Don't give up your momentum in combat just to pull off these moves.

ADEPT PARRY

COST 1

Your parrying window is increased. This makes it much easier to pull off parries, and thus get easy counterattack kills. Because this is useful and inexpensive, it's a required element for a combative player unless you're so good at the game that you're already getting parries

almost every single time. For this low cost, it's still a must-have for almost every brawler.

SNAP REACTION

COST 3

Time slows heavily when an enemy first spots you. This is usually a combative ability (because stealth players don't get spotted much), yet combative players start larger fights that roll from target to target. You don't usually need the break to figure out a plan. You have a plan already; use your combative abilities to kill everything in the area. This bonus adds a quality-of-life improvement to your Reflexes, but it isn't worth three points early in the game, when you're still getting your most important abilities set up.

For stealth players that aren't trying for perfection, Snap Reaction gets more powerful. If you don't need to keep a Ghost rating, Snap Reaction allows you to quickly target a Guard that spots you. Hit them with a sudden Sleep Dart to avoid having a real fight break out. You save yourself from needing to survive a large rush, and use far fewer resources as a result.

Agility helps with your character's mobility, both in and out of combat. It's one of the few advantages that both major types of players might consider. This initial purchase gives you higher jumping. Several places in the game are harder to reach without Agility. It's a good idea to try out Agility (with Rapid Sprint) before you commit to it. This is more of a fun purchase rather than a necessary one, so make sure you like what you're getting before you spend all those Runes and continue with the story.

If you fall in love here, consider adding Far Reach/Blink upgrades to get the most out of your enhanced mobility.

RAPID SPRINT

COST...2

The speed of your sprint improves. This is useful for crossing cleared areas, charging distant foes without giving them time to react, and for making the game itself generally feel faster and more responsive. This Agility bonus is best for combative players. Stealth players can't normally afford to move out in the open this boldly (or to create that much noise). However, you can get some later game upgrades for silent sprinting. Once those are purchased Rapid Sprint becomes viable for stealth players. They'll be able to charge through safe areas, along rooftops, and anywhere else that keeps line of sight minimal.

CAT FALL

COST...1

Take less falling damage. This is not essential, but can be nice for impatient players who like to run off edges without taking the time to find safer routes.

Blood Thirst

COST 2

What the? Stop!

Build up Adrenaline during combat. Killing and parrying your enemies raises this internal stat. When it reaches its limit, the screen turns darker and you can automatically kill a target with a fast attack. Blood Thirst is fully in the combative line of abilities. Even there, it can be divisive. The autokill you gain is useful, and finishes large melee encounters that much faster. But Adrenaline's visual effects are distracting and take time to build. You don't get constant free kills out of the bonus. It's best for players who want to dedicate to their Sword-fighting. They'll get the most Adrenaline and thus the most free kills. Ranged killers should look elsewhere.

ADRENALINE BURST

COST...1

Adrenaline builds to mid-level when you're outside of combat. This means your first Adrenaline kill comes much earlier in each battle. If you get Blood Thirst at all, this bonus is absolutely necessary for getting the most out of it. You can get autokills even during smaller fights.

GREATER BLOOD THIRST

COST...3

Blood Thirst becomes stronger, allowing for two deadly swings. If you purchase all of Blood Thirst's bonuses, you end up putting six Runes into this line. That's quite a bit, so get the most out of it by specializing in Reflexes and Vitality, and then make sure you have good Bonecharms for melee combat and survival.

Bonecharm Crafting

If you want to make your own charms, this is a required ability. You're then able to take Raw Whalebone and carve it into Bonecharms that you have some control over. This is discussed in the Gameplay chapter of this guide.

TRAIT SYNERGY

COST 3

Use the same trait up to four times. This lets you focus heavily on the traits you need and enjoy the most.

WITCH CRAFTING

COST 2

This bonus lowers the chance that your Bonecharms will be corrupted. Corruption adds negative effects to your charms, so this is very useful once you get farther into the game and have more materials for making powerful charms. Pair this with Trait Synergy so that you can make incredibly strong Bonecharms. Almost all players should get this combo.

MASTER CRAFTING

COST 2

A charm with three traits has no chance of becoming corrupted. This also further lowers the chance of corruption for charms with four traits.

CRAFT RUNES

COST 4

Convert Runes into Raw Whalebone, or turn Raw Whalebone into Runes. This is a late-game powerhouse that really pays off if you're a good collector. People who have gotten a large amount of both Runes and Raw Whalebone can examine their build, find out which resource they have in excess, and convert it into the other. Expensive builds with tons of abilities benefit the most from this.

Shadow Kill

When you kill unaware enemies, they turn into ash. Shadow Kill is most effective for stealth players who want a Ghost run but don't care about Merciful status. It's not important for combative players because they're high Chaos under any real circumstance.

Shadow Kill is for players who don't want to be seen, but who are happy to slaughter their victims. In this context, Shadow Kill is nice because you don't have to worry about hiding bodies, or having them discovered. It's a big time-saver, and if you're really frugal with kills, it can keep your Chaos rating down a fair bit.

GREATER SHADOW

COST 2

Turn all enemies into ash when they die, so even enemies engaging you in direct combat disappear. This isn't a very powerful addition to your arsenal, because even Shadow Kill can't keep you from getting high Chaos if you're seen by tons of people and are fighting them out in the open.

BLOODFLY SWARM

COST 3

Slain enemies burst into Bloodflies that attack nearby foes. Though cool to watch, this is an expensive option for a line that isn't trying to be combative. Only go up this far if you think it's cool or fun. For pure utility, there are better uses for your Runes.

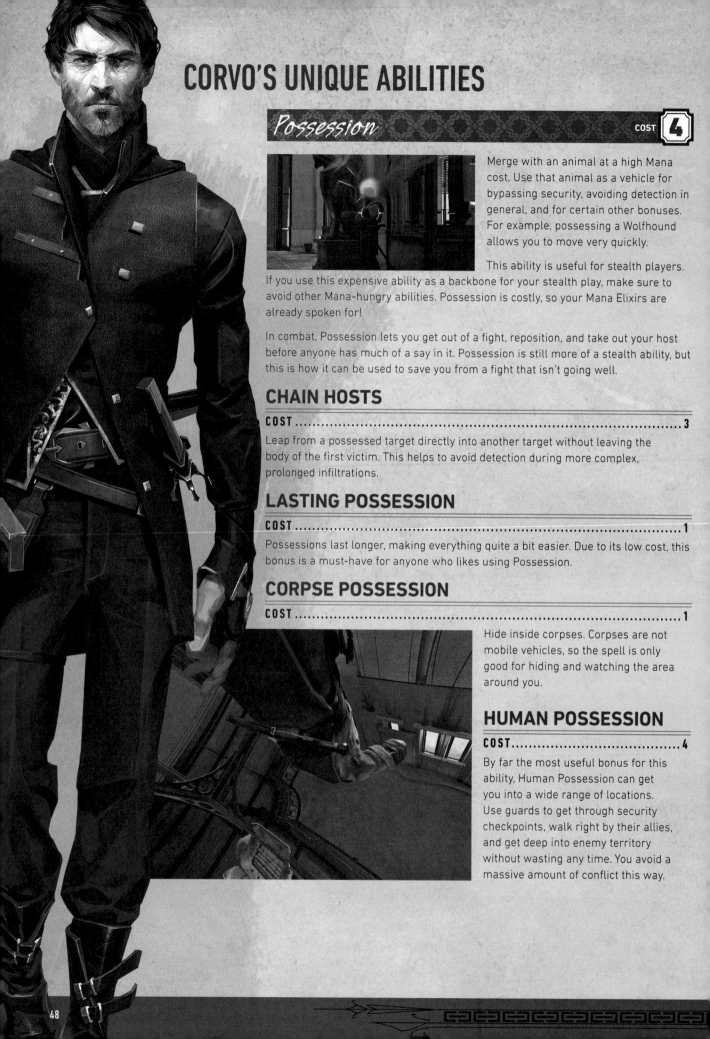

CORVO'S UNIQUE ABILITIES

Possession COST 4

Merge with an animal at a high Mana cost. Use that animal as a vehicle for bypassing security, avoiding detection in general, and for certain other bonuses. For example, possessing a Wolfhound allows you to move very quickly.

This ability is useful for stealth players. If you use this expensive ability as a backbone for your stealth play, make sure to avoid other Mana-hungry abilities. Possession is costly, so your Mana Elixirs are already spoken for!

In combat, Possession lets you get out of a fight, reposition, and take out your host before anyone has much of a say in it. Possession is still more of a stealth ability, but this is how it can be used to save you from a fight that isn't going well.

CHAIN HOSTS

COST...3

Leap from a possessed target directly into another target without leaving the body of the first victim. This helps to avoid detection during more complex, prolonged infiltrations.

LASTING POSSESSION

COST...1

Possessions last longer, making everything quite a bit easier. Due to its low cost, this bonus is a must-have for anyone who likes using Possession.

CORPSE POSSESSION

COST...1

Hide inside corpses. Corpses are not mobile vehicles, so the spell is only good for hiding and watching the area around you.

HUMAN POSSESSION

COST...4

By far the most useful bonus for this ability, Human Possession can get you into a wide range of locations. Use guards to get through security checkpoints, walk right by their allies, and get deep into enemy territory without wasting any time. You avoid a massive amount of conflict this way.

Blink

Blink is an amazing ability. Every character has some version of this, and it's never worthless. Blink gets you into hard-to-reach places, helps you avoid being spotted when you're out in the open, and helps you quickly move around the world.

Hold down the Ability button when Blink is selected. Watch for the icon that appears ahead; that shows you where you're going to Blink. Aim carefully so that you get where you want to go. This lets you Blink down and avoid falling damage, Blink up to higher balconies, or Blink behind people. The uses are myriad.

GREATER BLINK

COST 4

Extend the range of Blink. This is expensive, but you get so much out of Blink that it's really worth taking for most players. Some combative players can skip this, because they'll focus more on deadly abilities. But players who like to kill with assassination attacks can often clear an entire room with good Blinking. Because of that, even killers enjoy Greater Blink unless they're intentionally getting into large Sword fights.

REDIRECTIVE BLINK

COST 3

Time stops as long as you stand still while aiming your Blink spells. This is helpful when making more complex maneuvers, like Blinking during a fall or a fight, or when jumping, turning, and Blinking around a corner.

You can set up some amazing drop assassinations/takedowns with this ability.

BLINK ASSAULT

COST 1

For players who aren't afraid of kills, this is a wonderful bonus. Blink and automatically knock down alerted targets or assassinate unaware victims. The latter is ludicrously nice when combined with Shadow Kill—Blink, attack, and have a target go down into ash in almost no time. This allows you to get in, kill targets, and leave before anyone has a chance to turn around and see what you're doing.

Bend Time

This versatile ability improves your survivability, lethality, and stealth. It's a cornerstone of either stealth or combative builds, but you have to dedicate a huge number of points to it. As such, this requires a sacrifice. If you use Bend Time heavily, avoid other expensive purchases like Possession, because it takes way too long to get both of them off the ground. Using both is also rough on your Mana!

Use Bend Time during big fights to give yourself time to destroy your targets, reposition, and avoid incoming attacks and ranged fire. For stealth, Bend Time when your enemies aren't looking and quickly cross through protected areas without being seen. Use a thrown object to get people looking one way, and then Bend Time and move in another direction to cross a large distance without anyone being the wiser.

STOP TIME

COST 6

Other people and objects don't move at all during Bend Time. It's possible to advance time within the spell, if you need people to continue moving; otherwise, the world around you is frozen unless you interact with it.

For combative players, this is an unnecessary luxury. You already gain a massive edge by slowing time, so the six Runes this bonus costs are often better spent elsewhere. Stop Time is a much greater benefit for stealth players because you don't have to worry nearly as much about messing up while under the effect of Bend Time.

LASTING BEND TIME

COST 2

If you purchase Bend Time, get this bonus. Every use of Bend Time is expensive, and you must get the most out of it. Longer duration means you can avoid bigger areas, defeat larger groups of enemies, etc. There is no reason not to get this bonus.

RELATIVITY

COST 1

Your movement, relative to the slower or frozen people around you, is much faster. Like Lasting Bend Time, this is a must-have bonus for anyone who uses Bend Time.

Windblast

Use wind to deflect slower projectiles, shatter doors, and throw enemies around. This gives you time to recover in the middle of a big melee, and it also causes quite a bit of noise and distraction. Useful more often for heavy combative purposes, this is a good ability for people who like to fight larger battles out in the open. Once you upgrade Windblast with its bonuses, you gain an ability that is lethal, defensive, and knocks around targets in a moderate area of effect.

GREATER WINDBLAST

COST. 3

Windblast deals lethal damage against targets thrown into anything. Go around bends in a corridor so that pursuing enemies clump together near a wall, and then hit them with Windblast as they approach.

SHOCKWAVE

COST. 3

Windblast becomes a modest area-of-effect attack. If you become surrounded during a fight, this is one of the best ways to clear out opponents and buy yourself time to flee or at least kill a couple more enemies and regain the advantage.

Devouring Swarm

Devouring Swarm is a fun, thematic power. Call a swarm of Rats that attack your enemies (if any targets are present). The Rats are lethal to individuals or small groups, and they are also a massive distraction against those targets, who have to fight for their lives. If you have Possession, you are allowed to use summoned Rats as targets.

In general, Devouring Swarm is a fun combative ability. You usually get more oomph from other combative powers, but not all of them are as flashy.

GREATER SWARM

COST 2

Your swarm grows in size, making it more likely to kill multiple targets with a single use.

RAT PIPER

COST 2

Your swarm follows you, giving it a bit more utility by chaining between multiple small encounters.

TWIN SWARMS

COST 3

If you want to throw an entire room into anarchy, this bonus makes Devouring Swarm much more effective. You get to choose two areas where the swarms appear, so they attack more people and cover more territory. This is best used in large rooms that have defenders in various positions that you can't overwhelm quickly. Distract or kill two groups with your spell, and charge any other targets to kill them on your own while your Rat buddies do the rest of the work.

EMILY'S UNIQUE ABILITIES

Domino

COST **4**

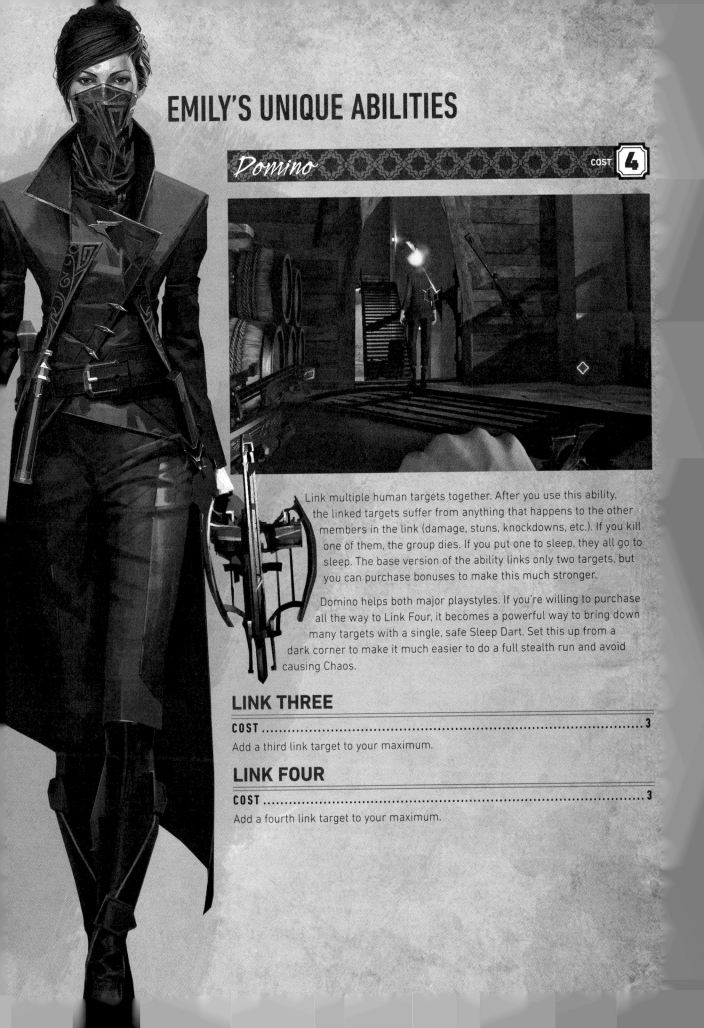

Link multiple human targets together. After you use this ability, the linked targets suffer from anything that happens to the other members in the link (damage, stuns, knockdowns, etc.). If you kill one of them, the group dies. If you put one to sleep, they all go to sleep. The base version of the ability links only two targets, but you can purchase bonuses to make this much stronger.

Domino helps both major playstyles. If you're willing to purchase all the way to Link Four, it becomes a powerful way to bring down many targets with a single, safe Sleep Dart. Set this up from a dark corner to make it much easier to do a full stealth run and avoid causing Chaos.

LINK THREE

COST 3

Add a third link target to your maximum.

LINK FOUR

COST 3

Add a fourth link target to your maximum.

Doppelganger

Cast this spell to summon a Doppelganger of yourself. The shadow distracts enemies, can trigger alarms, and gets into trouble by running away until it's killed. At that point, the enemies in the area return to their previous patrols. Use that distraction time to slip through areas unmolested. This is a decent stealth ability, but the bonuses you get later on turn it into a much more combative choice.

Unless enemies see both you and your Doppelganger, they'll assume that all is well after your clone dies. This causes them to return to their posts as soon as the clone falls.

BAFFLING SHADE

COST 1

Your Doppelganger's death causes confusion for several seconds in a moderate area of effect. This gives you even more time to leave the area and avoid detection. It's quite helpful for stealth, but it also gives you a moment to attack your enemies if you're using the Doppelganger aggressively.

TRANSPOSITION

COST 2

Trade places with your Doppelganger. It's tricky to use this bonus to its fullest. With considerable setup time, you can create your Doppelganger, rush into foes, kill a few, and then switch places. Then, start sneaking again to get easier kills as the guards return home with reduced numbers, thinking all is well.

DEADLY SHADE

COST 3

Here is a very strong bonus for Doppelgangers. They kill unaware targets and fight to protect themselves. They become a longer, deadlier distraction. Send one of them to kill enemies who haven't seen you yet, and use this time to flank the victims. Murder them from behind as they rush to aid their allies under attack from the Doppelganger.

TWIN SHADES

COST 3

Finish off the Doppelganger line with Twin Shades. As a trio, you and your shadows can fight massive groups of opponents. This is an incredibly powerful crowning piece of a combative build for Emily.

Shadow Walk

Reduce the range at which enemies realize you're a threat. Move without being detected unless you get very close to your targets or spend a huge amount of time out in the open. Shadow Walk is a great purchase for stealth purposes, and gets to be a wonderful assassination tool as well. If you mix Shadow Walk and Shadow Kill, Emily becomes a silent killer who has little trouble wading through targets without direct battles. For non-lethal play, Shadow Walk, Shadow Run, and Rat Shadows provide better methods for traversing areas without knocking out and hiding as many guards.

Normally, you pop out of Shadow Walk after killing/disabling one target. However, this ability has bonuses that let you increase that number. The minor unavoidable downside is that Shadow Walk changes your perspective. Emily gets low to the ground in this form, and that makes it harder to see around her. If that is a problem for your style of play, avoid this ability.

Note that Shadow Walk is also a powerful tool for non-lethal takedowns. Because you can avoid detection and take out targets without killing them, this ability is a very nice choice for Merciful players.

IMPROVED SHADOW ATTACK

COST 2

Kill or incapacitate two targets before popping out of Shadow Walk.

RAT SHADOWS

COST 1

Move through Rat tunnels while Shadow Walking. This enables Emily to bypass more enemies through several sections of the game. Ignore this if you're a combative player, but purchase it eagerly if you prefer full stealth.

SHADOW RUN

COST 2

Your movement speed is increased while you use Shadow Walk.

GREATER SHADOW ATTACK

COST 2

Kill or knock out up to three targets before leaving Shadow Walk.

Mesmerize

Completely enthrall and distract up to two nearby targets (upgradable to four with bonuses). You gain more than enough time to then murder the targets or hurry past without them remembering you were ever there. Due to the high cost of this spell and its bonuses, you're best off taking this for stealth purposes. There are cheaper and easier methods for killing people. Instead, use Mesmerize to distract enemy checkpoints or rooms of targets as you wander through.

Merciful players get many benefits from being able to distract groups of targets using this ability. It's a solid choice if you don't fall in love with Shadow Walk. Both of them are reliable!

MESMERIZE THREE

COST 3

Influence up to three targets.

LASTING MESMERIZE

COST 2

This bonus ncreases the duration that targets are mesmerized.

MESMERIZE FOUR

COST 3

Influence up to four targets.

Far Reach

Far Reach is similar to Blink. It's learned early in the story and helps constantly as you travel around the world. Use this to reach out-of-the-way places, set up attacks on unaware targets, or get out of trouble during battles. Far Reach is wonderful whether you're interested in stealth or fighting.

Far Reach has a somewhat different feel compared to Blink. You don't disappear and reappear at your target location. Instead, you aim Far Reach at a specific object and then trigger it. You're then kind of pulled toward the object, arriving very quickly. Enemies can certainly spot you when doing this, so avoid their line of sight whenever possible. During battle, they'll turn if you Far Reach behind them, because they can see you pass by them.

If you walk or run forward before Far Reaching, you can get more distance out of it. This technique is effective for crossing large gaps or fleeing from enemies.

PULL OBJECTS

COST 2

Bodies and inanimate objects are pulled over toward Emily. Step aside to have them zip past you, or catch the object as it arrives.

DECELERATE

COST 2

Time pauses if you start to fall while using Far Reach. This gives you time to aim carefully and either land safely or teleport to a distant ledge.

PULL ENEMIES

COST 4

Your Pull Objects bonus applies to enemies as well. You can kill or knock out the people you grab this way, but it's a costly maneuver. You need quite a few extra Runes to get to this point, but you gain a valuable combative power as a result. Pull Enemies doesn't cost any more Mana than Far Reach's base ability. As such, all your Mana regenerates afterward if you have enough time to let it reset. With this in mind, use Pull Enemies during battle to get practically free kills. Fight normally and let your Mana regenerate in between, and repeat to make your fights much easier.

ENEMIES OF THE CROWN

It's always wise to know your enemies. In *Dishonored 2*, there are many categories of foes, each with their own strengths and weaknesses. We discuss these here so that you have a good understanding of the tactics you need to survive. We talk about techniques that defeat enemies regardless of the supernatural abilities you choose, which means you can use these methods with any character build.

GUARD

Health: Moderate	Weapons: Sword	Special Attacks: None

Regular Guards don't have much Health or armor, so they don't take many hits to kill. Any type of assassination kills them instantly, and you can also parry and counterattack to eliminate them without much fuss.

At range, Guards are defenseless. They have to close the gap and engage you in melee combat. This means shots from your Pistol or Crossbow have a major advantage and can kill Guards before they respond. Use this to thin the ranks of groups by killing one or two of them at range while you back up and lead the rest into a narrow area where their superior numbers can't be used against you.

You only get into serious trouble with Guards if there are multiple attacks on your flanks. This makes it hard to block them, and your character can take damage quickly. Instead of fighting to the bitter end, use Blink/Far Reach to flash out of the way and get to range while you look for a better place to fight.

Later in the game, you start seeing Guards with extra armor on their chests or head. This protects them against some of your ranged attacks. Avoid shooting at the armor, whenever possible. Helmets can be knocked off with a first shot, leaving the target vulnerable to a lethal second blast.

ELITE GUARD

Health: Decent	Weapons: Sword and Pistol	Special Attacks: None

Elite Guards have red coats to show their greater status in the military. These enemies fight similarly to Guards, but they carry Pistols and are better at blocking to protect themselves. You can't easily spam Sword attacks against them, because they avoid the damage and sometimes parry you, leaving your character exposed to counterattacks. To win in melee, you must learn to fight defensively yourself! Wait for them to attack, parry their blows, and counter with instant kills. That's how it's done!

Preferably, kill the Elite Guards in a group before they set up a substantial melee defense against you. Accomplish this by assassinating Elite Guards before they're aware of your presence. If there are six targets in a room, use your initial assassination attacks on these enemies even if they're harder to reach than generic Guards.

Ranged attacks are still effective against Elite Guards. Pistol shots to the head kill them instantly, and Crossbow attacks are wonderful too. If you're discovered before you assassinate the Elite Guards, equip your Pistol and shoot these enemies in the middle of your skirmish. Stay close while doing this so that you can dispatch them with your Sword if you miss the headshot and only wound them.

Elites wearing helmets are called Veterans. They're similar in fighting style to usual Elites, but they're certainly harder to get with headshots. They'll also have Explosive Bullets for their Pistols. This makes it easier for them to hit and hurt your character.

Always remember to search Elites' bodies. They're better paid and frequently have money or Bullets.

OVERSEER

| Health: Moderate | Weapons: Sword and Either Pistol or Grenades | Special Attacks: None |

Overseers are the people who hunt down heretics and apostates within the nation. They're violently opposed to the use of Bonecharms, belief in the Outsider, and anything that seems too magical in nature.

Spot Overseers by the masks they wear. They're often found in groups, investigating buildings where Runes might be hidden. It's good news to see Overseers, because it usually means treasure is close by.

Overseers attack you on sight. They have Swords and either Pistols or Grenades, so either engage them in direct melee combat, or use speed to shoot them before they shoot you. Failing that, retreat around corners so that Overseers don't have the chance to shoot at you from long range. That way, they have to approach your area, losing the advantage of their ranged weapons.

If you invest in Reflexes and take Superior Deflect, you gain the option to parry Bullets and Bolts. This really helps to limit your risk when you fight groups of Overseers. Even Reflexes by itself makes your life much easier. Block when you see Overseers aiming at you, and then re-engage as soon as you block their attacks.

Aim for the body when you shoot Overseers; their masks are extremely well-made, so headshots don't take them down. Instead, use faster shots to ensure you disrupt your targets easily, and then kill them with follow-up melee strikes.

Warfare Overseers appear late in the game; they're the ones with music boxes made to counter those with the Mark of the Outsider. Your abilities get disrupted in a wide circle of effect around Warfare Overseers. If you get closer and are in front of them, you take damage as well. These are always primary targets for assassination or avoidance because they're such a pain for you. If you have to fight them, use heavier weapons (Special Crossbow Bolts, repeated Pistol shots, etc.). Major attacks can disrupt the Overseers' music.

WOLFHOUND

| Health: Low | Weapons: Bite | Special Attacks: Grapple, strong sense of smell |

Wolfhounds are deployed to patrol areas and sniff out intruders. They're fast and extremely aggressive once they detect someone. It's not wise to play defensively against them; they attack too quickly and hold on to you if they get a chance. Wolfhounds are doubly effective when Guards come forward at the same time. You're soon flanked and killed.

Avoid that scenario by attacking Wolfhounds without mercy. They can't dodge or block your Sword strikes, so they drop quickly under your assault. Use your Pistol as well to kill incoming Wolfhounds at range before they become a threat. By taking the initiative, you are able to stop the beasts and then focus on any of their handlers in a more traditional fight.

Remember that Wolfhounds are able to smell intruders, so they detect you by sight, sound, and smell. If they get close to your position, either attack or Blink away so that they don't realize you're there.

GRAVEHOUND

| Health: Low | Weapons: Bite | Special Attacks: Grapple, strong sense of smell |

Gravehounds fight like Wolfhounds, except they look a bit smoky and magical. In addition, they respawn after six seconds. This makes them a huge threat if you don't know what to do. Destroy the skull that appears when a Gravehound goes down. Pick it up and throw it, or smash the skull directly as soon as you can. This prevents the resurrection.

Sleep Darts don't work on Gravehounds, so they're even more of a pain for stealth players. Avoid the entire areas where these dogs are wandering, or wait until they're isolated. Then, shoot them with a regular Crossbow Bolt to get a kill. Crush the skull, and move away. No body will be left behind, and Gravehounds (like all animals) don't count against your kill tally. So you won't get any extra Chaos.

NESTKEEPER

| Health: Very High | Weapons: Fist | Special Attacks: Call Bloodflies |

Nestkeepers are uncommon enemies only found inside Bloodfly-infested buildings. The higher your Chaos rating is, the more you see these terrifying foes. They aren't attacked by Bloodflies, for whatever reason, so they move among the nests and talk to their disease-ridden friends.

If they detect your character, they charge you immediately and make weak melee attacks against you. However, they also alert the Bloodflies in the area. The insects swarm and do substantial damage over time if you can't get away or deal with the threat. To make matters worse, Nestkeepers explode into a swarm of Bloodflies if you sever their arms in melee combat. Between this and their high Health, it's just not worth getting into close range with these monsters.

It's usually effective to hit Nestkeepers at range before they see you. They almost never appear in groups, with two Nestkeepers being a "large" encounter for their kind. That makes them easy to kill with a Bolt or knock out with a Sleep Dart before they see you. The Bloodflies won't freak out about that.

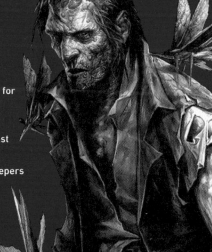

Then, destroy the nests in the area, loot the building, and move on without fear.

Bloodbriars appear in areas that have a Witch presence. They are animated plants that can detect and attack your character. They're defenseless at any decent range and can be killed with Bolts or Bullets. Up close, Sword strikes work well against them, but you have to dodge their swiping attacks to avoid damage.

Sidestep to dodge Bloodbriar vertical attacks, and jump if they try a horizontal swipe. A strong offense makes it much easier to win, because it only takes a couple of hits to lay the Bloodbriar low.

CLOCKWORK SOLDIER

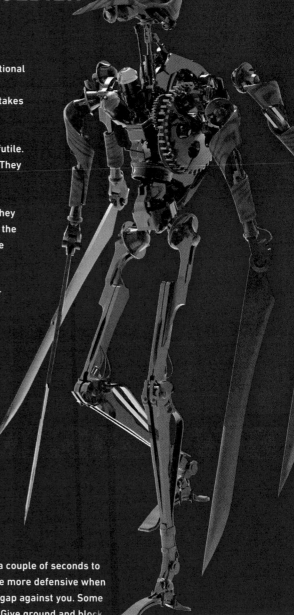

Health: Special   Weapons: Claws   Special Attacks: None

Clockwork Soldiers are powerful opponents. They aren't killed by many conventional attacks without a great deal of setup. A Drop assassination is the only type of assassination that works against them. Even then, the first Drop assassination takes out the head, and you need a second Drop assassination to finish the job.

Attacks that try to disrupt, blind, or put the Clockwork Soldiers to sleep are all futile. So too are abilities that try to disorient the machines. They can't be possessed. They don't feel pity, or remorse, or fear.

When sneaking around Clockwork Soldiers, avoid both of their cones of sight. They see directly in front of themselves AND behind as well. Their blind spots are on the flanks. Also, you can't see these guys with regular Dark Vision; because they are security devices, you need Greater Dark Vision to detect them.

Kill Clockwork Soldiers with Drop assassinations, by destroying all four of their arms, or by taking out the Whale Oil Tanks on their backs. Given time and some stealth, you can also open up their security panels and use a Rewire Tool on them. This turns a Clockwork Soldier into your friend. They avoid attacking you, and will go after any of your enemies (including other Clockwork Soldiers).

To destroy the head and arms on these enemies, target those areas directly with Sword strikes or ranged attacks. The armor paneling breaks off rather quickly, and then you can sever the limb. If the head gets severed, Clockwork Soldiers can't see. They then attack based on sound alone. If you use thrown objects, you can get them to run off or attack other targets. Standing on tables lets you target the soldiers' heads in melee without needing to get above them.

A pair of Stun Mines also does the trick. These weapons disable Clockwork Soldiers. Save Stun Mines for Clockwork Soldier encounters.

During battle, Clockwork Soldiers stop to vent heat periodically. This gives you a couple of seconds to attack them aggressively. Make your shots count while the machines recover. Be more defensive when they return to full power. Clockwork Soldiers have a leaping attack to close the gap against you. Some of them have four arms, and these soldiers also have a wicked spinning attack. Give ground and block to defend yourself while avoiding these heavier strikes.

Health: Moderate	Weapons: Sword, Crossbow (not always)	Special Attacks: Howling Bolts

Howlers are a strong gang of criminals who operate out of Karnaca. They're at constant odds with the Overseers, who violently stomp out most gangs. Your character has problems with the Overseers too, but the Howlers aren't overly sympathetic. They're nasty folks.

Thus, you often have trouble with the Howlers. All of them are adequate Sword users, but most of them also have Crossbows they use at range. You take Bolts from them as well as occasional Howler Bolts. This gives your enemies a chance to disrupt your hearing and sight with each ranged strike. Masked Howlers usually have a hallucinogenic powder as well. They toss that at you with similar disrupting results.

Negate this either by knocking out Howlers before combat so that their numbers are highly limited, or by using blocking and superior Reflexes to protect yourself from these attacks. If a Howling Bolt hits you, back away while you give the effect time to fade. Take cover to avoid additional strikes, and recommence the battle when the Howlers come after you.

It's easy to tell which areas of the city are under Howler control. The game is named for the constant yelling and howling they do to intimidate civilians and Overseers alike. If you hear people yelling like that, you know Howlers are on the prowl.

WANTED
HOWLERS

WITCH

Health: Decent	Weapons: Sword	Special Attacks: Teleport, magical spells

You only see Witches in a few parts of the game. That's good, because they're troublesome to deal with. All Witches can teleport, so they sometimes guard areas that are higher up or otherwise difficult to reach. They're harder to knock out with a takedown in these cases, so bring plenty of Sleep Darts.

Up close, Witches rely on Swords to attack, block, and dodge. They don't have the skill to parry and counterattack, so they're not too deadly as long as you're good at your own defensive techniques.

Each individual Witch has a second type of spell they'll mix in with their teleportation and swordplay. They can either shriek to disrupt your character, fire spikes at range, or summon a Bloodbriar so you have to deal with those nasty plants in addition to the Witch.

If stealth fails and a major fight breaks out, use Pistol and Crossbow attacks to punish Witches after they teleport. Swing your blade and press the fight to your advantage, and then immediately fire a shot if your enemies try to escape with their magic.

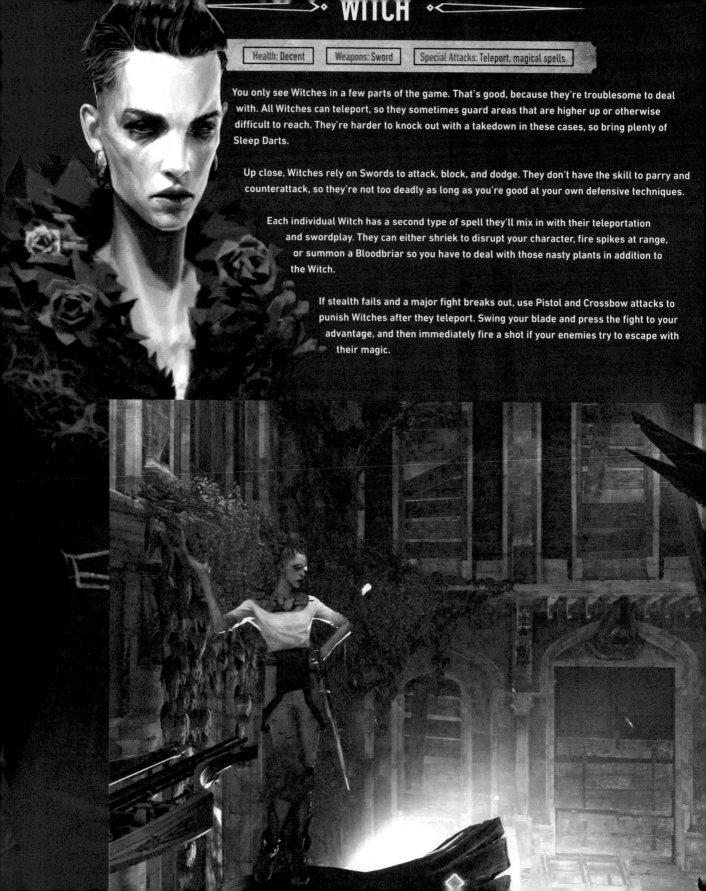

THE INNOCENT

Health: Low	Weapons: Sword or none	Special Attacks: None

All sorts of civilians inhabit each part of Dunwall and Karnaca. These are not your targets or your enemies unless you make them such. At worst, these are more people who might detect you and get you into trouble with the soldiers of the area.

Some civilians, like Beggars, are practically on your side. They don't summon Guards even if you cause trouble around them. At most, they flee.

Shopkeepers and house owners are a tier of threat up from that. They don't aggressively seek to cause you trouble, but they absolutely go to the Guards or Elites if they see you for too long or if you do anything extreme around them. Don't use takedowns or abilities in their presence. If they start to look at you for too long and say anything, walk away. Staying in their line of sight for a long time triggers a problem.

Workers are the most dangerous type of civilian because they're armed. If they freak out around you because you bump into them too much or stay near them too long, they may draw their weapons. In that case, flee or fight them.

Avoid all these problems by keeping violence away from civilians, and by moving past civilians quickly and quietly. This isn't their struggle, and you have no need to drag them down into it.

DANGEROUS ANIMALS

Health: Very low	Weapons: Bite	Special Attacks: None

Several types of violent animals inhabit Dunwall and Karnaca. Most of them aren't a huge threat, but it's still important to know what they are.

Bloodflies infest areas filled with disease and death. The creatures lay their eggs inside people, and a new generation of these monsters bursts forth after a short period. By the time you find an infested area, it'll have nests all over the place.

Bloodflies attack anything that gets too close to their nests. They do a fair amount of damage over time as they bite at you in swarms. Swinging your blade dispatches them, but it takes many blows to get all the individual Bloodflies. Cutting them down with melee attacks is more of a last resort than a solid strategy.

Instead, use bottles of alcohol to blow up nests and burn the Bloodflies. Pistol shots are also effective at range. If you can't find any of these items, rush up to a nest and destroy it with a couple of Sword strikes. Then, run away while the Bloodflies disperse. You take damage from doing this, but if you're really fast, it won't be that much and the area becomes safer to travel in the future.

Note that Bloodflies do not count against you in terms of Chaos or a loss of your Merciful rating. You can kill them at any time, because they're absolutely horrible creatures and you're doing a good deed by destroying them.

Some types of Fish are aggressive too. If you're in deep water, they attack you and do a modest bit of damage. Get out of the water as soon as you can to minimize this. Don't try to fight the Fish. Areas with carnivorous Fish will eat bodies you throw into the water. If you need something disposed of, that's always an option.

And speaking of flesh-eating, there are the Rats. They eat bodies, and swarms of the creatures even attack adult humans. Stay at range, and

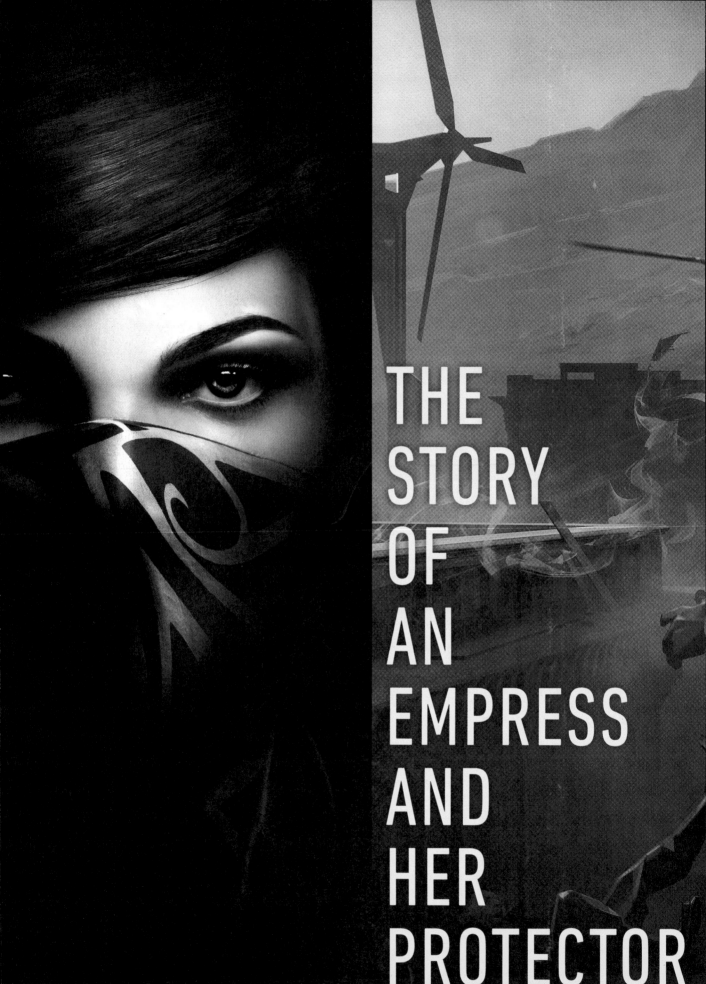

THE
STORY
OF
AN
EMPRESS
AND
HER
PROTECTOR

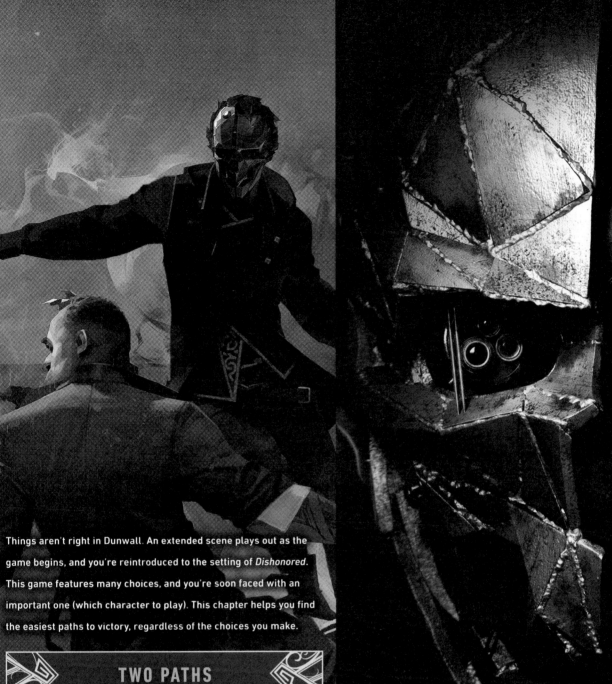

Things aren't right in Dunwall. An extended scene plays out as the game begins, and you're reintroduced to the setting of *Dishonored*. This game features many choices, and you're soon faced with an important one (which character to play). This chapter helps you find the easiest paths to victory, regardless of the choices you make.

 ## TWO PATHS

This chapter delivers two full Walkthroughs through the game. The first one lets you complete the story without harming anyone. It's a very low Chaos style that ensures you get the happiest conclusion. It emphasizes stealth, non-lethal solutions, and heavy supernatural-ability use. We play as Emily Kaldwin in this section.

The second run is bloody. It focuses on high Chaos, weapon use, gadgets, and doesn't even consider the word "mercy." Vengeance will be ours. We suggest you play the game at least twice so you get the full experience of both styles, because they change many aspects of the story. We play as Corvo Attano in this section.

A Long Day in Dunwall

Today marks the anniversary of the death of Empress Jessamine Kaldwin, assassinated 15 years ago. Visitors from across the Empire of the Isles have journeyed to Dunwall Tower for the occasion.

COLLECTIBLES

Runes	N/A (1 from the Void, after the Mission)
Shrines	N/A
Bonecharms	N/A
Coins	1490
Blueprints	N/A
Paintings	2

SPECIAL ACTIONS

Freedom of the Press	Go to the upper level of the Dunwall Courier and knock out the Guard there before he slaughters the paper's editor
Jessamine's Words	Play an Audiograph from the old Empress
Time Capsule	Find a room boarded up since the Rat Plague
Coin of the Realm	Take the gold from the safe inside the tower's Safe Room
Dr. Galvani's Safe	Open the safe inside Dr. Galvani's laboratory and take its contents
The Ramsey Fortune	Lock Mortimer Ramsey inside the Safe Room

STEALTH WALKTHROUGH

Take a calm breath and begin your quiet pursuits. Justice is nothing without compassion, so we use a gentle hand to uncover the truth and save our family. Instead of fighting, we use guile, deception, and patience as our most powerful weapons.

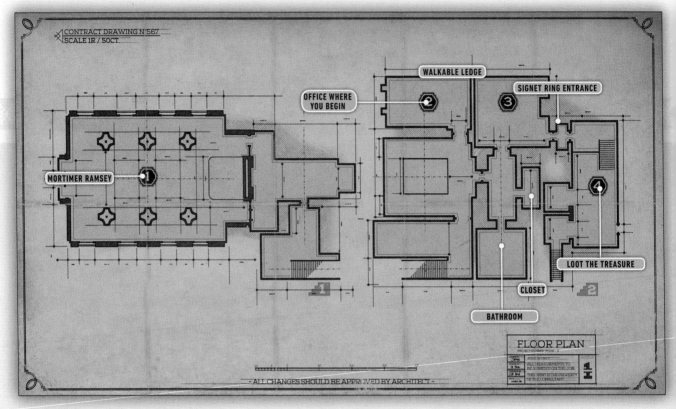

CONTRACT DRAWING N°567
SCALE 1R / 50CT.

WALKABLE LEDGE

OFFICE WHERE YOU BEGIN

②

③

SIGNET RING ENTRANCE

MORTIMER RAMSEY

④

LOOT THE TREASURE

CLOSET

BATHROOM

FLOOR PLAN

ALL CHANGES SHOULD BE APPROVED BY ARCHITECT

DUNWALL TOWER

Escape the Imperial Chambers

Select Emily Kaldwin as your character during the introduction. Observe the scene in the throne room and wait to get control of your character. You're brought to a small room in the upper level of Dunwall Tower. That is where our game truly begins.

Look around the room when you have control of your character. There are several items of food close by. Eat all of those to regain your health. You also get to read some Documents on the desk.

Look for a window on the far side of the room. Open it and climb out. Sneak over to another window farther down. The first window you reach is locked, but the second one is wide open. Crawl into it.

Check on Alexi Mayhew

You're now in the adjoining hallway. Alexi Mayhew is on the ground close to you.

She's in horrible shape and won't last long. Talk to her. You get yourself a blade, though you don't need it. Afterward, look in the bottom of the cupboards for some spare change. You may be Empress, but it looks like you need everything you can get your hands on. There is also an Audience Request lying next to Alexi.

Knock Out Mortimer Ramsey

Start creeping down the hall. There's a bathroom at the other end. You don't find much of importance there, but a few items are worth money. You can also listen to an Audiograph Corvo left.

Sneak into the other room along the main hall. A Guard there has his back turned. Creep up to him and choke him out. This takes much longer than assassination, so remember to be careful if your target is observed by anyone else. In this case, you're totally in the clear.

Grab the Key from the Guard's body once he's down. Stay crouched, because another Guard is close enough to hear if you make any loud noises. Unlock the room to your right; that's where you were being held earlier, and now you can go back and forth at leisure.

Then look for the stairs that lead down, and take those. Sneak up on the lower level's Guard and choke him as well. Either wait until he turns away, or make enough noise to lure him toward you while you're beside the doorway or around a corner. With a quick ambush, you can knock him unconscious without being spotted.

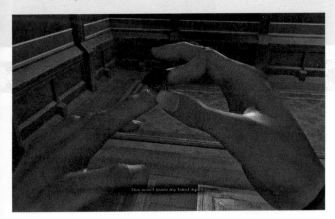

Open the door that leads away from the Guard's room and into the throne room. Mortimer Ramsey and two Guards are inside, but they're farther into the chamber and can't see you enter. Hide behind the pillars on the right while they talk, and then wait for Mortimer to split off from the other two men. He walks over to the door you used to enter the room. Stay crouched behind those pillars until he's fully past you. Then sneak up to him and knock him out. Loot his body for your Signet Ring afterward.

Open the Safe Room

Carry Mortimer out of the room. Go back upstairs. The entrance to your Safe Room is near the beginning of the area, near Alexi. Use your Signet Ring to unlock the Safe Room, and go inside. Drop Mortimer there. Use the button by the door to lock Mortimer in the room so he can't wake up and escape later.

Search the room for the following:

▶ **Health Elixir**

▶ **Documents to read**

▶ **Bullets (3)**

▶ **Your Pistol**

▶ **Spyglass**

▶ **Money from a safe**

When you have everything, exit the tower. A door at the other end of the Safe Room takes you out toward the streets.

DUNWALL STREETS

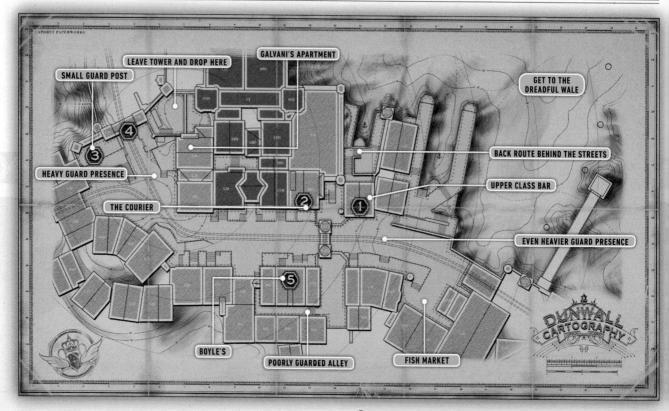

- LEAVE TOWER AND DROP HERE
- GALVANI'S APARTMENT
- SMALL GUARD POST
- GET TO THE DREADFUL WALE
- **4**
- **3**
- HEAVY GUARD PRESENCE
- BACK ROUTE BEHIND THE STREETS
- UPPER CLASS BAR
- THE COURIER
- **2**
- **1**
- EVEN HEAVIER GUARD PRESENCE
- **5**
- DUNWALL CARTOGRAPHY
- BOYLE'S
- POORLY GUARDED ALLEY
- FISH MARKET

Reach the Streets

Exit the tower and go through a short passage with a couple of books and some coins. A collectible **Painting** hangs on the right side of the passage. Unlock the door at the end of the route and head into the fresh air.

Carefully descend from the tower, using the ledges on your right to drop lower without taking any damage on the way. A lone Guard is below, farther down. Use a non-lethal takedown from above against him. A tutorial pops up to advise you that this is a good spot to practice it.

DROP TAKEDOWNS

The biggest advantage of Drop takedowns is they're way faster than normal chokeouts. When you can afford to set up these dropping attacks, they're very effective. They also break your fall, preventing damage to Emily.

Go over the next wall and drop onto a lighting rig on the other side so you can observe the men in the streets nearby. You find many Guards here, so it's time to get cautious again.

Reach the Boat

You don't have any supernatural abilities yet, which means your options are highly limited for avoiding all this trouble. Instead of taking everyone out, use discretion. Wait for people to split up and move apart. The buildings below and behind you are filled with ammunition and trouble. You don't really need either in a non-lethal playthrough.

However, the building on the left side of the street contains some great loot if you can spare the time and risk.

THE PAINTING AND SAFE IN DR. GALVANI'S BUILDING

Sneak into the laboratory on the left when no one is looking, and choke the Guard inside. The man is clearly a murderer, because there are already bodies in there.

The lab is in the second room. Grab a Painting off the wall, and look for a code scratched into the frame behind it. Use that code to open the safe there. You receive 150 coins and more Bullets for your time.

The building on the right houses a single Guard. Quietly knock him out if you want more coins; that building has a few decently valuable lootable pieces.

When you're done looting, proceed along the main street. Tons of Guards patrol the next area, but you split off before you bump into them. Approach the man making his announcement, but stay crouched and split off to the right before you reach him. Get onto the upper ledges and knock out a patroller up there. He's by himself and is likely walking away from you. But don't leave him where he falls. Another patroller will see the body if you do.

Instead, carry him into the nearby building and leave him behind a fallen display case. If you're patient, wait and get the next patroller that way too, and leave the two together.

A small route goes forward from here, beside the main road. Take it carefully and quietly; Guards are very close to you. Climb up some pallets beside a Dumpster and into a yard.

Don't knock out the Guard you see, because other people in the main road are watching him. Instead, pass him and use the alley on your right. It's just up ahead.

There are civilians here, but they're not a problem and don't rat you out. However, there is also a Guard. Wait for him to patrol toward the far end of the adjoining alley. Ambush him when he's far away from the civilians, knock him out, and carry him into the next yard, which is an abandoned fish market. There's a Dumpster here, to your left as you enter. If you leave him on the ground, civilians can walk up here and freak out.

You passed a building by doing all this. Unless you're very comfortable with your stealth skills already, consider leaving this one alone. It contains three Guards, and getting the coins sometimes involves making a lot of noise (smashing display cases, opening cash registers, etc.). The Crown Killer has been there, so a gruesome display is on the first floor, but you don't need to see that or do anything with it.

From the fish market, go to the edge of the area and look out over the next street and the harbor. Jump to an overhang and quietly drop onto a mattress below.

Creep to the end of this area below the street and go under a large vat to choke out a guy sitting on a crate.

Continue into a worker's yard (all the men have been slaughtered). Leave and return to the main street—you're now at the far end and have avoided most of the Guards.

Knock out one more and carry him back into the worker's yard to keep him out of sight.

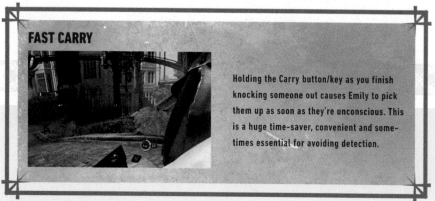

FAST CARRY

Holding the Carry button/key as you finish knocking someone out causes Emily to pick them up as soon as they're unconscious. This is a huge time-saver, convenient and some-times essential for avoiding detection.

Don't run out into the middle of the main street. The patrollers sometimes watch even this part of the road. Wait for the route to clear, then cross the road, leap down into the water, and swim out to the ship.

Climb up the left side of the ship and talk to the captain to complete your mission.

MORE TO SEE

This route takes you through most of Dunwall, but you went on the other side of the road from the Dunwall Courier and a tavern. You can backtrack and explore these if you're playing for maximum coin completion and to see everything. However, if this is your initial stealth run, it's way safer to complete the mission and keep your Ghost status intact.

The usurper Emily Attano and the murderous Royal Protector have been arrested.

THE VOID

Cross the Floating Island

You wake up in your cabin aboard the ship, but something is very off. Try to open the door to your cabin, but turn around afterward. The wall fades away, and you see the Void. It's just like Corvo described.

Walk forward until you meet the Outsider. He speaks with you briefly, and then asks if you want to receive the Outsider's Mark. If you refuse, you go through the game without the use of supernatural abilities. This makes the game a bit harder, but it's an interesting way to play. This style is far more viable for combative players rather than stealth players, because you can still focus on your weapons and equipment.

We highly suggest you accept the Mark. You immediately learn Far Reach and go through a tutorial that shows how to use this ability. Though similar to Blink, this ability has more motion to it, so get used to the arc that determines your destination.

Empress Emily Kaldwin, I'm a friend of your father's from the past old days.

Look up when you reach the second gap. Far Reach up to a higher platform, then jump and Far Reach to cross the divide. You find a dark scene on the other side.

Run to the end of the area and collect a Heart. You see an apparition and listen to it for a short time. You then are able to equip the Heart, which helps track down Bonecharms and Runes.

Let the Heart guide you to a **Rune** farther ahead. It's out in the open, so it's easy to find. The level ends after you pick it up.

ABOARD THE DREADFUL WALE

Meet with Meagan Foster

You wake up aboard the Dreadful Wale again. This time it's in the real world, so get up and search your cabin. Write in your log, if

you wish. A Crossbow hangs by the door. Take it and the Note next to it. Captain Foster tells you about the hidden stores throughout the region (marked with two hands, to let people know the black market is nearby).

Getting a new weapon is nice, since your loud and deadly Pistol isn't of much use. But your Crossbow is quiet and can eventually be armed with Sleep Darts, once you get a few. These non-lethal devices are a blessing for a stealth/non-lethal player.

Open the door to your cabin and explore the lower level.

A blocked cabin lies on the other side of the floor. You can't force it open. Instead, go into the briefing room and climb out an open porthole. Crawl along the outside of the ship and jump into another porthole on the right. This takes you into the barricaded cabin.

You find Notes, money, and a Mana Elixir (also called Addermire Solutions). There are some Incendiary Bolts too, but they're not of use to you.

Follow the objective marker toward Captain Foster and talk to her. This starts your briefing for the next mission. Listen to the captain, and then search the room and the private berth behind it for more goodies. You get a couple more Elixirs! There are also Documents all over the place, and an Audiograph to listen to.

Go to the upper levels of the ship and head out onto the deck. Meet the captain again there, and tell her you're ready to go ashore. This starts the next stage of the mission.

Edge of the World

Find Addermire Station, and take a carriage to Addermire Institute. It is the best lead you have
for tracking down the "Crown Killer."

COLLECTIBLES

Runes	7
Shrines	1
Bonecharms	6
Coins	3334
Blueprints	1
Paintings	3

SPECIAL ACTIONS

A Fresh Grave	Snatch a body for Mindy Blanchard
Black Market Heist	Rob the black market
Hypatia's Apartment	Explore Dr. Hypatia's apartment
Try to Unlock Me	Win the safe contest in the Winslow building
The Nest Keeper	Put down the Nestkeeper in the Bloodfly-infested building

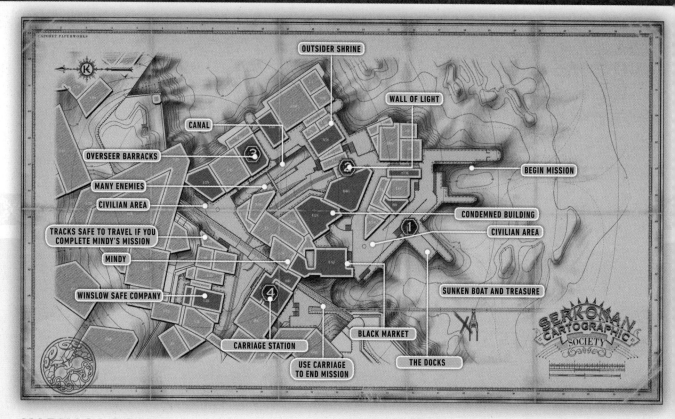

KARNACA DOCKS

Locate the Black Market Shop

Captain Foster takes you to the coast. She can't get you all the way to your destination because of a Watchtower that guards against strange vessels, so that has to be disabled at some point. You make landfall in neutral territory. You're not attacked or harassed unless you cause trouble.

Go all the way to the left while staying by the coast, and then climb up through the buildings above the wharf. Two levels up, you find a small yard you reach by climbing through a window. This is directly behind the black market shop, so if you find the yard, you know you're close. Talk to Mindy, and she tells you about a corpse she needs retrieved.

Agree to this and then turn around to unlock a side gate. This allows you to return here more easily, without going through the main thoroughfare.

MINDY'S QUEST

We walk you through the quest after visiting the black market. It's possible to roll this side task into your normal collection of Runes and Bonecharms so it doesn't waste any time.

Speaking of the black market, now is a good time to visit. The building that houses it, above the wharf, is marked with the two-hand symbol. See if you can afford anything good! If possible, pick up some Sleep Darts.

TO SAVE CASH, STEAL FROM THE BLACK MARKET

To get all the black market's items free of charge, you have the option to rob the place. Pay for any item upgrades ahead of time, because those cannot be stolen, and the shop closes for several minutes after anyone robs it (or forever if you kill the shopkeeper).

To rob the market, clear out the infested building nearby of its Bloodflies; it's not far from the market. Destroy all the nests on the first few floors. The staircase leading to the top is blocked. Look for a barricaded area near a piano room. Jump and crawl through the gap in the barricade to reach the top of the infested building.

A Nestkeeper—an infected person who lives with the Bloodflies—is up there. It's easy to miss the guy, and this upper apartment in general. Use a Sleep Dart to knock out the Nestkeeper before he sees you. A glass aquarium with more Bloodflies contains the Black Market Key.

Return to Mindy's yard. Open the back door to the market, walk in, and then close the door behind you. Knock out the shopkeeper now that you're alone and can't be seen from Mindy's yard.

Steal everything. You get way more than 1000 gold's worth of items. In addition, there are coins in the storage part of the shop. You find more weapons there too. This place is loaded.

BLACK MARKET GOODS

ITEM	COST
Crossbow Bolt	20
Pistol Bullet	30
Sleep Dart	30
Grenade	70
Stun Mine	70
Spring Razor	50
Addermire Solution	150
Health Elixir	75
Location of Sunken Supplies	250
Rune	400

Do Some Collecting

After exploring for a few minutes, equip your Heart and search for collectible items. The black market shop contains a **Rune**. If you don't steal it, purchase it for 400 coins—well worth the expense for the majority of players. A whale carcass along the wharf holds a free **Rune**. It's not far from where you begin this level.

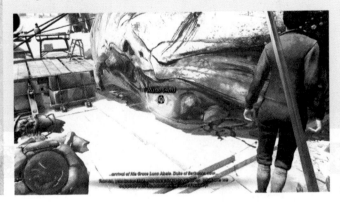

The black market map, purchased for 250 coins, leads you to a downed boat in the harbor. Walk to the end of the farthest point on the docks, then swim out to retrieve several items there. It's at roughly two o'clock from the front of that pier. You gain a couple of Sleep Darts, Spring Razors, Bolts, and other goodies. This is mostly advantageous for more combative players.

If you're wondering how to get into the locked door on the floor above the black market, try this: Go outside and around to the right side of the building. Far Reach up to an open window above you. There isn't too much inside. Far Reach again out another window to get back into the black market building one floor higher. Explore that locked room to get a pile of extra equipment. Unlock the door on your way out for easy access in the future.

If you're wondering how to get into the locked door on the floor above the black market, try this: Go outside and around to the right side of the building. Far Reach up to an open window above you. There isn't too much inside. Far Reach again out another window to get back into the black market building one floor higher. Explore that locked room to get a pile of extra equipment. Unlock the door on your way out for easy access in the future.

Get Help from Mindy

Let's resume our mission. The path above the wharf continues to the right from the black market building. Proceed toward a Wall of Light—a defensive structure meant to kill anyone who tries to cross without proper access.

There are many ways to avoid this dangerous trap. Emily should use the apartments above to skip the area entirely.

Look for the condemned building you looted earlier for the Black Market Key. Go in again!

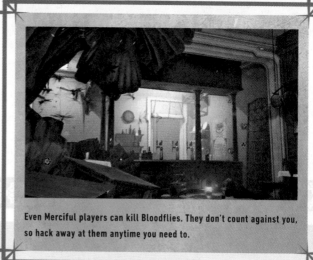

Even Merciful players can kill Bloodflies. They don't count against you, so hack away at them anytime you need to.

Crouch and go through the infested house. When you get close to a nest, race forward, smash it, and retreat. This avoids most of the swarms, so you're unlikely to take much damage. There is food in here (ick), and a Health Elixir too, so even if you get hurt, it isn't a lasting problem.

There are more active nests on the second floor. Search for a crate of flammable liquor, and toss it into nests to destroy them from a safe range. Whenever you find flammable items in Bloodfly areas, remember this technique, because it's fun, fast, and easy.

Grab the **Bonecharm** on the second floor. It's behind one of the nests, and you find it almost instantly with the Heart's help.

Climb to the third floor, explore it, and then use a second staircase on the other side of the building to get back down a level. Break open a door and step onto the balcony. You're safe from the Bloodflies, and have gotten all the way around into Canal Square.

And boy, is this place well-guarded. There are people at the bottom of the street, at the top, and more than a few in between. On the far side of the area are Overseers as well (what a nice group). They may not like the Grand Guards much, but that makes no difference to you, because they don't like you either.

How do you tackle this situation? The answer is simple. Don't. That street is misery, so go above it. Walk left along the balcony and use Far Reach to get over to a balcony across the street. It leads into a doctor's apartment. From the other side of it, Far Reach onto one of the balconies of the Overseers' building. There's much to do inside, so this is where you need to be.

Choke out an Overseer on this second level, and then Far Reach to the third-floor balconies to get inside. Look for the window into an office where an Overseer is writing. Knock him out, but be both quiet and still. There are two more Overseers in the room to your right, and any sign of trouble draws them both. Collect a **Blueprint** (Fire Hardening Treatment) from the Overseer's desk.

Far Reach across the hall to avoid detection, and grab a **Painting** off the wall. The other part of this area contains a safe. Obtain the safe combination by reading the Note and the Book close by. Search this room and the desk near the Overseer. The Mission Clues that reveal the combo appear once you read enough of the materials. Unlock the safe to gain Raw Whalebone and another **Rune.**

Look through a door to find the stairs. Climb up one flight. A Corrupt Bonecharm is on the next floor, but it's inside a locked room. One Overseer is in a side room, and another patrols throughout this floor. Hide and wait for the patroller, knock him out, and then do the same to the man in the small room. The latter has the Interrogation Room Key.

Unlock the door close by and go inside. Collect the **Corrupt Bonecharm** you've been detecting, and loot a few other minor items as well. The body Mindy wants you to retrieve is here. Once you're done with the Overseers, and carry the body outside. Climb out the window and use Far Reach to get to the right. Wait for the patroller below to wander away, and then Far Reach down and away from the building. Enter the next part of town and immediately turn right. Mindy is in a basement here (not back at the black market).

Follow your waypoint marker to get down to her, and deliver the body. She gives you a modest reward and directs one of her people to kill the power to the carriage station ahead. With that down, it's easy to infiltrate.

 MOVING ON

Skip ahead to the section "Go to Addermire Station" if you're not a completionist. Read on to get the rest of the collectibles nearby.

At ground level, outside the Overseers' building, is a table with some Raw Whalebone, a **Rune,** and a **Bonecharm.** These are tough to get as a stealth player, but it can be done. Head onto the balconies over the Overseers' building and drop down at the far end of the alley near the Overseer who's giving his eternal sermon. There are two civilians over there, but they don't alert anyone. If you upgrade your Far Reach to pull objects, steal the items from the table. Otherwise, Far Reach onto the table and take everything. It's scary as heck, but still doable. Far Reach to safety as soon as you're done.

Down in the canal, another **Rune** sits inside a drainage area, and you can't directly reach it. Drop down into the canal from the less-patrolled upper end of the street. To get the Rune, use your Crossbow and shoot the wooden board partially blocking the flow of water. This brings the Rune to you without causing much noise.

From the Overseers' interrogation room, exit onto the awning and Far Reach onto the roof. Use your Heart to detect a Bonecharm not too far away. Far Reach over the rooftops to get to it, but don't relax. There are two Overseers in one section, and you have to quietly avoid them. Jump up high enough to spot the two, and wait for the patrolling one to look over the roof's edge (toward the street). Far Reach between the two Guards to get off the roof in seconds. Don't stop to choke them. The **Bonecharm** itself is on a roof a bit farther along, unguarded except by a tiny group of Bloodflies.

There is a building near the Wall of Light's Windmill. Take the main street from the black market to approach. Use Far Reach to get onto the balconies as soon as you hit the secure zone, and Far Reach behind the lone Guard up top to choke him out.

Hide the body farther down the street, or it will be discovered soon enough.

Enter the building on the left, not that far away. There are two Overseers inside. Climb to the second floor after a civilian finishes talking and leaves the area. Lean around the corner to watch for when the first Overseer turns his back. Choke him out, and then Far Reach behind the other to clear the place out. This building contains an **Outsider Shrine** and a **Bonecharm** on the second floor. There are also multiple valuable items, including a **Painting** right next to the shrine, and a Mana Elixir as well. Slot your Bonecharms so you get their bonuses!

The Outsider in Conditional Dreams

Take

Go to Addermire Station

After finishing your collection work, return to the balcony of the Overseers' building. Far Reach over the patroller below, if you haven't knocked him out, and get into the civilian area ahead once again. If you Far Reach to the upper walkways, you soon arrive at a railway that feeds directly into the station. Don't cross it yet, but note where it is.

Carriage (90m)

Far Reach to the right, jumping between balconies until you reach the entrance to the Winslow Safe Company.

Jump in at the front door and stay inside so the Guards don't see or bother you. The guy working inside is a good fellow and isn't a problem.

Search for the Key to Dr. Hypatia's apartment at the back of the building. Grab it and find the stairs. Climb up a few floors and unlock the apartment. Snatch a **Painting** inside, on the main hallway. Search for money throughout the apartment, and listen to an Audiograph in the back room.

When you're finished, return to the Safe Company's main floor and open the big safe in back. The cash register by the front door contains the combination. Inside the safe is a **Bonecharm**, a Pistol, and more Bullets. Oh, and 300 coins too! Worth taking, eh?

You've now gotten everything that isn't nailed down in this region. Far Reach back up to the railway, and cross it to reach the carriage. It's marked as your objective, so it's easy to find. Head past the objective, staying in the rail area underneath the platform. Keep quiet, because two final Guards are on the platform. Far Reach up there and sneak into the carriage so they don't spot you.

The Good Doctor

Eliminate the Crown Killer, who's been murdering your enemies to make you look guilty. Find your ally, Anton Sokolov, last seen being carried toward Addermire. Alexandria Hypatia, who runs the place, should know more.

COLLECTIBLES

Runes	5
Shrines	1
Bonecharms	4
Coins	2206
Blueprints	1
Paintings	2

SPECIAL ACTIONS

Sunken Wreck	Swim out to the submerged boat
Abandoned Basement	Find the basement
Release the Hounds!	Let the starving Wolfhounds out
Three Witnesses	Save Hamilton, read Valiente's letter, and talk to Vasco
The Counter-Serum	Craft an antidote

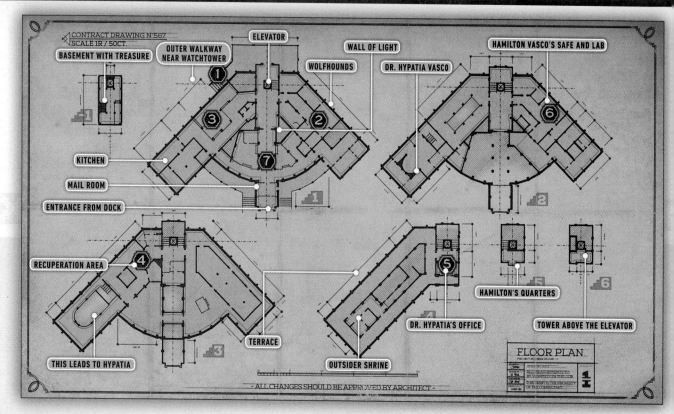

THE ADDERMIRE INSTITUTE

Get a Map of Addermire

The carriage quickly takes you over to the institute, which is on an island that looks creepy, isolated, and miserable. That's not far from the truth. If you read the Documents around the place, you learn that even the people who work here totally hate having to be here.

Once you disembark, go to the edge of the landing and look for a pipe below you. Drop onto it and seek a recess underneath the stonework. A **Bonecharm** is hidden there, and your Heart makes it fairly easy to find once you know about the pipe to land on.

Far Reach back up, and climb the steps toward a small building above.

Three Guards are congregated in a mail/storage room. You pass a pool with fish in it along the way. If you like Possession, turn a valve nearby to raise the water level, and Possess a fish afterward to get farther into the complex.

Otherwise, watch the three men talk. One Guard leaves early to start his patrol. Follow him and take him down. You don't need to move the body right now. Wait for the second one to leave (he goes in the opposite direction). Knock him out and then come back for the guy who stays in the mail room. With this trio down, you have the run of the initial area.

The route to the right doesn't go far, but it leads to a piece of Raw Whalebone. These are useful later on, so grab it. Then take the path on the left. You hit a series of cliffs, but it's possible to walk on them (carefully). Take them around until you find a window into the facility. Going in this way bypasses some serious trouble.

You arrive in the pantry and kitchen. There isn't too much to loot, so crouch and move out to the dining hall. There are patrollers and relaxing people everywhere. You're looking at multiple mobile Guards, some Elite Guards as well, and a challenging stealth situation. To make it worse, a Rune is in the middle of the dining hall. Combative players have it so easy; you have to work for this one!

Use noise to lure out one of the dining pair. They're the biggest rub, so choking a single person from that pair makes everything else quite doable. Make the noise behind the curtain on the left, and hide until the person investigates and then starts to return. Once that's done, get an angle on the other two diners and hit them with Sleep Darts. It's much easier than luring yet another person off for a choking session.

Knock out the lone guy on the right side of the room. He's easy to sneak up on. Get the **Rune** from the placard in the middle of the hall, and put the bodies somewhere safe and out of the way. The rear of the pantry where you entered will do.

Open the gate to the right; it leads to the front of the area, but you can assault it from a safe position now. Knock out the Guard near the gate. Lure him toward you with sound if need be. Then sneak up behind the patroller and give him more of the same.

Use your Heart to find a **Bonecharm** in the room. It's a freebie, and isn't hard to grab. With control of that room, loot a **Painting** near a Wall of Light. Far Reach up to a higher level to grab a Whale Oil Tank. This brings down the Wall of Light instantly.

Stay on the upper level and search the entire flank. There are tons of minor items to pick up. The most important goodies are inside one of two safes. Find the combination near the wall, not far from where you encounter the safe. Read the Documents to get the code.

Inside the safe is a **Blueprint** (Combat Sleep Dart Formula).

Go through the Wall of Light and take a look at the map in the main corridor. This completes one of your goals here, and it shows you a solid layout of the region.

Go to Dr. Hypatia's Office

Head to the main stairs and wait for a patroller to come down. Once he exposes himself, take him down and bring him back to either of the cleared areas. Leave him there and climb the stairs to the upper floors.

Get off at the second floor and look for an Elite Guard ahead. Knock her out while she's relaxing, and leave her there. Return to the stairs and take the open route to the side. A Guard working in that balcony area can also be choked without difficulty. Search for several valuable monetary items.

The rest of the second floor is locked for now. Go the stairs and make a tiny bit of noise. This lures one of two Guards down to your area. Hide on the lower steps until he turns around, and then take him! Far Reach to the chandelier above the second Guard and use a Drop takedown on him for extra cool points.

Climb up to the fourth floor, but slow down near the top. Wait for two Guards to head out on their patrols. They go onto the upper terrace and split up. If you want, follow each and knock them out in turn. This nets you some extra goodies. Equip your Heart and look for the **Outsider Shrine** on this level. It's in a room off this upper terrace. Have a nice little talk with your dark buddy. Afterward, Far Reach onto the roof. It's high up, but explore there until you see a window into a tower. You can't reach this part of the building internally without riding the elevator to the top and Far Reaching up and out of it. That way is slightly more fun. Anyway, Far Reach inside that window and get a **Rune**!

Jump back to the roof where you were, but don't leave. Get onto the smokestack and Far Reach to the absolute highest rooftop. A bird's nest is filled with a **Black Bonecharm**. Return down to the terrace once you find it.

Dr. Hypatia's office is on the other side of the level, by the stairs where you came in. Approach and read the notice on her door. Enter and search everything. Look in a bookcase to the right of the door to find a hidden Gold Ingot (sweet)! Dark Vision really helps for finding goodies like this.

Read a journal on the floor and retrieve Dr. Hypatia's Key from her desk. Also, listen to an Audiograph to learn more about what's happening here.

Talk to Hamilton

Descend to the second floor and unlock the doors to your left. The Key you just grabbed opens them without a hitch, but take cover. There are more Guards in there. The closer one is a regular Guard who looks easy to take, but he's watched by an Elite Guard farther back. Don't give in to temptation and rush for the "safe" choke.

Wait for the two to meet, talk, and split up. When the Elite Guard is totally gone, choke the closer guy and bring him back to the hallway. The Elite Guard is now alone, so stalk her at leisure.

After you deal with her, use the Key again to get into the room with Hamilton, as marked on your HUD. Talk to him to learn more about the Crown Killer.

Get Hamilton's Quarters Key when you leave. It's in a small pan behind the patient.

Search Hamilton's Quarters and Find Vasco

Take the staircase to the top. A separate, private staircase is around the corner. Take that up, and watch out for a tripwire attached to a Bolt-thrower. Use the new Key to unlock the private quarters, and start looting. Among the items, you find a **Blueprint** (Memory Vapor Distillation). In the back of the room, you get to read Hamilton's diary.

This leads you toward the Recuperation Area. Go to the third floor and unlock the doors on the right. Bloodflies have taken over, so you get to do a little fighting.

Destroy the nests as you go, and look in the remains of the first nest's debris for a **Rune**. A Bonecharm is also in the region, but it takes a moment to find. Use your Heart to get close, and look for a few tanning tanks. Open these to reveal a path into a subroom that is otherwise blocked off. Crawl through to nab your **Bonecharm**.

Follow the waypoint to the Recuperation Area, and get away from those Bloodflies. Descend the stairs as you arrive, and search for a **Corrupt Bonecharm** at the bottom. Behind it is a **Painting** on the wall. You've come to a series of labs. There aren't any Guards to bother you, and Dr. Hypatia is close by. Talk to her now.

Go through the area and loot everything. Vasco is a patient in the back. Things proceed quickly once you talk to Vasco, so don't

do that until you're ready to face the Crown Killer. Once you talk, a cutscene plays, and you have some new goals to work on.

Find Vasco's Journal

Sneak away from the Recuperation Area and go back to the second floor, near Hamilton. If you explored there already, you might remember a safe in one of the offices back there that didn't have any codes. Well, now you can use that. Vasco gives you the proper code when you first talk to him. Open the safe and retrieve the Notes inside.

Unlock the lab practically next door, and get a Syringe from the counter. Listen to an Audiograph there as well. Take the Syringe and use it on a dead body in the Bloodfly area, a short distance away. Obtain your sample, bring it back to the lab, and make a special Serum. Collect this final product and return to the Recuperation Area.

Eliminate the Crown Killer (Non-Lethal Version)

Dr. Hypatia is in real trouble. You have to save her now, and the only way to do that is to destroy the Crown Killer. Don't worry; this solution doesn't hurt your Merciful rating.

Follow the waypoints to the Crown Killer. They don't know you're coming, so stealth is still on your side. Hide behind the columns of the area for cover, and use Dark Vision if possible to watch the Crown Killer's position so you can sneak up behind them. Failing that, watch the objective marker, and wait for it to move away before you break cover and approach the target from behind.

Use the Syringe on the Crown Killer. This completes the primary mission. If something went wrong and you didn't get to talk to Dr. Hypatia earlier, you still have to find out where Dr. Sokolov has been taken.

Head into the laboratory and look for a **Blueprint** on the main working counter (Dispersed Incendiary Release). Take it, and listen to an Audiograph in the corner room. That gives you Sokolov's location if you can't get it any other way.

...people of the Empire fodder for their nightmares.

Explore the Basement

Your primary task is done here, but take a second to explore the last part of the institute that you haven't seen yet: the basement. To get down there, climb up to the roof, Far Reach on top of the terrace, and enter a tower area through a window. Look for the top of the elevator inside. Shoot the red canister on the elevator cable, and listen as it barrels down through the shaft. Follow it (safely), and hop down at the bottom to access the basement.

There, search for a **Rune**, a **Painting**, and some spare money.

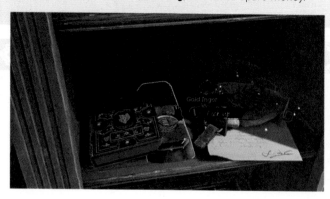

Shut Down the Watchtower

With the Crown Killer dealt with and the area looted, leave the institute. Captain Foster is ready to pick you up, but she can't dock with the Watchtower still powered. Take it down to get out of this crazy place.

Return to the kitchen area on the first floor. Unlock a door that leads outside. One of the men there is an Elite Guard, and the other is a normal one.

Make a small amount of noise, or almost let yourself get spotted so one of the Guards comes toward the building to investigate. Ambush and choke them as they arrive, and leave the body inside. Sneak up behind the second target, and knock them out. No one else can see this part of the walkways, so you're in the clear.

Far Reach over to the Watchtower close by. Open the Whale Oil Tank's container, remove it, and then you're good to go. Captain Foster arrives in about a minute. Far Reach down toward the lower docks, meet her, and leave (unless you have anything else you'd like to do here)!

ABOARD THE DREADFUL WALE

You wake again on the Dreadful Wale. Get up and go out into the hallway. Read a maintenance list for a small table, and then talk to Captain Foster. Don't follow her when she heads up on deck. Instead, enter the briefing room on that level and look for a wheel. Take it from a large table at the back of the room and then follow your new waypoint into the boiler room.

Get down there and install the wheel on a pipe. Turn it to shut off the water and keep the ship in good shape. Read the nearby book, and then find the captain on deck. She's standing by the skiff, ready to take you out into the city again.

When you're ready, tell her to head out.

The Clockwork Mansion

Anton Sokolov is being held at the mansion of Kirin Jindosh, Grand Inventor to the Duke and creator of the Clockwork Soldier. Get inside, rescue Sokolov, and eliminate Jindosh before he builds an army of Clockwork Soldiers.

COLLECTIBLES

Runes	4
Shrines	1
Bonecharms	7
Coins	4802
Blueprints	3
Paintings	3

SPECIAL ACTIONS

Ghost Between the Cogs	Reach Jindosh without revealing your presence
Hidden Repository	Discover Jindosh's hidden repository by manipulating the walls of the mansion
Flawless Extraction	Free Sokolov without alerting the Clockwork Soldier in the Assessment Chamber
A Man of the People	Kill Paolo, the Howler Leader (Once)
Black Market Heist	Blast your way into the black market
Looted Aventa Station	Rob the ticket booth in the station

AVENTA DISTRICT

Enter the Carriage Station

Captain Foster takes you into the Aventa District. You pass through two guarded parts of the city before you reach the mansion. Luckily, there are quite a few items to collect along the way, so your time is far from wasted!

There's some money where you begin, and a Health Elixir on the right side. Grab these small goodies and then take the way forward to enter the city.

The initial street has patrolling Guards and a good number of civilians. Wait for an opening in the patrol, which doesn't take long. Then turn left and approach the quiet end of the street (near the civilians). Find a small entrance to an abandoned building there. It's filled with four Bloodfly nests, but it's nothing new or difficult to handle.

Search the second floor for basic loot, and the third floor for an **Outsider Shrine**. To get to it, bypass a locked door. Jump through the open window beside the door to reach the locked areas.

Leave the building and stay on the upper walkway where the civilians are congregating. This keeps you far away from the Guards. Progress along the street, then turn into an alley to the left. Another building is accessible from the alley, behind a metal shutter.

Climb to the second floor and search around for many items.

The room on the third floor is locked. To access it, return outside and Far Reach onto a nearby building. Climb to the top and Far Reach back onto the upper balcony of your current building. Steal everything, including a **Black Bonecharm** and more money inside the apartment. A **Painting** hangs on the wall, near the balcony.

The open yard ahead conceals a trap. A woman calls for help, but she's part of the same gang as the patrolling man. If you approach her, she summons all her buddies, and they come in with steel bared. Far Reach onto the balcony to the left while you observe them. The **Rune** you want to steal is toward the back of the yard. Spot it with your Heart so you know where to Far Reach. Having Mesmerize or Shadow Walk really helps. Steal the Rune and then back away, the way you came in.

Go to the main street of the district and cross to the other side. Far Reach on top of a small wall near another building. Far Reach again to reach the balconies above it, and go through an unlocked door into the higher floors. The Guards shouldn't see this as long as you crouch while you work.

Exit to the balcony and move carefully around the corner onto a lower, small roof. Wait for the patroller to move farther away, and note the post beneath you where another Guard is standing duty. Far Reach ahead and to the right as far as you can to avoid these observers. Then sneak into the unwatched yard ahead. A beggar is there, but he's a good fellow. He gives you a warning if you pay him five coins. It sounds like there are even more disreputable fellows lurking in the region.

A basement entrance from this yard gains you access to the black market shop. Talk to the woman inside, though she can't sell you anything yet. After she tells you this, try to leave, but stop when the woman speaks again. She says the nasty sorts are here. Use a brick pillar at the side of the room to hide. Crouch there while the merchant talks to her visitors.

Don't move while the criminals are in the shop. Once they're gone, you can buy goods without any issue.

Break into a china cabinet to get a **Bonecharm**. Loot the desk for a valuable Medal, and steal a **Painting** from the wall. All in all, quite a bit of money for a quick job.

BLACK MARKET GOODS

ITEM	COST
Crossbow Bolt	20
Pistol Bullet	30
Sleep Dart	30
Grenade	70
Stun Mine	70
Spring Razor	50
Addermire Solution	150
Health Elixir	75
Rewire Tool	200
Rune	400
The Key to Unlock the Ticket Booth	250

As long as you have cash to spare, buy the Key. It's useful within minutes. Beyond that, get the **Rune**, a Rewire Tool, and whatever else you like. It comes out to under 1000 for the big-ticket items, and you've probably pulled in over twice that since your last time at the market.

Finish shopping and exit into the street. Use the balcony area across from the market to gain a higher vantage. Far Reach from there, on the balconies above the black market. You have to get up to a fourth-floor entrance to access the locked building on this side of the road.

Go in through the balcony and explore. You get a bit of money on the Bloodfly-infested fourth floor. There is Raw Whalebone and some minor loot on the first floor. Approach the basement entrance with care (it's outside the house, but still within the locked gate's area).

Enter the basement and crouch while you listen to two criminals talking about explosives. Let the two split up after they're done talking. That's when you can go after them safely, and quietly.

 ## VICIOUS PROFIT

If you knock out these two criminals, you can get some major cash. The women here have set up two Whale Oil Tanks by a brick wall. Bring a third one from the carriage station, and put it with the others. Blowing them all up (together or on their own) destroys the wall. Looting her safe and goods is worth a massive amount of money.

Once you're done, take your Rewire Tool back to the front street. Clear the patrollers when they're at the far end of their route (closer to the shady area you just explored). Leave their unconscious bodies back in there, and then rewire the Security Panel to the right of the Wall of Light.

You can safely walk through the wall now, and into the carriage station. If you bought the Ticket Booth Key, use it to open the booth ahead. It contains an unlocked safe with almost enough money by itself to cover the cost of the Key. Open a cash register for even more, and take the free **Blueprint** on the nearby desk. Good stuff.

Climb the stairs to the second floor of the carriage station and Far Reach from the steps onto the other side of the second level. Guards are watching the primary way up, but their backs aren't protected. Knock out the Elite Guard when the other patrols toward the stairs, and then follow suit with the patroller.

Search for a **Bonecharm** here on a few small cages. Then take the carriage to the next district.

A Veteran at the top of the building holds a Side Gate Key. He's resting on the new Gate Code Document as well. But he's almost asleep. As long as you didn't start a huge battle, he's a joke. Creep into his office, knock him out, and loot the place. You now know the gate code.

Just outside that office is a **Blueprint** sitting out in the open. Take it when you leave.

UPPER AVENTA DISTRICT

Enter the Mansion

Crouch as soon as you get to the next station. Turn right and advance toward a soldier's barracks. The door isn't too far away. Far Reach past the main desk when you get inside, and sneak behind the two men. They're both working and are easy to ambush and knock out. Hide them in the tiny internal room behind the front desk.

Climb to the second floor. Both men here are in the same room, so they're a little harder to deal with. Make a bit of noise to lure one out. Ambush him for a knockout, and then sneak up on the guy left in the typing room. As before, hide the bodies far away from the stairs, in case anyone patrols in here later. Search there for a **Bonecharm** before you go.

Return to the carriage and go the long way around to the left side of the yard. Avoid the patrollers by staying at a good range from them. The side alley is locked with an iron gate, but you've already discovered the Key to it. Go through here, where it's much quieter. This circumvents the Wall of Light.

Now that you're behind it, crouch and go around the periphery of the next yard. To avoid the patrols, enter the first building you can; it's across from the iron gate. Look for a **Rune** at the back side of the second floor. There are only civilians inside the building. Also grab the Hound Figurine from the room at the end of the hall. It's worth a fair amount.

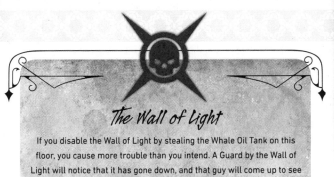

The Wall of Light

If you disable the Wall of Light by stealing the Whale Oil Tank on this floor, you cause more trouble than you intend. A Guard by the Wall of Light will notice that it has gone down, and that guy will come up to see if something is wrong with the tank. You could ambush him while he's away from his post, but we'll find another way through instead!

Leave the building and slip around the corner when the patrollers are away. You can see the mansion ahead, but this isn't how you get to it. Climb down a chain at the end of the route for a little more money, then immediately come right back up. Use your Heart to locate one final building, which is actually a bit behind you when you come back up the chain. Open a window to get inside, and clear out its Bloodflies. A **Corrupt Bonecharm** awaits you inside.

Go all the way back to the carriage and enter the code from the soldiers' outpost into the console next to it. Re-enter the carriage, and use it to approach the Clockwork Mansion. When it stops, go up to the main doors and enter the building. This is the estate of Jindosh, one of the two greatest inventors in the Empire. He's helping your adversaries seize control of the throne.

We'll see what can be done to remedy this situation honorably and decisively.

THE CLOCKWORK MANSION

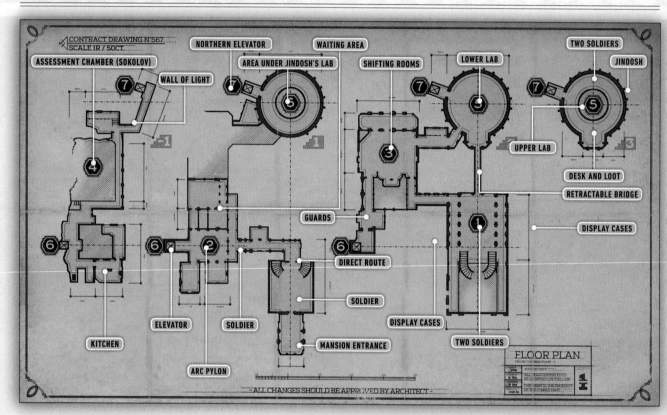

Rescue Anton Sokolov

The first two rooms of the mansion are lovely and barren of dangers. Walk into the large room adjoining the entrance, and use a mechanism to the right of the door. This lets you change the room to access the rest of the house. A Clockwork Soldier is ahead, but it isn't on duty. It doesn't detect you or attack. At least, not yet.

After the room finishes its transformation, head to the upper floor and look the display cases on each side of the chamber. The right side contains a Mana Elixir, a Stun Mine, and a Rewire Tool!

After grabbing the goodies, activate the transformation mechanism again. This time, turn left and Far Reach up to get onto a display case and then the ledge above it while the room is engaged in its transformation. If successful, you reach the inner workings of the room before it finishes. This lets you avoid Jindosh's sensors, re-establishing your advantage of surprise.

Follow this internal hallway until you approach a group of windows. Open the one on the right and emerge into a carpeted hallway. Two Elite Guards are on one end of it, talking. Head in the opposite direction.

If you wait around the far corner, one of the Elites comes to you on her patrol. Knock her out and leave her there. Now you can go where the two were talking, because the other is off on his patrol too.

Search the rooms here for loot. A Clockwork Soldier is in the hallway you just explored, but it doesn't activate unless a fight breaks out. Use Dark Vision to track down the other Elite Guard, and knock him out before he can uncover you. A third Elite comes into the main room (with the piano) from time to time, so don't leave the bodies out in the open. Put them to the side and wait for your final target. Once he's knocked out, your task becomes much easier.

Go into the elevator at one end of this route. It connects three levels, and you're on the middle one. Select the Assessment Chamber, the lowest. That's where Anton Sokolov is being held. Wait for a patroller to approach the elevator, and knock him out.

Look through the kitchen and go around the back of the area. A mechanism lets you pull the waiting room down here to be searched. It doesn't hold too much of interest, but you don't have to deal with the Guards protecting it as you do if you examine the place from the level above. A small connecting area between the two floors of the waiting room grants you access to a special place. Get in between the floors and use the Configuration Mechanism inside to send the floor up. At the top, exit into another recessed space. A **Bonecharm** is hidden there, on a body. Use a hatch to get back onto the elevator and escape from this place.

When you're done, continue deeper into the level. No matter how you approach the Assessment Chamber, you bump into it quickly because it's huge. Stay on the upper walkways above it for now.

Hide until you spot the Elite Guard at the other end of the chamber. She's usually on the other side of an open doorway. Far Reach over to ambush her, and choke her out. The tiny room behind her contains a **Bonecharm** inside a desk drawer.

Get back over the Assessment Chamber and look for a metal staircase that leads down. Descend the stairs. A mechanism opens the Assessment Chamber, and the place is a bit of a puzzle. Each golden square you step onto changes the configuration of the walls. If you don't take the perfect route, you bump into a Clockwork Soldier and are spotted.

Open the front door and then take the following path:

- ▶ **Step into the puzzle and move onto the first square**
- ▶ **Far Reach forward and right to skip a Clockwork Soldier**
- ▶ **Step on a square ahead, as you continue forward and right**
- ▶ **Let the walls finish shifting, and then look around the corner ahead and left of your position**
- ▶ **Break a set of wooden boards on the floor**
- ▶ **Step on the revealed square**
- ▶ **Anton Sokolov's cell opens**

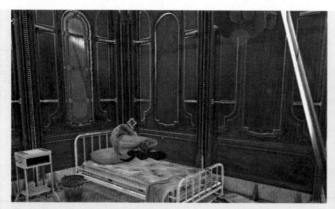

Wake up Sokolov. Finding him is good news. Take the **Painting** inside the cell, and then break another set of boards over a square. Pick up Sokolov and step on that square. This opens the cell again. Far Reach out of it, and use the square outside to change the walls. Head toward the exit door, careful not to alert the Clockwork Soldier still in the area.

Use a square to the left (if you're facing the exit) to open the tiny entrance area. It's pretty clear from here, so hurry out and get Sokolov back to the elevator.

Ride the elevator back to the middle level. You already knocked out the Guards, so follow the waypoint back through the cleared room and hallway beyond. Use the Configuration Mechanism at the end to open the way out.

Leave sleepy Sokolov by the door. He'll be fine.

Eliminate Kirin Jindosh

Don't leave yet. You have to stop Jindosh from being a threat to your rule, but you don't have to murder him. Instead, return to the Assessment Chamber and examine the Elite Guard's room. She's already unconscious, but there's a Wall of Light in there that you can't pass.

Use Shadow Walk and skitter into the Rat hole in the wall to avoid the Wall of Light, and disable it from the other side. You also discover an elevator that goes right into Jindosh's laboratory from underneath. No more Guards or Clockwork Soldiers stand in the way.

Press Button 2 in the elevator to ride up to the lab. The top floor is much harder to sneak into. Leave the room by a side hallway with a red carpet. The adjoining hallway takes you past a small room with some Documents, and then into a room with a spinning internal mechanism. Use a Configuration Mechanism and then ride the inner section while it spins into another room. Far Reach into a small door by the corner. The tiny room there has a secret below it; use a mechanism to lower the floor, collect a **Black Bonecharm**, and then retrace your steps back to the laboratory.

Sneak around to get the lay of the middle area. The Electroshock Machine you need is underpowered, so a few other things must be disabled before you can use it. Two Bay Control Panels are a few feet away from the Electroshock Machine.

Press the Optics button on Bay 1's panel. Press the Anatomy Platform button on Bay 2. A **Rune** is on the Anatomy Platform, which is now on the middle level. Pick it up as soon as you can get it without drawing attention from the Clockwork Soldiers patrolling above. If you want to explore and grab a couple more minor items, descend into the lower portion of the lab while the bays are changing.

Once the new platforms are in position, the Electroshock Machine receives its power. Use the elevator to ascend to the third floor, and Shadow Walk through the Rat tunnel to get close to Jindosh. He wanders, but gets pretty close to the Rat tunnel exit. Ambush him while you're still in Shadow Walk, knock him out, and Far Reach to safety with his body as soon as you can.

Bring him to the middle level and go around the outer edge to avoid visual detection. Place Jindosh in the chair and then turn on the machine. This effectively eliminates him as a rival, but he doesn't die.

If you're still in the mood to search before leaving, the upper tier of the lab contains a **Painting** behind Jindosh's desk. Inside the desk is a **Blueprint**.

A floorless hallway leads back to the beginning of the level. Use a lever beside it to raise the floor and give yourself an easy

escape. Take Sokolov out of this horrible place. Carry him through the main doors to reach freedom.

Ride the carriage back to Lower Aventa. Grab Sokolov and carry him back to the boat. Take the rear exit out of the station to avoid detection. Far Reach up onto the roof of the building around the next corner, and from there onto the balcony of the black market structure. Descend to the lower floor, exit the building, and from there it's a simple run to the end. The Guards don't see anything, and you don't even freak out the civilians this way like you would if you stayed on ground level.

THE VOID CALLS AGAIN

Emily wakes, but she quickly discovers this is another of her journeys into the Void. Get out of your bed and open the door. Follow the waypoint toward a meeting, not far away. Listen to what the other person has to say, then keep following the

waypoints to learn about the past. There isn't anything you can do here besides walk forward and observe.

Soon, you find a way out and are taken back to the Dreadful Wale.

SAFE ON THE SEAS

Get up again, and write in your journal. When you're done, go to the briefing room and talk to Captain Foster and Anton. Look in the back room afterward and read a Document on the Bloodfly

tank, which gives you the secondary task of clearing out all the Bloodflies on the ship. Examine the painting of Delilah

in the briefing room for some extra background.

Progress through the vessel in search of Bloodflies. You find them in the boiler room. Walk down there and slash them to pieces.

Meet Captain Foster up by the skiff to start the next mission.

The Royal Conservatory

While held captive, Anton Sokolov learned the identity of one of Delilah's chief allies, Breanna Ashworth. An architect of the coup that took the throne in Dunwall, Ashworth is powerful and full of secrets. She is building a mysterious device for Delilah. Breanna Ashworth must be eliminated.

COLLECTIBLES

Runes	6
Shrines	1
Bonecharms	9
Coins	3813
Blueprints	3
Paintings	3

SPECIAL ACTIONS

Shrewd Negotiations	Get the best price for the Roseburrow Prototype
Parley with Delilah	Talk to the statue in Ashworth's office after eliminating Ashworth
Witch No More	Sever Ashworth's connection with the Void
Black Market Heist	Rob the black market
Spying Overseers	Find Vice Overseer Byrne's outpost

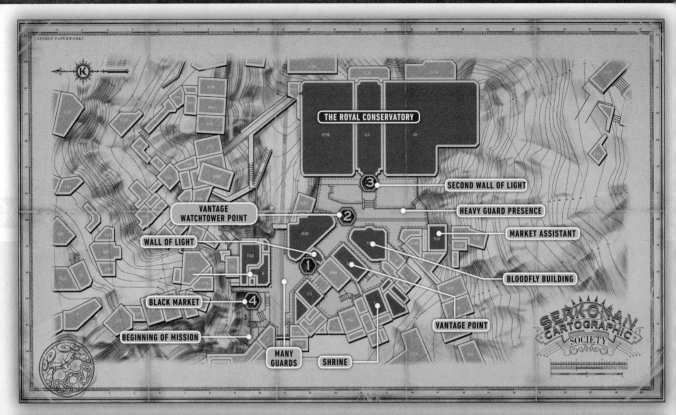

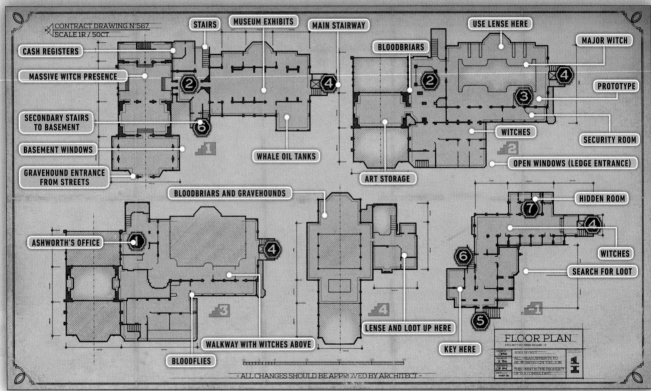

CYRIA GARDENS

Find Out What Vice Overseer Byrne Knows

Breanna Ashworth runs the Royal Conservatory, but you also discover she's a secret ally of Delilah. Your next task is to find out more about Breanna and then stop her. Captain Foster takes you to a dock in Cyria Gardens, where she drops you off.

Before approaching the Conservatory, find out more information from the Overseers (and take a fair sum of collectible items).

Grab some supplies from a tiny room on the right as you leave the boat behind and advance toward the main town. Another boat is docked ahead, and that holds even more minor items.

Finish looting, crouch, and look to the right. A Guard is up on a higher tier, patrolling over the docks. When he turns toward the stairs, Far Reach behind him and knock him out. This is a quieter area, and he's the only patroller in sight. Looking ahead, you see far more Guards by the next few buildings.

Use Shadow Walk to move quickly and without catching their attention. Stay to the left and watch for the basement entrance to the black market. Talk to the shopkeeper inside to get another mission and to buy more items.

Stock up, and leave the store with care.

A BIT MORE STEALING!

There is a valid way to rob this store without killing anyone. We explain how to do this here, but consider waiting until your mission is complete. That way, you can do the side task for the shopkeeper and retrieve a machine for him. Afterward, use the following steps to steal from the store:

Take a wheel from the rear of the shop, and carry it with you when you're ready to rob the place. Buy the upgrades you want first, but don't spend anything on items. Look for a window with steel bars on the right side of the shop. A heavy cable is suspended on the other side. Target a red canister on the cable and shoot it with a Crossbow Bolt.

When the red canister pops, leave the store. Put the valve you stole onto a small metal stand back at the canal. Turn the wheel to open a gate and allow access to the area underneath the store. A chain hangs there. Climb up and rob the black market.

BLACK MARKET GOODS

ITEM	COST
Crossbow Bolt	20
Pistol Bullet	30
Sleep Dart	30
Grenade	70
Stun Mine	70
Spring Razor	50
Addermire Solution	150
Health Elixir	75
Rewire Tool	200
Safe Combination	250
Rune	400

Far Reach along the left side of the street when the patrollers are away. You leave the Guards behind as you cross over the small canal, but slow down on the other side. The people in the next alley look like civilians at range, but they're all armed criminals. Ick.

The criminals on this side of town are still hanging around. Because they like to shout and call out frequently, people tend to call them Howlers. This group has several members patrolling around the area. None of them have much treasure to their name, so back away without being spotted and leave them be.

Return to the canal. Stay on the upper walkway above the water and crouch as you return to the pawnshop. Guards are easily close enough to see you, but the short half-wall there is enough to block line of sight. Be quiet and look for a door into the pawnshop's building. There are three soldiers up top (two Guards and an Elite); because they spend most of their time looking out over the street, you can choke all of them with ease.

Use an open vent in the roof to drop into an Overseer's chamber. Knock him out (he's sleeping already), and loot the place for a massive amount of intel. An Audiograph completes your mission goal.

Search the Associate's Last Known Location

The black market shopkeeper wanted some help from you (as long as you didn't rob him). Why not do the guy a favor, especially since you steal his inventory later. Your next goal, then, is to find an associate of his. There's also a good number of collectibles on the way, as you search the remainder of the district.

Cross to the building on the other side of the street. Use a large pipe to do this quickly and easily. The ground level has way too many Guards to deal with. From there, Far Reach to the area above the Wall of Light, and then over to another balcony. That building has trivial loot (money and a Mana Elixir) if you take the time to rob the place.

However, you can get onto its roof with some jumping or Far Reach. Follow the rooftops on the other side as you move around the Wall of Light below. The next important roof you reach includes an Elite Guard and a civilian. The two of them talk for a short time, but either or both are easily knocked out once they separate. Note that you come back to this rooftop multiple times; it's a hub for this entire half of the level.

Search the building. The bar in the upper floor contains a **Bonecharm**. Only a single civilian is sweeping the place, so stealing is easy whether you knock him out, avoid him, or ignore him. An Elite Guard and a regular Guard are outside and can be knocked out or avoided as well. Go with your preference.

After the search, Far Reach from the outside roof into another building. Bloodflies are all over the place. Be careful. The nests here are normal, but a Nestkeeper lurks among them, living with them but overtly unharmed by them. If you missed the one Nestkeeper earlier, this is a new threat. Hide until you spot this guy, and then use a Sleep Dart on him so he can't call the Bloodflies to attack you. Clear the house normally after that (but don't use fire anywhere near his body, just to be safe).

Once you've cleared the infestation from this large building, grab the **Painting** and look for a safe. Use the combination from the black market to unlock it and collect a substantial amount of money and some Bullets. On the floor close to the safe is a **Corrupt Bonecharm**.

Far Reach back to the previous rooftop (with the maid and Elite). Get onto the roof and use your Heart to find a Rune on the edge of the map, inside a faded teal house. Use Dark Vision to spot a number of traps as you head in. Disarm them and Far Reach to an upper floor. Use the **Outsider Shrine** up there.

Yet again, return to the maid's roof. Far Reach to the gray building across the big street. Use the second balcony to get on top of a Watchtower. Disable the Whale Oil Tank to shut it off (nobody notices). Then get a good perch to examine the enemies below.

Use Sleep Darts on the patrollers on the lower side. Your targets are the ones patrolling through a gated room under the stairs. Take one out, Far Reach down there, and Sleep Dart the second during his approach. Remove another Whale Oil Tank from the area, and then Far Reach up to the Wall of Light above. Stealth your way through quickly, using Shadow Walk, and turn left. Far Reach up the hill on your left to get onto the upper ledges of the Conservatory. These lead all the way across the building and onto another ledge. Take that to get onto a balcony. It's a roundabout route, but it lets you avoid many Guards by the bottom entrance.

Once you enter the building, search the desk. A Document guides you to the next stage of the shopkeeper's mission. You also gain a **Bonecharm** and a **Blueprint**.

Uncover Ashworth's Role

Get back to the ledges and enter the Conservatory through a partially open window.

Crouch and walk through a lab. The room ahead has two talking women. Listen in on their conversation and wait for them to part ways. Both of them are Witches; they have the Outsider's powers, but they still go down quickly if you get the drop on them. The one who splits off down the hallway is your first target. When she puts her back to the wall, approach and quietly choke her. Pull her into the lab area while you do this, and leave her there when she's unconscious.

The other Witch is still sitting on her bed. Though you could Far Reach to her for a takedown, it's much easier and safer to plop a Sleep Dart into her at range.

Look for food, Documents, and a Mana Elixir in the lab area. A body there hides extra Sleep Darts as well. Stock up on them before you proceed.

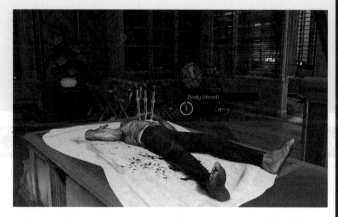

Use your Heart to find the **Rune** on the left side of this level. It's unguarded now. Take it and look for the Roseburrow Prototype waypoint. It's on this level, and you don't have to go far.

Traverse the main hallway and use Dark Vision to find a Witch patroller inside a massive room. She patrols on the outer edges. Choke her and drag her to the cleared area you've made.

The other side of the main Conservatory room is the harder part. Multiple Witches guard and patrol that end. Use bookcases for cover while you approach closer to the Oraculum. Be patient, and let a couple of Witches come toward you. When they start to turn around and walk away, knock out both. Drag them behind the bookcase for disposal.

Watch out for the Witches on the upper tier of the room. They can see you down there, so stay behind cover as much as you can. The only other Witch on this floor is stocking books, and can be knocked out easily while you finish your circuit of the chamber. With her down, you gain somewhat free rein to explore.

Crawl up the stairs by the end of the room, and wait for a patroller to approach the summit. Choke her and put her halfway down the steps, where no one will find her.

Explore the third floor (you were on the second before). The front of the building has Bloodfly nests everywhere, but no Nestkeepers to bug you. Destroy the nests as you pass them. Look for a **Bonecharm** on a chalkboard as you clear everything out.

Return to the stairs. Press the button on the elevator, but hide as it comes up. The ring of the elevator arriving briefly draws a Witch's attention, and you don't want to be spotted. Enter the elevator once the coast is clear, and Far Reach above it through a hole in the top. A **Black Bonecharm** is hidden in a crawlspace just a few feet away.

Stay up here. Your Heart points toward another Black Bonecharm on this floor. Head toward it, across a small upper ledge for the library below. Go through a window at the other side and into a room on your right. The **Black Bonecharm** is there.

Outside that room, you hear a conversation coming up from the lower floor. Eavesdrop for some interesting information.

The office and lab on the other side of the hallway contain a bunch of good stuff. You find **Lenses** (very important), Raw Whalebone, a Mana Elixir, and plenty of money. Take it all.

A door leads outside onto a large ledge filled with two Gravehounds and a few Bloodbriars. A **Rune** sits on a small altar to the right. You can Far Reach past the Bloodbriars, but the Gravehounds are right there. Killing them isn't a good idea. They return from the dead and make plenty of noise, making it a poor for Ghost players. Instead, destroy the Bloodbriar in front of you with ranged attacks.

Far Reach past the plant's body, and come at the altar from the other side. Far Reach onto the altar, take the Rune, and back off the way you came. The Gravehounds don't wake up, and that's a good thing.

Go back into the building carefully to make sure no patrollers can see you (if a Gravehound comes up from the lower level, wait it out). The half-floor down the stairs holds a **Painting**. As long as the Gravehound is far away, you can steal it without repercussion.

Search the office at the bottom of the stairs, doing everything in your power to avoid the gaze and detection of the Gravehound. You need the Documents from the main desk. Everything else here is just a bonus. Watch out for the statue of Delilah; it's more than it appears and should be avoided.

There is an Audiograph downstairs that you also need, but it can wait for you to clear the whole place out while you explore.

Eliminate Breanna Ashworth

First, backtrack all the way to the second floor that you cleared while looking through the library. When you arrive, use the Lenses on the Oraculum. After installing everything, pull the lever on the right, and watch the end of your adversary.

Acquire the Roseburrow Prototype

Head to the other side of this level and look for the Prototype. It's clear on your HUD because of the waypoint, but a locked door prevents you from reaching it. Instead, use Shadow Walk and go through a Rat hole to the left of the device, when you're still in the library. Search with Dark Vision if you have trouble finding it.

From the other side, look for a Security Panel and rewire it. Now you're able to steal the Prototype without causing any alarms. Go into its cubby, take the machine, and back out. When you are almost done with the town, deliver the machine to the black market shopkeeper. Receive your reward, and consider robbing him afterward if you're really in a dirty mood!

Retrieve Breanna Ashworth's Audiograph

You're almost done. Descend onto the first floor and look for the stairs down into the basement (not the elevator stairs, the ones on the other side of the building). With Ashworth's power broken, this building is much safer to explore. The quartermaster's room is by the bottom stairs. Jump through an open window to get outside, and then turn right around to go into the window of the quartermaster's room. A **Bonecharm** is inside. Take it and the Archive Key from the room, and then get back into the basement.

Grab a few pieces of Raw Whalebone

from a table, and explore the one path that leads deeper into the basement. Destroy a few small Bloodfly nests, and follow your Heart toward the last Rune in the level. The Archive Key opens a door back there, and you find the **Rune** and the Audiograph you're looking for. Take both. Far Reach onto the bookcase behind the Audiograph table. Crouch, get up there, and find a small hidden room in between the bookcases. A **Painting** is in there.

This completes the side tasks and missions here. Get out of the building quietly and return to Captain Foster. Visit the black market again on the way to finish the side task if you haven't already.

Dust District

You must travel through the Dust District to Aramis Stilton's Manor, which contains more of Delilah's secrets. Vice Overseer Byrne and his religious followers are at war with Paolo, leader of the Howler gang. Either Byrne or Paolo will aid you, for a favor.

COLLECTIBLES

Runes	5
Shrines	1
Bonecharms	8
Coins	3973
Blueprints	3
Paintings	2

SPECIAL ACTIONS

The Jindosh Lock	Solve the Jindosh Lock on your own
Childhood Home	Explore Corvo Attano's childhood home
Power of the Streets	Side with the Howlers
Theocratic Support	Side with the Overseers
Book of the Fallen	Add Byrne's name to the Book of the Fallen
Another Solution	Eliminate both faction leaders
Black Market Heist	Rob the black market
Uninvolved	Don't take sides with either faction

Between missions you get some more time aboard the ship. Talk to Sokolov in the briefing room. He has some ideas about what you can do next. Afterward, meet him up by the skiff. There isn't much else to do right now, so start the next mission pretty much immediately.

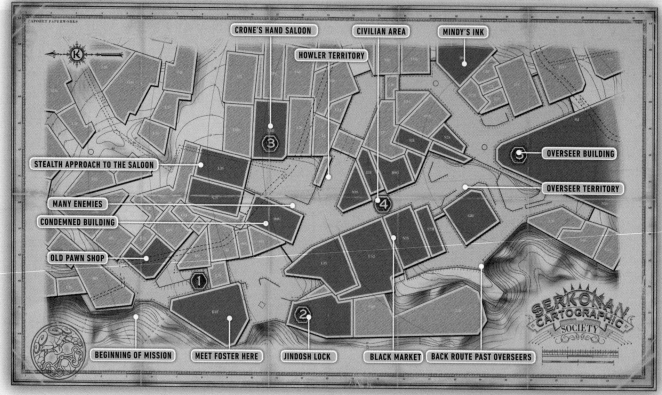

OLD BATISTA DISTRICT

Finding a Way

Aramis Stilton is your next target. He's a man of wealth and power. Self-taught, he's not some noble dandy you can break with a few moments of effort. You might need help, but Sokolov knows the area and the people. His plans should be of use. Make your way out of the submerged basement where you begin. Treasure is minimal, though there is a piece of Raw Whalebone on a desk before you leave the first greater chamber. Pick it up and follow the waypoint toward Captain Foster.

Far Reach across the street to the left as you emerge into the sunlight. This avoids a few Guards who are busy chatting. Go into the damaged building and climb the steps. Two regular Guards are at the top. Wait for one to patrol away. Far Reach to the other, extract your Sleep Darts quickly, then Sleep Dart the farther target and choke the first.

Grab the **Blueprint** from the bottom of a wooden table, and then shut down a Wall of Light by disabling the Windmill up here. When the patrols are by the front of the street, Far Reach down and stealth your way past the group. Go through the Wall of Light and turn right to reach another damaged building.

Far Reach to a higher level of the building and look for Captain Foster. She gives you a bit of information. Nab more Raw Whalebone from the small apartment, and then hop out of the building from an opening nearby. Turn around and smash a wooden barricade to enter the lower part of the same building. A **Rune** is hidden in that room.

Leave the building and brave the dust storm that's starting to rage throughout the district. Visibility is horrible, but that's kind of in your favor. So, no big deal.

The streets funnel you through a chokepoint ahead. A number of Overseer masks are nailed to a signpost, letting people know that this area isn't so safe for their kind.

Hug the wall to the right as you pass the sign, and look for a Winslow Safe Company store. Loot it if need be, and continue right afterward to find the black market, which is in a lower part of the district. Descend the stairs and pass some workers until you find the store entrance. A couple of Howlers are already there, so give them time to clear out before you shop.

BLACK MARKET GOODS

ITEM	COST
Crossbow Bolt	20
Pistol Bullet	30
Sleep Dart	30
Grenade	70
Stun Mine	70
Spring Razor	50
Addermire Solution	150
Health Elixir	75
Rewire Tool	200
Map of Stilton's Home	100

After buying the upgrades you want, it might be time to steal from the market again.

Look for a locked door on the same floor as the black market. There is a keypad beside this door. Enter the code after you find it.

The code is located upstairs, in the shopkeeper's private quarters. You can't get in at first because the door is blocked. Break the barricade by going outside and shooting through the barred windows to destroy the wooden planks that are holding the door. Now you can get inside quite easily.

Read the Note up there near a wedding silvergraph. This gives you clues about the shopkeeper's wedding anniversary. Then, look at a calendar on the wall. You see a day circled during the month of rain (the 4th month). That month and day are your code to the market door.

Enter 4xx (with xx being the day marked on the calendar) into the black market back door. It unlocks the door and lets you into the rear of the store. Look for a **Bonecharm** inside a desk, and take everything else.

Return up to the main boulevard and search for a condemned building. Break in through a barricaded door and destroy a Bloodfly nest by the entrance. Climb to the second floor and search for a **Rune**. It's in a side room, contained in a dresser. There are more nests, but this is a fairly safe house compared to some.

Use an open window at the top of the building to climb outside. Far Reach to a pipe and examine another open building. This one has Bloodflies too, plus two Nestkeepers. Foul people. Use Sleep Darts on them at long range so you aren't spotted or attacked. They don't usually stay in the same room, so neither notices when the other goes down if you're patient.

Destroy the nests in the building and look around. Grab some minor loot and use another set of windows to exit outside afterward. The Heart shows a **Rune** just a few feet away, so snag that next.

Look outside for an awning on your left. Far Reach onto it, and enter a new structure. Knock out a lone Howler on the floor you enter, and silently go down to the lower floor. Two patrollers are below, so don't run for any reason. Stay quiet and hide in the stairwell. When one approaches, open the door into the stairwell, choke them, and drag them into that area as they fall unconscious. Repeat this for the next patroller, and the building is yours.

Search for two **Paintings** and an **Outsider Shrine** on the lower floor. You're inside Paulo's apartment; he's the guy running all these criminals you've practically bumped into a few times. His bedroom is loaded with money, inside an unlocked chest. You also get a **Blueprint** from a metal case in the living room. Stealing from him is gutsy, but so what? He's a jerk.

Investigate Durante

Now that you're close to the Howlers' apartments, it's time to investigate their actions. You might be able to get the information you need from these people without helping the Howlers or the Overseers to kill each other.

Far Reach from the balcony of Paulo's place onto a railed balcony one tier down. Look for a Note tacked onto a door. Take it and read it.

The man who owns this apartment is named Durante. He's been taken to the Overseer Outpost, so that's your next point of call.

Retreat all the way into neutral territory between the Overseers and the Howlers. Near the black market is a soup kitchen where miners get their food. Look for a damaged brick wall about 12 feet away, around a cement pillar. Break the wooden repair beams underneath that wall and crawl through.

This gets you into Overseer territory from a side route they don't guard well. Silence their lonely patrollers with Sleep Darts or normal takedowns. The outpost isn't far up the hill, but you're not in good shape yet. There are many Overseers by the main building.

Far Reach onto the scaffolding on the second level of the outpost you're approaching. Jump around up there until you get to a window, and slip inside. A Rune is in this direction, but be patient. Far Reach from the inside of the window to the left; there aren't many patrollers there. Stay on this upper level, and look for a barracks where Overseers are sleeping. Sleep Dart the only alert Overseer to keep that room clear. Pickpocket a resting Overseer to get the Confiscation Room Key. With that in hand, move in toward you Rune. It's really close now.

Choke out the Overseer in the far hallway, and then the next one inside the small room to your left. Both are easily ambushed. Unlock the door nearby with your new Key and take the **Rune** and money inside.

Climb down the stairs and Sleep Dart an Overseer at the main desk. Dump him in the room behind there so no one can see he's down. Durante's cell is back there (throw the body in the cell if you think it's funny). A Document on the cell explains that Durante is dead and his possessions were moved.

Return up the stairs and then keep moving until you reach the elevator and another set of steps. Go to the third floor. Two side rooms contain weapons and a Mana Elixir. The main route forward leads toward the Vice Overseer's office.

THE FOURTH FLOOR

If you climb to the fourth floor, you find a mostly destroyed area. A Painting is hidden on the right side of the level, and is reached by crawling through windows along the internal walkway. This is also a useful alternative route to reach Byrne's room, by dropping down into it.

Far Reach through a small window in the side rooms to get behind an Overseer Guard and knock him out. A doctor on the left side of the hallway is just as easy. There are several more Overseers in the level—the Vice Overseer and his buddies. A group Mesmerize takes care of them really well if you combine it with Sleep Darts and some choking for the last fellow. However, making noise and taking out the investigators works too.

When everyone is down, take Durante's Key from a desk in the Vice Overseer's office. Look for a **Bonecharm** in the same desk.

Exit the building and return to neutral territory. Far Reach on top of a simple building close to the Overseer checkpoint. Our screenshot shows you which one we're talking about.

Break through the wooden boards on the second story and slip into the house. Search for the **Bonecharm**, some Raw Whalebone, and other items of lesser importance.

Head to Howler territory again after leaving the house. Use the upper pathway you took earlier to reach Paulo's apartment, and then Far Reach again to get to Durante's office without being seen. Unlock his door with the Key from the Vice Overseer's room.

Enter and read everything there. You get a Silvergraph Studio Key while taking Durante's Documents. Look behind a bottle of booze to find a **Bonecharm** before you go.

The only other collectible in this mission is underground. Spot it with the Heart and then go to the other side of the balcony when you leave Durante's office. Far Reach to enter the alley below the balcony (otherwise you make way too much noise when you fall).

Crouch and go around the corner when no one is looking, and Far Reach down into a basement entrance. The cellar contains a **Blueprint** and a **Bonecharm**. If you want, knock out a Howler keeping an Overseer captive.

Exit the cellar and get away from the Howlers' territory. Retreat almost all the way to the beginning of the district, where the large statue is located. Your waypoint leads toward the Jindosh Lock.

When you arrive, input the answer to the riddle you receive, from left to right. Ignore the hints to the riddle found next to the door. Instead, put in the answers you found in Durante's study. The combo changes each time you play the game, so you can't just memorize the answer and use the same one in the future.

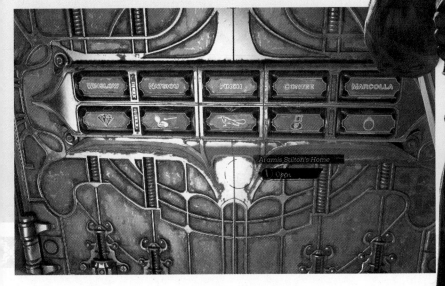

The door unlocks when the correct code is entered. Proceed to the Stilton Mansion.

A Crack in the Slab

A strange ritual was performed three years ago in Aramis Stilton's Manor, involving Delilah Copperspoon and her followers. Once inside, find out what you can about Delilah's secrets.

COLLECTIBLES

Runes	3
Shrines	N/A
Bonecharms	3
Coins	3334
Blueprints	1
Paintings	2

SPECIAL ACTIONS

Under the Table	Steal the Master Key while hiding under the dining room table
Temporal Investigator	Reach the study without using the door code
A Mind Made Whole	Save Aramis Stilton from going insane
Leaky Basement	Fine the Rune in the basement
Collapsed Balcony	Manipulate time to collapse the balcony
A Better Today	Visit Aramis Stilton's office in the altered present

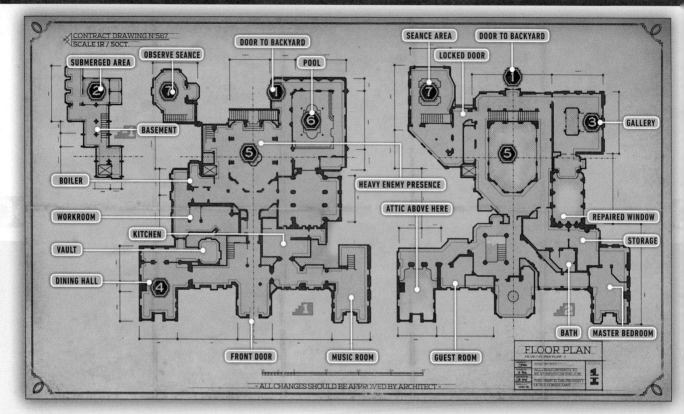

SUBMERGED AREA

OBSERVE SEANCE

DOOR TO BACKYARD

POOL

SEANCE AREA

LOCKED DOR

DOOR TO BACKYARD

BASEMENT

GALLERY

BOILER

WORKROOM

KITCHEN

VAULT

DINING HALL

HEAVY ENEMY PRESENCE

ATTIC ABOVE HERE

REPAIRED WINDOW

STORAGE

BATH

MASTER BEDROOM

FRONT DOOR

MUSIC ROOM

GUEST ROOM

FLOOR PLAN

1/1

— ALL CHANGES SHOULD BE APPROVED BY ARCHITECT —

ARAMIS STILTON'S MANSION

Discover Delilah's Secrets

Stilton's mansion isn't really guarded at the moment, so you're free to explore the place. Only a few items show up as collectible when you equip your Heart, but this level has a few tricks up its sleeve, so there are more items than you expect.

Walk upstairs and turn toward the right. A **Rune** is on the floor, not far from the top of the stairs. Grab it, then approach the noble's private quarters, and drop down through the floor into his music room. Talk to Stilton and the Outsider. You receive a new tool: the Timepiece.

THE TIMEPIECE

With this new item, you can switch between the mansion as it stands right now, and the mansion as it was three years ago. This allows you to explore, find more collectibles, and proceed through the story. Most of the puzzles and problems in this level revolve around jumping back and forth to avoid various obstacles.

When the cutscene ends, you're left in the music room. Try out the Timepiece, and switch back and forth between time periods. Raising and lowering a lens on the device lets you catch a glimpse of the other timeline without switching, but it obstructs your vision of the current area and should be kept down most of the time.

Exploring and Collecting

Venture to the past and listen to a conversation between two Guards. They're on the other side of the door. When they leave, return to the present and approach the barricade just outside the main door. Switch timelines again to find yourself in the corridor outside the music room. Now you can move freely again.

Walk quietly down the hall and examine the Guards in the distance. The doors to the right lead into the kitchen, where two civilians are working. You can't get through the door at the back without the Kitchen Key. Return to the present and look in a cabinet (almost across from the door you entered) to find the Kitchen Key. Retrieve it and switch to the past timeline.

Unlock the kitchen door, head through, and switch to the present. Hop through a damaged window to enter an open yard. Go through the doors on the left and get out your Crossbow. Two Wolfhounds are resting in the adjoining area. Shoot them at long range.

Another door takes you back to the right side of the mansion. A few Bloodfly nests are in there. Destroy those as you explore. With that room clear, go back to the Wolfhounds' area and climb up the debris to reach the higher tier. Jump over the railing and continue clearing nests. Have your Sleep Darts out, because a Nestkeeper patrols this part of the level. Dart him the second you see him.

Go back downstairs. Another set of steps close by leads into the basement. Watch out for Rat swarms, and look for a submerged room. There is a **Rune** inside, but it takes some work to acquire: Go into the past and ambush two Elites working nearby. When they're down, get a wheel off the shelves in the corner. Throw it into the room that becomes submerged in the present. Jump forward in time, attach the wheel to a pipe in the watery area, and then jump up to obtain the Rune.

Don't leave the basement yet. Go to the other end and look for an elevator. Jump to the top lip of it and open a hatch. Climb inside and maneuver around until you find a place to go into the past.

A **Bonecharm** is on top of the elevator ceiling. Most spots to transition there are blocked, but shift and reposition until you find enough room. Get it and leave the elevator.

Return to the ground floor. An iron gate held with a wooden board offers another exit from this major set of rooms. Destroy the board and open the gate. Go around the new bend on the right, and examine a collapsed pile of debris.

Switch to the past timeline and loot a desk in the same spot. Crawl underneath the desk afterward and find a place to transition. By doing this, you avoid the barricade and can enter the locked boiler room ahead. In the past, there is a **Black Bonecharm** in there, inside a safe. You also get 135 items' worth of money. To obtain the loot, take the body of a dead Wolfhound in the past and put it into the furnace. Press a button to turn on the furnace and wait for it to finish cremating the body. When you return to the present, the safe has the correct combination on its door. Record it, and go back to the past to open the safe.

In the past, there is another collectible on the left side of the mansion. Above the dining room are three chandeliers. Hop onto the farthest one while in the past, transition, and then leap up to a broken set of joists in the present. The **Bonecharm** is in an attic area above the dining room.

Transition in Tim

Unfold Timepie

Down below, one of the Veterans is carrying the Master Key. Hide under the dining room table while in the present, and shift to the past. Pickpocket the Master Key without being seen (this counts as a special action).

Find the Combination to the Study

That's enough gathering. Return to the kitchen, pass through into the large hallway beyond, and walk by the area where you defeated the two Wolfhounds. Climb to the upper tier of the room again and get right next to the waypoint (it says "Combination").

Switch to the past there. You end up right behind a Veteran, but he doesn't know you're near him. Use the marked door to exit the mansion and enter the backyard.

STILTON'S BACKYARD

The backyard isn't too large an area. Go to the edge of the railing ahead and use your Spyglass to look out over the yard below.

Creep down the unguarded right hallway. Climb onto some wooden supports at the end of the hall, and crouch while you advance. You can get close to your waypoint by doing this. Eavesdrop on Stilton for a while.

Get out your Crossbow and transition to the present. There are a few Wolfhounds in the yard, but they can be killed without costing you your Merciful rating. Hit them with Bolts, and then head to the gazebo where Stilton was pacing around.

Climb onto the railing of the gazebo, at the back, and transition. Immediately grab the combination and transition back without being spotted. If you just read the codes in the present, you don't get the full amount of info.

Many things about the present change depending on what happens to Stilton that dark night three years ago. If you do nothing to him, the present ends up being what you've already seen. Choke him unconscious and he won't have to witness the terrifying events that drove him insane. Kill him and his story will end there.

The three paths change the look of the mansion and the creatures that are still inside of it. In this walkthrough we'll leave Stilton as he is.

Get into the Study

Return through the yard and follow the waypoint to the doors. Transition to the past to go through them.

Two Elites are near this entrance into the mansion. Lure the first over when the other patrols away. Knock him out, hide him behind the screen where you began, and then do the same for the other. If you get nervous using yourself as bait, Sleep Darts work well too, but you might be getting low on them by now even if you use Bonecharms to help salvage them after use.

The study is your marked waypoint now. Approach with care, and transition to keep yourself from being seen when you cross the big room and head upstairs. You need to be in the past to get the door open, because the lock is broken in modern times. Switch back once you're hugging the door, and input the code to unlock it.

Go through the study and the séance room below. You witness a couple of events, and everything you see is important. When it's finished, retreat from the mansion and try to return to the Dust District.

Visit a Very Old Place

When you walk out the mansion's door, you're transported somewhere else. The Outsider explains what you've seen, and he walks you through several places in the Void. There aren't any challenges or tricks here, so just watch and learn.

Look around you, a crumbling island at the very edges of the Void.

When he's done, you return to the world.

Return to Your Allies

Run back through the Dust District. Your waypoints are marked, and there are few Guards. It only takes a minute or two to find Sokolov and Captain Foster back by the skiff.

PREPARING ABOARD THE DREADFUL WALE

You get some rest back on the ship, and then wake up a few hours later. Meet Captain Foster on deck and talk to her. She and Sokolov are figuring out what needs to be done during the assault on the Duke's Palace.

There's a new Audiograph down in the briefing room as well, if you're interested.

After you finish with everyone, head to the skiff and tell Foster you're ready to go!

The Grand Palace

Self-serving and corrupt, Duke Luca Abele rules Serkonos, and orchestrated the Coup against you. Enter the Grand Palace
to find and eliminate the Duke, who protects himself from assassins with a body double. You must also locate Delilah's

COLLECTIBLES

Runes	5
Shrines	1
Bonecharms	7
Coins	4430
Blueprints	3
Paintings	3

SPECIAL ACTIONS

Through the Pantry	Enter the Vault through the secret pantry passage
Sunken Storage	Swim into the submerged storage room beneath the Palace
Friends in High Places	Place Duke Luca Abele with his body double
Haunted by the Past	Steal the broken gazelle from the Vault
Black Market Heist	Steal yet again from the black market
Addressing Karnaca	Use the speaker in Duke Abele's chambers

RAVINA BOULEVARD

Find a Way to the Grand Palace

Climb the stairs above the docks after you land. There's Raw Whalebone over by some fish stalls, but that's about it for the dock area. Follow the only path away from the docks and through this civilian area. Two smugglers down on the beach are talking about their work. Listen in for a moment as you pass above them.

You can't board their boat without the Delivery Boat Key. If you get it later, return for some money and quite a few minor weapons inside.

Take out your Heart and get an idea what's spread around this map. Your first target is a Black Bonecharm. It's the farthest collectible on the right. Follow the docks until the path finally splits. Take the route to the right, through an alley. Pass a beggar and stop a few feet later. Far Reach onto a wooden scaffold above you, and then keep going up with Far Reach until you reach a pipe way higher up.

Crawl through an open window at the top. Go inside and open a vise to collect the **Black Bonecharm**. You also find Raw Whalebone.

Watch the street below the other side of the apartment. Far Reach down and into the Winslow Safe Company store when the Guards are patrolling the other way. Inside, you find a code for the gate in the adjoining alley and an Apartment Key from the register. Knock out the clerk in the store to make sure he doesn't freak out while you're taking everything. Steal the Key afterward.

ANOTHER ROBBERY

To rob the black market here, unlock the gate by exiting the Winslow building and slipping into the nearby alley. Open the gate using the code you obtain in the Winslow Safe Company store. Sneak up on a woman trying to use the black market. Pickpocket her to get the Key to the boat back in the harbor. When you arrive at the harbor, the boat has been robbed (although there is an instance where, after getting the boat key, if you're really really fast, you'll find the guards in the process of robbing the boat). To find the missing Audiograph, search the first floor of the building with a windmill on its roof. Use the password at the back door to the market, and then you're inside. Steal the Key from the shopkeeper, knock him out, and take everything you want. Grab the special item that turns off the electricity to the carriageway. This helps in the next section.

BLACK MARKET GOODS

ITEM	COST
Crossbow Bolt	20
Pistol Bullet	30
Sleep Dart	30
Grenade	70
Stun Mine	70
Spring Razor	50
Addermire Solution	150
Health Elixir	75
Rewire Tool	200
Disable the Carriage Rail	250

Don't leave the black market area just yet. Go out the back door and hop up the embankment that overlooks the store. Crouch, creep past a bright light in the area above, and hug the wall as you turn right. You come to a wooden barricade. Break through it and look for the **Outsider Shrine** in the room within. You also get Raw Whalebone there.

Runes (11m)

You're done looting the right side of the region. Backtrack to the split in the path, before you met the beggar. The route to the left leads toward two Bonecharms. As soon as you start along that road, you spot Guards ahead. Don't approach them.

Instead, Far Reach up to the balconies above the road. Jump to them, and then onto a circular platform that surrounds a massive tree in the middle of the area. Far Reach from there onto a third-floor balcony, to the left side of the road. Toss the place for the first **Bonecharm** in this apartment block.

The apartment with the second Bonecharm is farther along the same street. Far Reach out to the Watchtower that overlooks the area and turn it off by removing its Whale Oil Tank. Observe the Guards from above, and Far Reach over to the next apartment building when they're away.

Climb to the third floor and use the Apartment Key from the Winslow Safe Company area to enter. Search for a **Blueprint** and some valuables inside. Head into the bedroom and slice a pillow off the bed. Underneath is the **Bonecharm** you've been tracking. The safe in the apartment has 225 coins and some Bullets. Search the area by the desk to find a picture of a man with a safe behind him. The combo is right there in the picture (123).

Use the door up here to get into the next part of the map at your leisure.

Outside, at ground level, is another **Blueprint**. It's down in an open-air store not too far away from the Wall of Light. Sneaking in and stealing it requires great stealth. Shadow Walk really helps here. Either use that and wait for an opening, or knock out all the patrollers. Both take some time.

If you want more collectibles, cross the street and enter another apartment building. This one has a Windmill on the roof.

Climb to the top floor and knock out two Guards protecting the Windmill. Turn off the Wall of Light now, if you wish, but that's not why you're here. Instead, stand by the Windmill and look over the edge. Far Reach to a balcony almost directly underneath you, on the right.

A **Rune** is tucked away in here, but several Bloodfly nests and a Nestkeeper protect the place. Use a Sleep Dart on the Nestkeeper before you go far inside from the balcony. Then take out the nests without worrying about watching your back. If you've knocked out enough Guards nearby, you might even be able to use your Pistol on the nests without triggering anyone. The Rune is in the bathroom area. You also get money from the bedroom and a **Painting** of an old acquaintance of your father.

You have everything in the district. Retreat safely to the upper apartment and use the door to leave the area. You're ready to approach the Palace itself.

Far Reach to ground level on the other side of the door. Sneak past two talking Guards, and Far Reach up onto the carriageway above. Use that to cross toward the Palace.

You can get to the other side easily, but there are still many Guards in between you and the main entrance.

THE PALACE

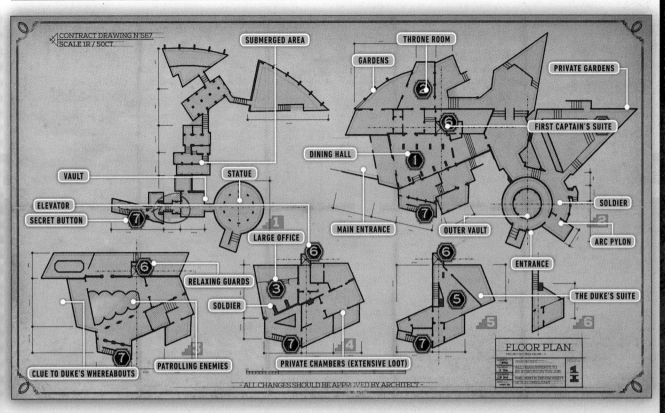

CONTRACT DRAWING N°567
SCALE 1R / 50CT.

SUBMERGED AREA

THRONE ROOM

GARDENS

PRIVATE GARDENS

FIRST CAPTAIN'S SUITE

DINING HALL

VAULT

STATUE

ELEVATOR

SECRET BUTTON

SOLDIER

ARC PYLON

LARGE OFFICE

MAIN ENTRANCE

OUTER VAULT

ENTRANCE

RELAXING GUARDS

THE DUKE'S SUITE

SOLDIER

CLUE TO DUKE'S WHEREABOUTS

PATROLLING ENEMIES

PRIVATE CHAMBERS (EXTENSIVE LOOT)

FLOOR PLAN

- ALL CHANGES SHOULD BE APPROVED BY ARCHITECT -

Getting Collectibles

Go through the first yard, clearing out the Guards ahead of you. Do this by luring the first couple forward; almost let them spot you, and then hide while they approach to see what's going on. Choke them out and leave them behind cover when they're unconscious. Far Reach past the next two Guards. Hit the Elite Guard in back with a Sleep Dart, and then knock out the closer one from behind.

Don't go up to the front door. The Wolfhound and Elite Guard there are an annoying combo to face. Instead, hop over the left wall and crouch as you descend into the garden. Two civilians are in the lower level, while a single Guard watches them from above. Far Reach up and behind him for the easy knockout.

When the civilians split up, knock them out too. It's not necessary, but it reduces the chance of complications.

Climb up the stairs toward the main building. There are many more civilians ahead, so watch your targeting. You can reach two rooms from here. The pool doesn't contain anything of importance yet. Ignore it. The Duke's throne room farther along contains loot, but it's guarded and hides a trap.

The lone Guard isn't a problem. He's in there with a maid and can be dispatched in so many ways. However, an electrical coil goes off on anyone who isn't supposed to be in there. To loot the Bonecharm in the room, you need to disable that trap.

Use Shadow Walk to enter and get behind the throne. Pull out the Whale Oil Tank back there to disable the trap. Turn on Dark Vision to watch the maid and Guard. When the Guard isn't close enough to notice, slip out and steal the **Bonecharm** on the throne. Then leave the room.

FINDING THE DUKE

We've taken you through the entire palace, even though you might have been able to find the Duke and his double already. The reason for this is that the Duke can be in several locations. Now that you've cleared a path through the main building, you can reach all of these areas even if you are still looking for the Duke.

He can be in one of these five locations: the private garden, the throne room, his 3rd floor office, his private quarters, or Delilah's chamber. Search these one final time if you're still tracking him down.

Get Far Reach ready and enter the pool for just a moment. Use Far Reach to zip past the talking civilians inside, and enter a room on the left. You go through a few small rooms afterward. This takes you near a closet, through a sitting room with a resting civilian (who should be knocked out), and then forward into a longer hallway. These are the First Captain's Quarters.

Two drunk Guards are in rooms to the right. Knock them out if you wish. Then sneak up on the Veteran at the far end of the office. Far Reach behind him for a knockout, or use a Sleep Dart if the proximity worries you. Grab all the Elixirs in the suite, and examine the safe. It contains a **Rune** and 300 coins, but the combination isn't here. It's in the Duke's quarters.

Backtrack to the sitting room. Dump the unconscious civilian in the First Captain's Quarters, and then look through the door to your left. This opens into the banquet hall. No one is paying attention here. Knock out the Guard close by, the resting civilian, and the Elite across the way without getting caught. Take them all into the First Captain's Quarters.

Cross the banquet hall and head toward the Bonecharm close by. Your Heart picks it up clearly. The item is inside a room on the right as you move away from the banquet. Save before you enter, because there are multiple civilians inside. Getting the Bonecharm from the inner bedroom without freaking them out is tricky.

Use Sleep Darts after the two women separate, or Shadow Walk to knock them out. This gives you much more time to nab the **Bonecharm** from the bed, and the Sleep Dart under a table in the front part of the suite.

Close the doors to the suite when you leave, and sneak along the wall to reach another exit, closer to the banquet hall where you started. This leads into a stairwell that goes both up and down.

Take the lower stairs and knock out the Guard at the bottom. Proceed through the lower kitchen and knock out the Elite as well. Those are the only two defenders down here. Then look for a small button near some heavy wooden paneling. We give you a picture of it so you know where to look.

Press the button and open a secret door. You enter a series of rooms with excellent treasure. Get a **Blueprint** for a long table two chambers into the secret passage, and a **Black Bonecharm** from a side room. You can't get through the heavy Vault doors from this side. You'll be back.

The side room with the Black Bonecharm has one more secret to reveal. Look for a screen placed against the wall. Slash it apart with your Sword to reveal an abandoned area within the basement. Swim into the water collected there, and take a fast dive underneath some stairs. If you move quickly, you can collect the **Rune** there and return before you drown.

Leave the secret chamber and return to the stairway. Ascend a few flights while using your Heart to locate your new target, a Corrupt Bonecharm. Knock out the only Guard by the landing, and then open the doors to your right. Knock out a civilian cleaning the room you've reached, but stay close to the walls. A Guard is in a second room, and he can get a line of sight on you if you're careless.

Follow the suite to the bathroom at the back. Knock out yet another maid on the way; she'll be fine. Take the **Corrupt Bonecharm** from a cabinet in the bathroom, and then back out. Examine a windowsill on your way out for two pieces of Raw Whalebone.

The other suite on the same level contains a **Blueprint** inside a dresser, but a maid and a Clockwork Soldier are in the room too. You don't have to fight anyone. Wait for the maid to look away, sneak into the room, and grab the Blueprint (turn right and hug the wall to locate it). Exploring the rest of the room nets you the code to the safe in the First Captain's Quarters.

Go out to the stairs and ascend another level. This entire floor is dominated by a single suite. Explore it for minor loot. An internal stairway leads to the top. That's one of the spots where the Duke or his double might be located.

No offer to bow or kiss my hand?

Skip

129

Double Cross

For this plan to work, you have to retrieve the Medal that Duke Abele carries. Get a Chest Key from the double before you leave, and loot the desk nearby for a pile of good materials.

Unlock the door to the outer balcony and go outside from the Duke's suite. Use Far Reach to safely descend and move toward the private garden. It's marked, but don't fully go to ground level. Use the wooden support beams to move out and over the private garden.

Private Garden (43m)

Use Dark Vision to find some cables below you. They're feeding one of Jindosh's Arc Pylons. Far Reach to the cables and follow them to a panel. Remove a Whale Oil Tank to disable the device, and then climb back up the steps toward the garden. Disable a lonely Elite Guard, and then the Duke is fully isolated.

Approach, surprise him, and knock the ruler out. Take his Vault Key, but don't pick him up yet. Leave him in the garden while you prepare the Vault. There is a patrolling Clockwork Soldier, and another Arc Pylon in front of the Vault itself. Shadow Walk to the machine's Whale Oil Tank and disable it from the shadowy corner. Wait for the Clockwork Soldier to leave on the far end of his patrol, and then bring the unconscious Duke to the Vault.

While passing through the Vault again, use the effigy to seal away Delilah's Spirit. This is important for your final mission. A short cutscene plays before you continue. Loot everything in the Vault for a massive amount of money and the Haunted by the Past secret action, and leave the Duke's body by the inner Vault door.

By yourself, return into the Palace and the secret passage. Unlock the inner Vault door so you can grab the Duke without having to carry him all the way through the more dangerous parts of the Palace.

Take him upstairs to his room. Place the Duke on the bed and watch an enjoyable cutscene.

That's it then. Now it's up to me. I'll take the medallion and call them.

You're done at the Palace. Exit and follow the waypoint to the Duke's private dock. Leave as soon as Captain Foster arrives to pick you up.

LAST TRIP ON THE DREADFUL WALE

Wake up on the Dreadful Wale and go to the briefing room. Talk to Sokolov and examine his most recent painting. Search the room behind it for a **Blueprint** on the worktable, then meet Captain Foster on deck and talk to her. Pickpocket a Cabin Key when the conversation is over, and go belowdecks again. Open her cabin (beside the briefing room), and steal two **Bonecharms** from a desk.

You now where to go to find Delilah, but how will you handle her? It's my hope that you have some sort of plan.

With all that done, use the skiff to go ashore.

9

Death to the Empress

You must confront Empress Delilah Copperspoon before she changes all the world with her will. Enter Dunwall Tower and find a way to reunite Delilah Copperspoon's spirit with her body to make her mortal again. Only then can you eliminate her and take back the throne.

COLLECTIBLES

Runes	5
Shrines	1
Bonecharms	9
Coins	2562
Blueprints	2
Paintings	1

SPECIAL ACTIONS

Captain's Quarters	Search Meagan Foster's cabin aboard the Dreadful Wale
World As It Should Be	Trap Delilah in her painting
Avenging Jessamine	Take revenge on Billie Lurk for her part in Jessamine's assassination
Heart of the Tower	Reach the Royal Protector's chambers
Saving Your Father	Rescue Corvo Attano
Saving Your Daughter	Rescue Emily Kaldwin
Black Market Heist	Sneak in one more robbery before the end
Your Daughter Is Safe	Take the throne as Corvo Attano, leaving Emily as a statue
Your Father Is Safe	Take back the throne as Emily, leaving Corvo as a statue
In the Coven's Wake	Use the street speakers to address the public

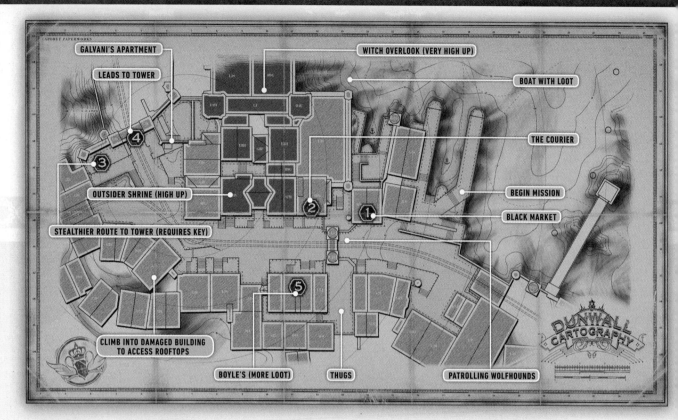

GALVANI'S APARTMENT

LEADS TO TOWER

WITCH OVERLOOK (VERY HIGH UP)

BOAT WITH LOOT

THE COURIER

OUTSIDER SHRINE (HIGH UP)

BEGIN MISSION

BLACK MARKET

STEALTHIER ROUTE TO TOWER (REQUIRES KEY)

CLIMB INTO DAMAGED BUILDING TO ACCESS ROOFTOPS

BOYLE'S (MORE LOOT)

THUGS

PATROLLING WOLFHOUNDS

DUNWALL CARTOGRAPHY

DUNWALL STREETS

Looting the City

You land in Dunwall again, but the streets are in even worse shape than when you left. Wolfhounds wander aimlessly, threatening anyone who gets too close. Keep your Crossbow out and ready, and kill any that wander near you.

BLACK MARKET GOODS

ITEM	COST
Crossbow Bolt	20
Pistol Bullet	30
Sleep Dart	30
Grenade	70
Stun Mine	70
Spring Razor	50
Addermire Solution	150
Health Elixir	75
Rewire Tool	200
Rune	400
Key to City Watch Armory	250

A Rune shows up when you scan with your Heart. It's close, near the docks. Follow the waypoint toward it, and you bump into the black market. See what they have for sale besides that Rune.

 ## ROBBERY

Get the Common Key found near the Courier (we explain where soon) and use it to unlock a door at the back side of the black market. It's roughly one floor down from the shop. Once you enter this small warehouse, look for a broken section of the ceiling. Blink up there to enter the shop, and steal whatever you like.

Listen carefully while you shop. If you haven't taken out both patrolling Wolfhounds, one of them might lumber in and chomp on you even while you're buying things.

Complete your purchases, and take a detour to search the boat that's gone ashore in the harbor if you want more cash. Go out behind the docks to find it. Clear out the boat and return to the main street. Pass between the broken gates on the road, and kill another Wolfhound in the next strip.

Look for Boyles, on the left as you advance. The front door is heavily barricaded, so go around back. Stay crouched, because two punks in the back alley hear you if you're running around.

Enter Boyles and knock out the handful of people from the Hatter gang who are robbing the place. There is more than enough money to go around once they're all unconscious. Using stealth, approach and eliminate everyone without making noise.

Leave Boyles and head over to the Dunwall Courier. Its main door is sealed too, but a small alley on the left lets you get closer

to the building. Climb over some debris, and use the Courier's side entrance. Talk to the editor up top to see what he's doing in the name of truth, and maybe loot the building a little too, because it has hundreds of coins' worth of goodies.

Leave the Courier; go to the first floor but take the building's safe door into a ruined alley. To your right is a metal shelf. Clear away a couple of bottles, and grab the **Common Key**, which is required for you to pull off the black market robbery.

Follow the street toward the tower. The City Watch Armory Key found in the black market unlocks the small Guard building near the end of the path. It has Raw Whalebone, weapon supplies, and a door that leads to Coldridge Canal. Don't use the door yet.

To unlock the door to Galvani's apartment, search the area for a maid corpse and take her key. This place is across the street from the City Watch Armory. A **Blueprint** is inside, on the worktable. You find an Elixir and some modest treasure along with it.

A smaller building beside the main road looks totally devoured. There's nothing in it, but the ceiling is damaged. Far Reach to get up a level, and stay quiet as you ascend all the way to the fourth floor of the destroyed place.

A Witch lives at the top, but she looks out over the street most of the time. Keep quiet and hit her with a Sleep Dart to disable her. Use the beams that lead out from the building to cross the street onto a balcony. Men are inside, stealing what they can.

Disable the one on the left, and Far Reach behind the one in the right room to knock him out too. If he's already approaching, ambush him when he comes around the corner.

Look for a Barometer in the second room. It opens a secret door. The next room contains an **Outsider Shrine** and plenty of items to steal.

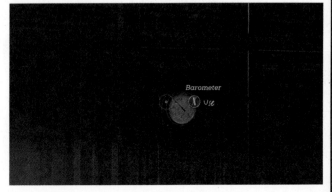

Barometer   ① Use

Return to the balcony and skirt the left side of the building. Walk over pipes to reach the back of the structure. Use your Heart to target a Black Bonecharm much higher up, and begin crossing the rooftops to get closer to it.

A Witch watches you from above. Hit her with a Sleep Dart once you get close enough to do so; she's on a stone ledge at the top of the ascent. If you can't get a good angle to shoot her, climb up the buildings on the right to reach her level and then hit her from the flanks.

Search inside the lofty place to obtain a **Black Bonecharm**.

Find a Way into Dunwall Tower

After getting the Black Bonecharm, return to street level and use the door into Coldridge Canal from the Armory. That key is purchased from the black market.

COLDRIDGE CANAL

You're directly outside Dunwall Tower, but at a weird angle. You're in the canal that backs up against the tower. This poorly guarded approach gives you a major advantage against your enemies.

Swim forward onto the small landing along the right wall, then use a mix of jumping and Far Reach to start a major ascent. You can comfortably reach the top of the walls with just a moment of climbing.

Get onto the walls and crouch to look around. To your left are two Witches and a couple of Gravehound skulls lying on the ground. Avoid that area.

Instead, hop off the wall and look for a small opening on the right (above ground level). Jump onto some pipes to get in. Several Witches are in the greenhouse. A **Bonecharm** is on the left side of the room. The Witches are distracted enough that a bold player can stealth over and steal the Bonecharm without mishap.

Take the far door out of the greenhouse and stealth between the two large groups of enemies to the left and right. This takes you directly toward the parapets. Jump over the wall and onto the hill below. Use your Heart to locate a Bonecharm. That's the direction you want.

A Witch and Gravehound patrol along the left, so skirt them by heading toward an infamous gazebo on the right. This is the long way around to your target, but it's safer.

Look out over the far wall of the gazebo. A **Painting** is on a lower terrace, but you have to deal with three Gravehounds to get it. Use your Crossbow Bolts and shoot each skull from above. The Gravehounds don't even get to spawn, and they don't start any alerts. There aren't any Witches to spot your actions, so you're in good shape.

Approach the large building where the other Bonecharm is located. You might remember this structure from the last game. This is the channel lock that lets boats approach Dunwall Tower without getting destroyed.

Stay low to avoid the gaze of a Witch near the corner of the building, but don't disable her. She can't spot you unless you're careless. Get onto the walkway on the right side of the building to advance.

Move around to the back of the building and use Dark Vision to spot the Witch watching your side of the structure. Jump up when she turns around, and choke her out. The Witch on the other side of the platform is even more vulnerable and can be disabled without care. Grab the **Bonecharm** from an open box.

Return to the gazebo and stay left as you creep along the walls and approach the pump room. A Rune is hidden inside, but there are several Witches along the way. The first is on some stairs near the pump room and looks isolated. Be wary. Another Witch just inside the room might see if you attack the lone enemy. Lie in wait and use Dark Vision to time your attack.

Go after the two remaining Witches inside the pump room once you down the outer foe. These Witches are spread out a little, which makes your life a bit easier. Get onto the walkway on the right side of the room and look for a tiny recess along the wall. Hop down into it to get under the walkway, and collect the **Rune** you seek.

Exit the pump room by jumping through a small window in the upper part of the room. Far Reach onto the walkway above the tower entrance, and only jump down when you're directly above the doorway that leads inside.

Enter the tower when you're ready.

DUNWALL TOWER INTERIOR

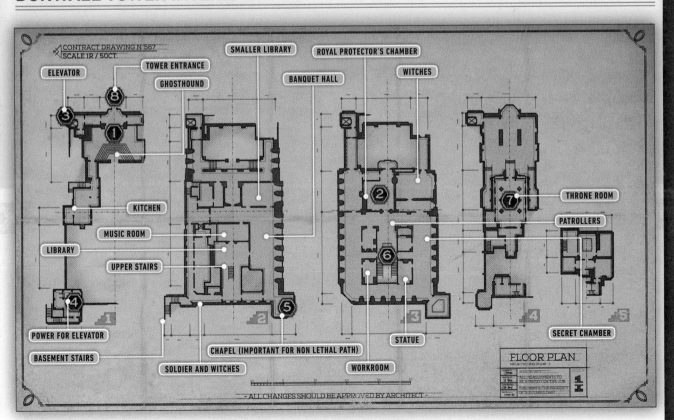

Search the Overseer Chapel

The first few rooms of the tower are somewhat quiet. Two Witches are to the left, in a room that doesn't have anything you need. Far Reach forward, over some debris, to avoid their line of sight and to reach the main foyer. Use your Crossbow at range to kill a Gravehound skull near the dead Overseer ahead. With that down, loot both a **Bonecharm** and a **Corrupt Bonecharm** from the corpse.

Climb the stairs at the back of the room and look for the only way forward that isn't locked. A statue of Delilah is in the middle of the corridor, and you can talk to her if you like without being formally spotted. We suggest that you don't interact with it at all.

Sneak into the next hallway. The number of defenders starts to increase, so be on guard. Open the door almost directly ahead to find a music room. Another statue is there, if you're feeling chatty. Again, say nothing if you want your confrontation with Delilah to be a bit easier when you two meet.

Back out and take the left side of the hallway. Another door is close by, along the other wall. Open it to explore a small library. You get a piece of Raw Whalebone for your efforts.

A banquet area lies ahead. Everyone there looks dead, but don't approach. First off, a Clockwork Soldier watches the room. Second, Witches are sitting among the dead, eerily chilling out. This is not a safe room.

Instead, back off for now and go down the right side of the hallway. It ends in a door to the kitchen. Listen carefully for two Witches inside to finish their conversation. After they split up, only one remains in the room. Sleep Dart her, then go around the right corner quietly to knock out her partner.

Crawl through a window on the left side of the kitchen and head toward the corner of the building. Two Witches watch the outer hall, so it's easier to stay inside the kitchen and pantry rooms while you advance.

Use Shadow Walk to slip by the Witches and Clockwork Soldier by the corner, and use the stairs there to head down into a security room. Steal a Rune from the pipes overhead, near a series of Whale Oil receptacles.

While you're down there, take an empty Whale Oil Tank from one corner and place it on a filling machine by the receptacles.

Use the lever on the right to fill the tank, and then load it into the only empty receptacle. This turns the power back on.

Two Witches come down to investigate, but they split up a little to do it. Use Shadow Walk again to bypass them (or to knock them out if you prefer). Get back upstairs and head toward the chapel in the other back corner of the building.

Listen to the Audiograph inside the chapel, read a Note next to it, and take two pieces of Dried Algae from the area. Pigments can be found in big bags on the left of the workshop. A Skull on the right is also required. When you have these items, interact with the workshop to place them there. Wait for a magical combining process to complete. When it does, pick up the Corrupt Rune that appears.

Get Two More Collectibles

Leave the chapel and enter the greater library, which is one room away along the hall. Sneak through to avoid the Clockwork Soldier on the first floor.

The top floor of the tower is extremely well-guarded. There are Witches in many rooms, and patrolling Gravehounds make it harder to hide and set up your attacks. Dangerous stuff. Turn left at the top of the stairs, and then pass through a tiny hallway. Use Dark Vision to avoid patrols, and enter the first room you can by turning left again. Knock out a Witch inside and gain a **Bonecharm**. On the other side of the stairs is a hidden room with the other **Bonecharm**. Enter by Far Reaching through an opening almost at ceiling level, from the tiny connecting corridor between the two hallways. The room also contains a survivor who has been hiding this entire time, so give him a few words of comfort before you leave.

Seek Delilah in the Throne Room

After collecting everything you want, head for the throne room. Turn right from the main doors and go through a tiny room to reach the elevator, which appears as your waypoint. It's right next to the entrance you used to get into the tower.

Ambush the Gravehound that rides down when you call the elevator, and then ride up to the throne room at the top of the tower. A door exits onto the rooftop, where you finish this once and for all.

DUNWALL TOWER ROOFTOP

Follow your waypoint into the throne room. Break the wooden boards at the entrance; Delilah is too busy painting and doesn't hear you. However, if you talked to any of Delilah's statues she'll know that you are coming and will meet you directly. She is on her throne when you enter, and is protected by Gravehounds. For this reason, we suggested earlier that you avoid her statues.

If you didn't, use Crossbow attacks to stop the Gravehounds, and then use your Heart on Delilah as soon as you can.

Otherwise, sneak up on her and use the Heart against her while she's busy. A cutscene plays, and she enters her painting. Do not follow yet. Approach the throne and use the Corrupt Rune you made to alter it. Enter the painting only after this is done.

Many replicas are spread around the alternate version of the throne room. Sneak around the area and look for clusters of statues. Each group has a replica hidden inside. As long as you keep choking these replicas from behind, you avoid detection and eventually find the real Empress.

Your status updates as soon as you find the real Delilah and take her down. Lethal players will happily cut her throat and end everything, but you've followed your own methods this entire time. After she's unconscious, carry her out of the painting and put her on Emily's throne. Then interact with Corvo's statue. This takes you through the end of the campaign.

A Long Day in Dunwall

Today marks the anniversary of the death of Empress Jessamine Kaldwin, assassinated 15 years ago. Visitors from across the Empire of the Isles have journeyed to Dunwall Tower for the occasion.

COLLECTIBLES

Runes	1 (During the follow-up)
Shrines	N/A
Bonecharms	N/A
Coins	490
Blueprints	N/A
Paintings	2

SPECIAL ACTIONS

Freedom of the Press	Go to the upper level of the Dunwall Courier and knock out the Guard there before he slaughters the paper's editor
Jessamine's Words	Play an Audiograph from the old Empress
Time Capsule	Find a room boarded up since the Rat Plague
Coin of the Realm	Take the gold from the safe inside the tower's Safe Room
Dr. Galvani's Safe	Open the safe inside Dr. Galvani's laboratory and take its contents
The Ramsey Fortune	Lock Mortimer Ramsey inside the Safe Room

COMBAT WALKTHROUGH

Shine and sharpen your blade. It's time for high Chaos and murder. In this Walkthrough, we cut a bloody path through the entire game. Expect large fights, more danger, and a grim ending. We wouldn't have it any other way.

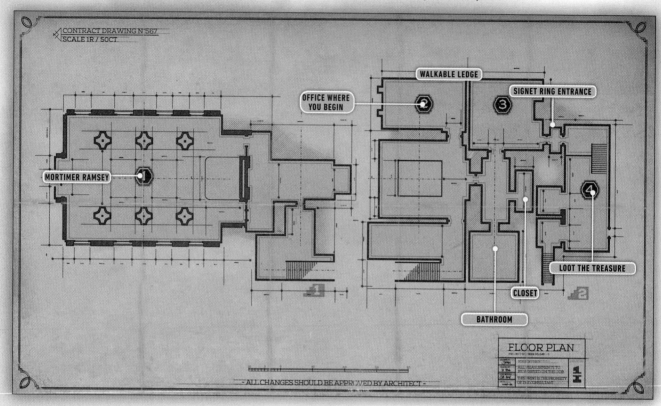

DUNWALL TOWER

Escape the Imperial Chambers

Choose Corvo Attano during the introduction of the game. You gain access to your character after watching the first few cutscenes. You're taken to a private room on the second floor of Dunwall Tower. There, you're locked inside a room and left to rot.

The rough treatment you've received has left you a bit low on health. Remedy this by eating the food on the right side of the room. Interact with it to eat everything, and then search for useful Documents. There's some interesting reading on the desk.

Check on Alexi Mayhew

When you're ready to leave, climb out the window on the left and emerge onto a ledge. Crawl from there over to another room, and go inside. Alexi Mayhew is collapsed on the ground close by. Talk to her. She's wounded and dying. As she expires, you take her Blade and an Audience Request Document.

The hallway ahead leads to two rooms. One is the bathroom. Listen to an Audiograph there for more information. You can also search for some minor items (for coins).

After looting the bathroom, sneak into the other room in the hallway and assassinate the Guard. He holds a Key to your room, which makes travel here easier in the future. Plus, killing him is your first piece of vengeance. To perform the assassination, crouch and creep up behind the soldier. When you're close enough for a melee attack, tap the Attack button and watch Corvo end the man's life in a mere second.

Look for another target in the side room, by the stairs. Kill him before he realizes you're there.

ASSASSINATION

People die instantly if you attack them when they're unaware; they're much harder to kill once they're alerted. There is a brief window of time between these two states. A Guard who starts to spot you doesn't immediately draw their sword and realize trouble is upon them. If you bump into someone, attack immediately. You can still score a fast kill even from the front if you're quick about it.

You've cleared the upper level of the Tower. Descend the stairs and search for a Paper and more fruit, if you need any more health.

Kill Mortimer Ramsey

Follow the only hallway back into the throne room, where the game began. Mortimer Ramsey is talking to two Guards inside. Sneak into the room and wait for Mortimer to approach the doorway you just used to come in. Ambush him from behind. Assassinate Mortimer and then sneak behind the pillars on the right to get behind one of the two Guards in the room. Kill him with surprise on your side, and then charge down his buddy for a proper swordfight.

PARRYING

Swordfights aren't clickfests where you simply outswing your opponents. This method kills lesser Guards, but it's a good way to get yourself killed when fighting a larger group. Instead, time your strikes to get the most out of Corvo's skills.

Parrying is essential! Block enemy strikes at the last moment and immediately counterattack while they're off balance. If you react fast enough, this often scores an animated kill against the target, taking them out of the fight without exposing Corvo.

Open the Safe Room

Loot Mortimer's body for a Signet Ring. You need that to exit the castle. Go back up to the second floor and follow the waypoint to a secret room. Your Signet Ring unlocks this, and a panel slides open to grant access to the chamber.

This room is a treasure trove. Look for Documents, a Health Elixir, Bullets, and your Pistol. This is a powerful sidearm that helps in larger fights. You also gain a huge stash of money if you search the safes in back.

Once you've gathered everything, use the far door to exit into the Dunwall Streets.

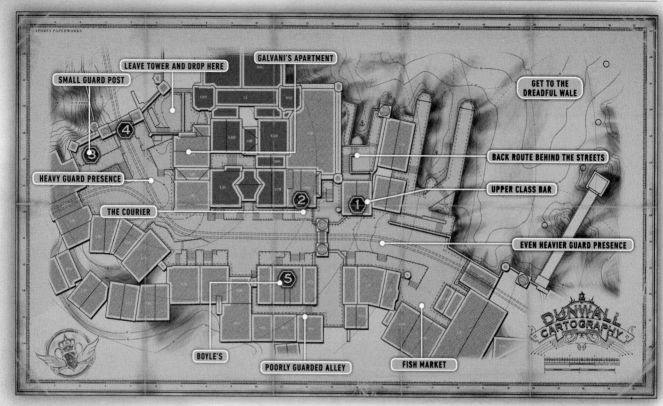

Reach the Streets

Take the passage that leads out toward fresh air and freedom. There are a couple of Documents in the passage, a collectible **Painting** along the right wall, and a few coins to loot as well. Unlock the door at the end of the corridor, and go outside.

You're now out on the rooftops. Climb down the stairs ahead and drop over the roof on the right. Many structures on the way down help you avoid damage. Continue right and look for a Guard in a small yard below. You learn how to do Drop attacks against him. Use a lethal attack to quickly bring the fiend down as you fall upon him from above.

Reach the Boat

Jump over another wall on the right, and crouch while you listen to four soldiers talking. Wait for the men to separate. In time, all of them face away from you, allowing for an excellent chain of kills. Crouch and sneak up on the captain, who was barking orders a moment ago. Slice his throat, do the same for his buddy ahead, and enter the building on the right. Another Guard is searching that house for you (probably for loot). He doesn't hear you if you're still crouching. Cut him down and search for fruit and a Health Elixir. Break the glass on the corner case to reach it. Another Elixir is outside, sitting on a container by the main road.

After clearing the area, enter the laboratory on the left. One Guard might still be inside, if he didn't hear the fighting. Kill him quickly and search around for a Health Elixir in the first room.

A lab is in the second room. Grab a **Painting** off the wall in there, and locate a code scratched into the frame behind it. Use the code (451) to open the safe there. You receive 150 coins and more Bullets for your time.

Search a couple of smaller buildings behind you, or proceed immediately to make it through the area quickly. In road ahead, six more men are clustered into a couple of groups. This is a good time to learn how to deal with larger fights.

Assassinate the first Guard and attack the one to his right immediately afterward. Use aggressive attacks or a parry plus counterattack to kill him before anyone is ready to respond. The other Guards begin to charge because of the noise, so give ground to buy yourself time. Use your Pistol to shoot the first fool who approaches, and cut him apart if he survives the ranged shot. For the others, practice parrying and scoring instant kills with your counterattacks. This is rather easy once you've got the hang of it. If you ever miss a parry or get into trouble, use the Pistol to wound or kill your enemies while backing up to retain your footing!

Today on this sad anniversary we mourn the tragic slaying.
Attention Dunwall citizens! As of today, Delilah Kaldwin is our new Empress. All hail Delilah, first of her name!

You've taken the main street. The Dunwall Courier is on the left. Many Documents are inside, and you can listen to an interesting conversation on the second floor between a soldier and the editor for the paper. Assassinate the soldier so he doesn't encourage any more propaganda in the future. Search the ground floor for a Health Elixir, inside the lockers.

A place called Boyles is on the right. Two men are talking inside, and you learn more about the Crown Killer. You don't need to go in, but it's interesting stuff. Sneak up on both targets to assassinate them without difficulty. A third Guard patrols the street outside and sometimes comes in to check up on things. Cut him down when he enters. Boyles has quite a bit of loot, so search well if you go in!

The main street leads toward the docks. Head straight after you finish looting the nearby buildings. Sneak up the street and assassinate both soldiers on the left. They're paired together, but fast work dispatches both before they scream. The real fight usually starts when you approach a tiny Guard station farther along the road. Lure the man inside back down the road to keep your enemies in the same direction (several more approach now that you're making noise).

As with the last fight, a mix of parries, counterattacks, and Pistol shots ensure you kill these adversaries without taking substantial damage. Even if you lose, it's well worth your time to practice and refine these techniques, because they form your combative backbone throughout the game.

A side yard on the right has minor loot and a Paper to read, and the Guard station holds an Order that comes straight from the Tower. Read these, and then go down to the docks. Walk to the end of the pier and then swim out to the ship marked as your objective.

Talk to the captain of the ship to complete your mission. Her name is Meagan Foster, and she's one of the only friendly faces you see this day.

Lord Protector, forgive me for saying it, but you look like death warmed over.

IN THE VOID

Cross the Floating Island

You wake up in your cabin aboard the ship, but something is very off. A familiar feeling stirs within Corvo, as he's taken to a distant realm he's seen several times before. Try to open the door to your cabin, but turn around afterward. The wall fades away, and you see the Void again.

Walk forward until you meet the Outsider. He speaks with you briefly, and then asks if you want to receive the Outsider's Mark a second time. If you refuse, you go through the game without the use of supernatural abilities.

This makes the game a bit harder, but it's an interesting way to play. This style is far more viable for combative players rather than stealth players, because you can still focus on your weapons and equipment.

If you accept the Mark, you immediately learn Blink and go through a tutorial that shows how to use this ability. Blink to the platform across from Corvo. Notice that you can jump across a gap and still Blink in the air to get even more distance!

Corvo, old friend, do I even have to say it? You've lost another Empress.

Look up at the second gap. Blink up to reach a higher platform, then jump and Blink to cross the divide. You find a grisly scene on the other side, but you don't have to do anything with it.

Instead, run to the end of the area and collect a Heart. Corvo meets and talks to someone. You can then equip the Heart, which helps track down Bonecharms and Runes.

Let the Heart guide you to a **Rune** farther ahead. It's out in the open, so it's easy to find. The level ends after you pick it up.

ABOARD THE DREADFUL WALE

Meet with Meagan Foster

You wake up aboard the Dreadful Wale again. This time it's in the real world, so get up and search your cabin. Write in your log, if you wish. A Crossbow hangs by the door. Take that and the Note next to it. Captain Foster tells you about the hidden markets throughout the region (marked with two hands, to let people know the black market is nearby).

Well, you're better armed than you were, and you have a fighting chance. It's almost time to leave the ship. Open the door to your cabin and explore the lower level.

Follow the objective marker toward Captain Foster. Meet her in the briefing room and talk to her. Listen to her, then search the room and the private berth behind it for more goodies. You gain a couple more Elixirs!

A blocked cabin lies on the other side of the floor. You can't force it open, so search for an open hatch inside the briefing room. Climb out onto the side of the ship and head right. You reach another hatch farther down, which leads you into the barricaded cabin. You find Notes, money, and a Mana Elixir (called Addermire Solutions).

Ascend to the upper levels of the ship and head out onto the deck. Meet the captain again there, and tell her you're ready to go ashore. This starts the next stage of the mission.

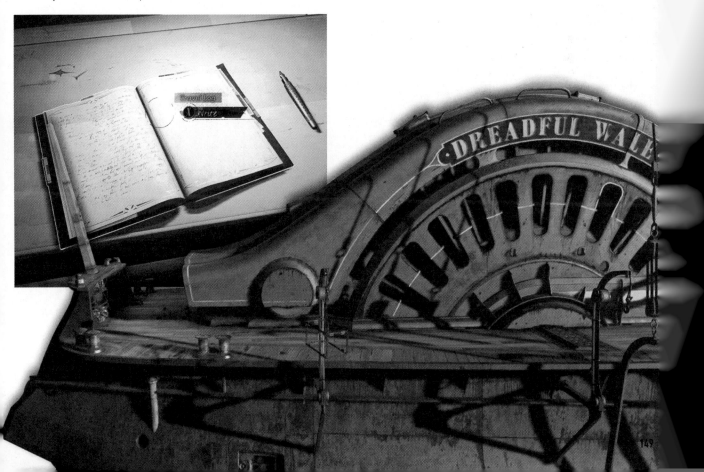

Edge of the World

Find Addermire Station, and take a carriage to Addermire Institute. It is the best lead you have for tracking down the "Crown Killer."

COLLECTIBLES

Runes	7
Shrines	1
Bonecharms	6
Coins	3334
Blueprints	1
Paintings	3

SPECIAL ACTIONS

A Fresh Grave	Snatch a body for Mindy Blanchard
Black Market Heist	Rob the black market
Hypatia's Apartment	Explore Dr. Hypatia's apartment
Try to Unlock Me	Win the safe contest in the Winslow building
The Nest Keeper	Put down the Nestkeeper in the Bloodfly-infested building

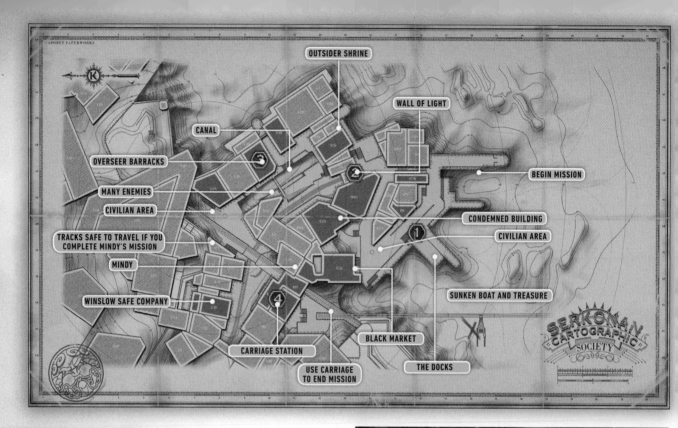

Map labels:
- OUTSIDER SHRINE
- WALL OF LIGHT
- CANAL
- BEGIN MISSION
- OVERSEER BARRACKS
- MANY ENEMIES
- CONDEMNED BUILDING
- CIVILIAN AREA
- CIVILIAN AREA
- TRACKS SAFE TO TRAVEL IF YOU COMPLETE MINDY'S MISSION
- MINDY
- SUNKEN BOAT AND TREASURE
- WINSLOW SAFE COMPANY
- CARRIAGE STATION
- BLACK MARKET
- USE CARRIAGE TO END MISSION
- THE DOCKS

KARNACA DOCKS

Locate the Black Market Shop

Captain Foster takes you to the coast. She can't get you all the way to your destination because of a Watchtower that guards against strange vessels, so that has to be disabled at some point. You make landfall in neutral territory. You aren't attacked or harassed unless you cause trouble.

Take the wharf all the way down to the end of the route. Enter a building and keep your eye out for the black market symbol (two hands). Search inside the building until you find the market. It's on an upper floor. See what you want to purchase, because they have pretty useful stuff!

Collect Items Before Starting Your Work

After you've explored for a few minutes, equip your Heart and search for collectible items here. Let's list where you find a couple things.

The black market shop has a **Rune**.

BLACK MARKET GOODS

ITEM	COST
Crossbow Bolt	20
Pistol Bullet	30
Sleep Dart	30
Grenade	70
Stun Mine	70
Spring Razor	50
Addermire Solution	150
Health Elixir	75
Location of Sunken Supplies	250
Rune	400

You have to purchase it for 400 coins unless you stole it from the market already. A whale carcass along the wharf has a free **Rune**. It's not far from where you begin this level.

The toughest collectible to get here is a **Bonecharm** inside an infested building of Bloodflies. The building is on the left when you start to get close to the Wall of Light. Going through there is dangerous (there are dozens of Bloodflies inside). You lose tons of health if you fight all of the insects without first destroying their nests. Crouch and move carefully to loot the place without drawing their ire. The Bonecharm is upstairs, and there are Elixirs and loose wealth all over the place too. Break a barricaded door on the other side of the house if you want to skip over to the canal area (on the other side of the Wall of Light).

The black market map, that you purchase for 250 coins, leads you to a downed boat in the harbor. If you walk to the end of the farthest point on the docks, you can swim out to get several items there. It's at roughly 2 o'clock from the front of that pier. You get a couple of Sleep Darts, Spring Razors, Bolts, and other goodies. This is mostly great for more combative players.

TO SAVE CASH, STEAL FROM THE BLACK MARKET

To get all the black market's items free of charge, you have the option to rob the place. Pay for any item upgrades ahead of time, because those cannot be stolen, and the shop closes for several minutes after anyone robs it (or forever if you kill the shopkeeper).

To rob the market, clear out the building infested with Bloodflies; it's not far from the market. Destroy all nests on the first few floors. The staircase leading to the top is blocked. Locate a barricaded area near a piano room. Jump and crawl through the gap in the barricade to reach the top of the infested building.

A Nestkeeper is up there. This is an infected person who lives with the Bloodflies. It's easy to miss the guy, and this upper apartment in general. Kill the Nestkeeper with Crossbow shots from a distance, and then slaughter any Bloodflies that remain. The Black Market Key is inside a glass aquarium containing more Bloodflies.

Return to Mindy's yard, behind the black market. Open the back door to the market, go inside, and close the door behind yourself. Knock out the Shopkeeper when you can't be seen.

Steal everything. You gain way more than 1000 gold's worth of items, and there are coins in the storage part of the shop as well. You find even more weapons there too. This place is loaded.

Go to Addermire Station

The path above the wharf takes you toward a Wall of Light. These are defensive structures designed to kill people who cross through them without proper access. There are many ways to avoid this dangerous trap. A stealthy player might use the apartments above to skip the area entirely. A brave adventurer could use the gutter below and deal with the Bloodflies there.

But that's not what we do!

Walk into the yard near the Wall of Light and attack the three Guards on patrol. These men are poorly armed and have little recourse when you go after them.

After the three are dead, climb to a higher area and look for a Windmill. Use your Blink to get up onto the device, and turn it off from a small platform higher on the machine. This shuts down the Wall of Light, making it useless against you.

Enter a building near the Windmill. Two Overseers are searching for heretical artifacts inside. Sneak in to assassinate them, because they're slightly tougher targets. Have your Pistol at the ready, in case they see you before you finish your work.

Afterward, search the back rooms for an **Outsider Shrine** and a **Bonecharm** (on the floor). There are also multiple valuable items, plus a Mana Elixir. Slot your Bonecharms to get their bonuses! Grab the **Painting** near the Shrine as well.

Go through the wall and into Canal Square. Kill the two soldiers below with a fast ambush and search a table for a small number of useful supplies. Do not approach the far side of the canal. Overseers above might spot you, and they carry ranged weapons. Blink up to take them out if that happens, despite the minor disadvantage. Otherwise, stay higher up and cross a bridge to reach these enemies. If you're bold, attack them directly, but in that case you must contend with their numbers and their Pistols. For a safer attack, shoot one of them at range and then retreat past the Wall of Light. Overseers are much easier to deal with when you lure them around corners. They can't fire at you until they're already within Sword range.

It's important to kill this group, because they have a **Bonecharm** and a **Rune** in their midst. Find these items on a table between the various Guards and Overseers.

Down in the canal is another **Rune**, inside a drainage area, that you can't directly reach. To get it, use your Pistol and shoot the wooden board partially blocking the flow of water. This brings the Rune to you.

Jump from a Dumpster onto a balcony overlooking the Overseer's area (where you grab the Rune and Bonecharm). Look for an awning and use that to get up another level onto the third floor. An open doorway leads inside the outpost there. Kill two Overseers before they react to your presence.

Another Overseer sits in the room to your left. Crouch and sneak up on him for an easy kill, and then loot the room for a **Blueprint** and two Elixirs. A **Painting** hangs close by as well. The side of the chamber contains a safe with 225 coins and a **Rune**. The combination shifts a little each time you play the game, so read the Note and a Book on this level to obtain the correct code. One is on the floor nearby, and the other is in a side room.

Go upstairs and sneak through that level to kill two more Overseers. They're talking at first but split up, in case you don't want to fight them directly. Steal an Interrogation Room Key from one of the men. Unlock the door to the interrogation area, or break through a window. Grab the **Corrupt Bonecharm** inside. These have stronger effects but carry a downside to their use.

Kill the two Guards on the roof and Blink over the other rooftops to reach another **Bonecharm** on a corpse not too far away. Kill the Bloodflies around it and take your prize.

Return to the canal area and continue up the main road. You get close to Addermire Station, but there are still a few sides area to explore if you wish. There are Guards and Elite Guards here; the tougher enemies have red coats, so they're easy to spot. Like Overseers, they can be armed with Pistols, so it's best to fight them at close range or to ambush them from a distance with a Crossbow shot to prevent them from shooting back at you! Kill a small cluster of these enemies as you approach the station.

The Winslow Safe Company has a building there. It contains a **Bonecharm** locked in a massive safe on the ground floor (use a combination found inside the register, near the front door, to open the safe). Higher up, Hypatia has her apartment. She's the alchemist you heard about back on the ship. However, her door is locked, so you can't just stroll into the place. Instead, after reaching her floor and locating the locked door, open an exit onto a small balcony next to it. Go around the balcony and jump over the railing toward the front of the building. Climb onto a pipe and take that over to her balcony to get inside without mishap. Take the front door Key, search for Elixirs, and steal the **Painting** in the main hall. Then leave.

Addermire Station is the last major building in the area. It boasts three sets of Guards, but none of them are much for cooperation, so deal with each group on its own. Sneak upstairs, using the steps on the right to find one group. There are three people upstairs. Assassinate the man in the chair. His two buddies rush over. Use your Pistol to shoot the Elite Guard, and then finish the battle with swordplay. Search around before retreating down the stairs.

The Wall of Light in back blocks your way to a carriage. Look right, inside an armory filled with Elixirs and supplies. It contains a few regular Guards. Kill the first and then back into the doorway to avoid being flanked. Then grab a tank of Whale Oil to turn off the circuitry for the Wall of Light (it's just inside the armory door).

Go outside, cut through the last two Guards, and use the carriage to proceed toward the next mission.

The Good Doctor

Eliminate the Crown Killer, who's been murdering your enemies to make you look guilty. Find your ally, Anton Sokolov, last seen being carried toward Addermire. Alexandria Hypatia, who runs the place, should know more.

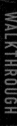

COLLECTIBLES

Runes	6
Shrines	1
Bonecharms	5
Coins	2206
Blueprints	4
Paintings	3

SPECIAL ACTIONS

Sunken Wreck	Swim out to the submerged boat
Abandoned Basement	Find the basement
Release the Hounds!	Let the starving Wolfhounds out
Three Witnesses	Save Hamilton, read Valiente's letter, and talk to Vasco
The Counter-Serum	Craft an antidote

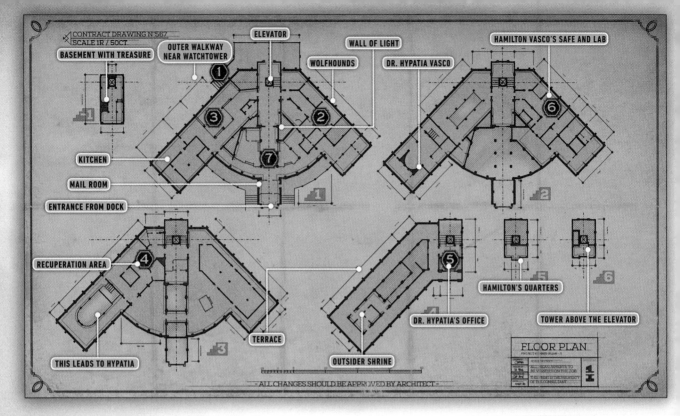

Floor plan labels:
CONTRACT DRAWING N°567
SCALE 1R / 50CT.

BASEMENT WITH TREASURE
OUTER WALKWAY NEAR WATCHTOWER
ELEVATOR
WALL OF LIGHT
HAMILTON VASCO'S SAFE AND LAB
WOLFHOUNDS
DR. HYPATIA VASCO
KITCHEN
MAIL ROOM
ENTRANCE FROM DOCK
RECUPERATION AREA
THIS LEADS TO HYPATIA
TERRACE
OUTSIDER SHRINE
DR. HYPATIA'S OFFICE
HAMILTON'S QUARTERS
TOWER ABOVE THE ELEVATOR

FLOOR PLAN

- ALL CHANGES SHOULD BE APPROVED BY ARCHITECT -

THE ADDERMIRE INSTITUTE

Get a Map of Addermire

Dr. Hypatia runs the Addermire Institute. It's a place where people of means have gone to recover from various ailments. You ride the carriage over there, hoping to find out more about the Crown Killer. You hope to meet Dr. Hypatia as well. For better, and for worse, no Guards greet you as you arrive at the institute.

Turn around and look over the wall behind your starting position. Drop onto a pipe below, and then look underneath the walkway above. A **Bonecharm** lurks in the dark recess there. Use your Heart if you have trouble seeing it. Jump back up the wall when you're done; it has handholds, so Corvo makes it to the top without mishap.

Walk toward the main building. You find your first sign of people when you turn a corner and approach a small receiving room. A patrolling Guard is close by, and two more men are talking inside. Kill the patroller quietly when he isn't looking, and ambush the men inside. At worst, you face one of them alone in a simple duel. Loot the room, and then enter the institute proper.

A **Bonecharm** is on the ground, a few feet inside the entrance. Take it! Turn left and enter a large room with many enemies. Sneak up to the guy on the left and kill him quietly. Stay crouched and repeat this for the lone patroller on the right. This thins the ranks fairly well, but the two men in the center of the room are more alert.

Instead of creeping up on them, line up a Crossbow shot against one, and then close as the other stands. Kill him with your Pistol out, and use that as an Elite Guard closes to assist him. If anything goes pear-shaped, retreat to the starting room and lure the enemies back to you so you know where everyone is.

Search the kitchen and pantry in the left corner for tons of food and some wealth. A **Rune** is in the Guards' area, hung up on the wall.

Head into the next hallway, on the right side of the dining hall. Multiple Guards aren't far from there. To be extra careful, pop out to kill a patroller, and then hide the body back in the last room to continue getting free kills. Otherwise, take the fight to them and retreat to the previous room to avoid ranged attacks while the incoming Guards approach.

A map hangs a few feet away in the new hall. Grab it, because it's an optional goal for this mission. Examine it closely before you pick it up, to get a decent sense of the place's layout.

Go to Dr. Hypatia's Office

Wolfhounds lurk in the next hall, if you continue forward. There are two of them patrolling, and two more inside a locked room. Ranged weapons or sneak attacks kill these enemies easily, but they're a pain in prolonged fights and dangerous if you attack them while Guards are still alive. Since Wolfhounds aren't good at defending themselves, spam your Sword attacks if they ever get close to you.

You can go around the Wall of Light without any trouble; it just connects the main lobby with the route you've cleared. However, if you want to bring down the Wall of Light, look for a ledge above it, on the lobby side. Blink up onto the ledge and get the tank of Whale Oil. This disables the circuit and turns off the Wall of Light. The second floor, around that spot, holds a code to a safe on a far-off desk. Find the code and search for the safe at the end of that wing to obtain a **Blueprint**.

Go back down after you get the items in the safe. Finish exploring the first floor, and then use the main staircase to start climbing.

Walk to the top floor. A couple of enemies are at the top. Shoot the Elite and finish them immediately afterward if necessary. The partner is a regular Guard and can't stop you alone.

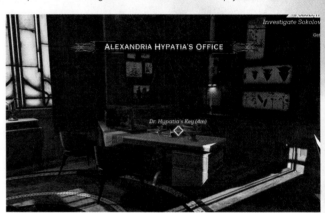

Open the doors into Dr. Hypatia's office. A Note on the door explains a little bit, but you learn even more when you read the doctor's journal. It's inside the office, near her desk. Also grab Dr. Hypatia's Key from the top of the desk. You now have access to way more of the facility. Look for a Gold Ingot tucked into the bookcase by the door.

Grabbing Collectibles

Stay up on the fourth floor and get out your Heart. **Runes** are stashed on an **Outsider Shrine** close by. Approach it and search a small unguarded room halfway through the level. Corvo gets a message from the Outsider after interacting with the shrine.

Return toward the main building, but don't go inside. Instead, look up! Blink onto the roof. It's high up, but explore there until you see a window into a tower. Blink inside and grab a **Rune**! Look around to locate the cables that hold up the elevator. Shoot either of the red canisters that power the device. This collapses the elevator, breaking it through into a locked-off basement area.

Go back outside and Blink to the middle roof, then onto some smokestacks. Turn around and Blink up to the highest roof to collect the **Black Bonecharm** in the bird's nest.

Return to the first floor and Blink onto a small ledge above the elevator entrance. Hop down onto the collapsed elevator, and from there into the basement. Grab a **Rune**, a **Painting**, and some money from the left side of the room.

Descend to the third floor and use your Key to open the door close by. You find a huge Recuperation Area where Bloodflies have congregated. A **Rune** is several feet from the entrance. Use flammable bottles to clear out the Bloodflies, or rush in, destroy their nests, and retreat to let them cool down. Either way, you score an easy Rune. Halfway through that room is a tank (like an iron lung) you can crawl through to reach a recessed room. A **Bonecharm** is inside.

Talk to Hamilton

Climb to the second floor. Look around for Joe Hamilton inside the area that was formerly locked. He's being held in a small room. Use Hypatia's Key to open that section and the door into Hamilton's holding area. Kill a lone patrolling Guard and make sure the coast is clear. Then get inside and talk to Hamilton. Obtain Hamilton's Quarters Key while you're there; it's inside a small container behind him, along with a huge stash of Bullets.

Grand Guard personnel: Anyone caught taking medicinal.

Return to the fourth floor and look for a small set of stairs that leads farther up. They're marked as long as you've talked to Hamilton. Disarm a tripwire by the top of the stairs.

Unlock Hamilton's room and take everything that isn't nailed down. Bullets, wealth, and information are everywhere. A diary on the far desk is what you need the most. Read that now.

Go to the third floor and walk all the way through the Recuperation Area. You hear a woman's voice as you come out the other side. Locate a staircase that leads down; it's a back set of steps. You can't get to this spot by walking through the second floor normally. Dr. Hypatia is in a laboratory.

Talk to Hypatia and then collect any items you need from the offices nearby. One small lab contains a **Corrupt Bonecharm**. Behind it, a **Painting** hangs on the wall.

A man named Vasco is lying down in a side area, behind where you first see the doctor. Talk to him last, because this starts a confrontation with the Crown Killer.

STOPPING THE CROWN KILLER

The Crown Killer is a powerful foe, possessed of high health and speed. Luckily, this engagement begins to your advantage, because the boss doesn't know where you are. Set a Stun Mine inside the doors to your area and then get out a ranged weapon.

Peek out and take a Crossbow shot at the Crown Killer's head to start the fight off correctly. Then retreat past your Stun Mine and switch to your Pistol to get faster, easier shots off during the coming brawl.

Ambush the Crown Killer when they step on the mine. Come forward with a mix of melee and ranged attacks to maximize your damage output.

This soon causes the enemy to stumble, and that gives you an opening for a killing blow. Take the shot and finish your enemy without mercy.

Though vicious, another method for this battle is to murder Dr. Hypatia before triggering the Crown Killer fight. If you attack her from behind while she's working, and then press the attack quickly, she dies. This prevents the Crown Killer from appearing and attacking you at all.

Heading Out

Retreat to the ground floor and follow the waypoint out toward a Watchtower. Open the door that leads outside, and use your Pistol to shoot a tank of Whale Oil sitting between two Guards. They blow up and leave the area clear.

Blink over to the Watchtower's control system, and pull out the Whale Oil battery. This disables everything and allows Captain Foster to approach the docks.

Blink down from the Watchtower and attack a Guard below. He's the last person standing between you and your extraction. The captain pulls up at the docks as you finish your work, so meet her and leave the area.

The Clockwork Mansion

Anton Sokolov is being held at the mansion of Kirin Jindosh, Grand Inventor to the Duke and creator of the Clockwork
Soldier. Get inside, rescue Sokolov, and eliminate Jindosh before he builds an army of Clockwork Soldiers.

COLLECTIBLES

Runes	6
Shrines	1
Bonecharms	8
Coins	4802
Blueprints	4
Paintings	6

SPECIAL ACTIONS

Ghost Between the Cogs	Reach Jindosh without revealing your presence
Hidden Repository	Discover Jindosh's hidden repository by manipulating the walls of the mansion
Flawless Extraction	Free Sokolov without alerting the Clockwork Soldier in the Assessment Chamber
A Man of the People	Kill Paolo, the Howler Leader (Once)
Black Market Heist	Blast your way into the black market
Looted Aventa Station	Rob the ticket booth in the station

THE DREADFUL WALE

Corvo takes a nap once he's back aboard the Dreadful Wale. You watch a cutscene, and then wake back in your cabin. Write in your journal after getting up.

Look for a crank wheel in Captain Foster's part of the ship, on the same level where you wake up. Pick it up from a table, and bring it to the engine room. Attach it to a valve at the bottom of the ship, and then turn the device. This finishes an optional goal.

Meet the captain at the stern of the ship, out on deck. Tell her you're ready to go, and she takes you to shore again. Your next task is to eliminate Kirin Jindosh while saving Sokolov. Both are in the same mansion, so you're working as both assassin and rescuer. Good luck.

SERKONOS: THE LOWER AVENTA DISTRICT

Gather Items

You're dropped off in the streets of Serkonos. Get your Heart out and walk forward to leave the shores behind; all the items ahead are higher up. You soon arrive in a guarded district of the city. Draw your blade and dispatch two enemies (a Guard and an Elite Guard) protecting the area. There are two more Guards out patrolling, but they don't come back for a while. Kill them later, when they're isolated.

The mayor's office is above this initial street. To reach it, Blink onto the roof of a small structure on your right, near the Guard post. Then Blink again to get onto a balcony higher up and around the corner. This leads onto the office. Smash a display case to find a **Bonecharm**. The opposite wall holds a **Painting**.

Next, return to ground level and locate a "Checkpoint Enforced" sign by a liquor store on the left. Jump over the sign and break into the building behind it. Bloodflies infest the structure, so move carefully. Look for some Raw Whalebone on the second floor, in a lab area. Climb the stairs to the third floor and jump through a window to get past a locked door. Turn right and use an **Outsider Shrine**. Poke your head out the window and Blink down to ground level safely, because you've gotten everything important inside.

A Black Bonecharm is here too. Go around the next corner after leaving the last building. You bump into a cluster of civilians talking about their problems. Blink onto a small building to their side. Rest to get your Mana back, and then Blink again onto a pillar higher up. From there, climb onto a roof and look for a balcony across the alley. Use your Heart to locate the **Black Bonecharm** inside. Jump or Blink over to the balcony, go inside, and claim your prize. Take a **Painting** from the wall by the balcony when you leave.

For more money, unlock the front door of the apartment and go to the second floor. Search for a safe inside the lower apartment, and use the code on the blackboard in the hallway to open it. Move the bottle to see the whole thing.

Follow the streets all the way to the back end of town. Another collectible is back there, plus the black market, so it's well worth your time. You find a series of dark, boarded-up buildings. Locate a basement entrance to these buildings near the corner. Descend to a lower door and look inside to find the black market.

BLACK MARKET GOODS

ITEM	COST
Crossbow Bolt	20
Pistol Bullet	30
Sleep Dart	30
Stun Mine	70
Spring Razor	50
Addermire Solution	200
Health Elixir	100
Rewire Tool	200
Rune	400
Key to the Ticket Booth	250

Before you shop, there are some problems. A few people arrive to threaten the shopkeeper. Equip your Pistol and talk to them to trigger a fast and enjoyable fight. Start it off with a Pistol blast to the first thug's head, and then slaughter his two bodyguards. Shop without any trouble after that's done. The leader of the group turns into a swarm of Rats when he dies. Maybe that means this isn't over.

VICIOUS PROFIT

Blink from the street outside the black market up to the fourth-floor balcony above the market. Go inside and climb down to the front door to find a basement entrance out there. Enter and slaughter two criminals inside.

The women here have set up two Whale Oil Tanks by a brick wall. Bring a third one (from the carriage station once it's cleared later), and put it with the others. If you blow them all up (together or on their own), it destroys the wall. You can loot the black market, steal from a safe, and collect a massive amount of money.

Take a Carriage to the Upper Aventa District

You can leave the district after you've purchased everything you want. Buy a Rewire Tool, and head to Aventa Station. Be careful if you go around to the rear of the building. The bandits hiding there lure you toward them, asking for help, then jump you as a massive group. Back into the alleys nearby to force them into a chokepoint, then savage the poorly trained fools. With them down, look for a **Rune** at the back of their yard.

To get into the station, approach the front of the building and locate a Security Panel. Open it, rewire the system, and walk through the Wall of Light at the entrance. You're clear because of the rewiring.

The ticket booth is on the first floor. You get the Key from the black market (either buy buying or stealing). Inside the booth is a pile of wealth and a **Blueprint**. You also find a Whale Oil Tank in a receptacle on the first floor. Bring it back to the basement near the black market to blow up the wall.

A **Bonecharm** is up on the second floor. Kill the Guards there before you search for it. Then, after collecting everything you need from this area, use the carriage to head into the Upper Aventa District.

THE UPPER AVENTA DISTRICT

Get the Carriage to the Mansion

Your arrival in this part of town isn't noticed, and you have time to look around for a moment. An Elite Guard is ahead, plus a watchful patroller, but that's about it. Get some food from a stand to your right, and then sneak up to the Elite for a fast kill. The other two Guards notice, but they are weak and can be dispatched with a Pistol shot and a Sword cut or two. Just make sure no one runs to the Wall of Light to get reinforcements.

The building to your right is a Guard station, with several men inside. Run through the front door and walk up to the front desk. This alarms two enemies, so shoot the guy at the desk and then block to counter and kill his buddy. Climb the stairs and search for a **Bonecharm** on the second floor as you clear the remainder of the building. No dangerous enemies lurk here, so the fights are super fast. A **Blueprint** sits out on a desk on the third floor. Find the gate code in a small, rear office.

On the way out, stop on the second floor and take the Whale Oil Tank from the wall. This turns off a tricky Wall of Light that blocks access to the mansion. Carry the tank outside, approach the chokepoint, and throw it into the Guards ahead. You get a decent fight out of this encounter, though there aren't enough special targets to threaten you much. After the tank explodes, charge forward and use a Pistol plus melee combo to kill the first two survivors of the explosion. Everyone else is farther back, and they trickle in.

Clean up the fight and examine the building ahead and to the left. Blink up to a balcony to enter the second floor. Destroy a couple of Bloodfly nests, and search for a **Rune** inside a desk at the back end of the building.

A much smaller area on the right, also contains loot. Go around the building and look for an open window on the other side. Crawl through, destroy more Bloodfly nests, and grab a **Corrupt Bonecharm** and a **Painting**.

Return to the entrance of this district. A machine controls the gate access for the mansion. Dial the number you found on the third floor of the Guards' building into the console to open the way. Re-enter the carriage and select "Go to the Clockwork Mansion" to continue your mission. You arrive at the estate soon. Walk through the front doors to proceed.

THE CLOCKWORK MANSION

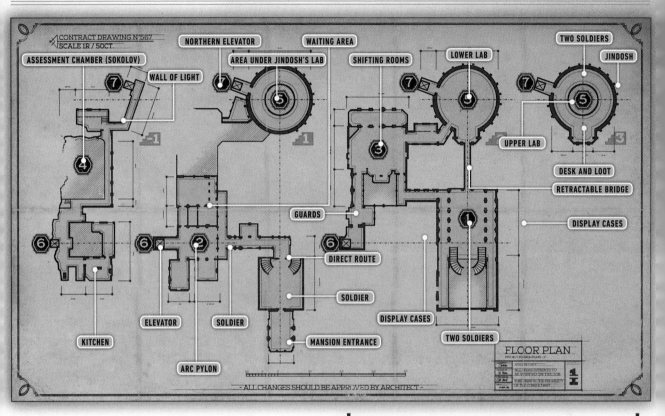

Locate Kirin Jindosh and Destroy Him

You're inside Jindosh's home, but it's a gigantic estate. You don't find him quickly. This place transforms, so several rooms have machinery that shifts things around, making them multi-functional. Stealth players have to worry about jumping into the machinery to avoid being seen.

You don't.

Instead, the plan is to face Jindosh's Clockwork Soldiers head-on.

DESTROYING CLOCKWORK SOLDIERS

Stun Mines are wonderful. They do substantial damage to Clockwork Soldiers and should always be reserved for fights against these tough opponents.

Even though Stun Mines take time to arm, you can plant one on a soldier during a fight. Block until it goes off, and then lay into the target.

Go for Drop assassinations whenever you can to instantly destroy the heads (or kill headless soldiers).

In a direct battle, swing for the arms and attack more aggressively whenever the soldiers overheat and shut down for a few moments.

Watch out when the Clockwork Soldiers lean over and start to spark. The good news is that you've killed them, but the bad news is that they explode. It doesn't do huge damage to you if you're close, but it's not fun.

Leave the initial room and enter the next chamber. Pull a lever to transform the room into a much larger area, and take a look at your first Clockwork Soldier. It doesn't attack (it's here on display), but there isn't anyone to help out if you trigger the attack here.

Put a Stun Mine on the soldier and then attack it viciously. The sooner you master your skills against Clockwork Soldiers, the more fun you have in here!

After the battle, search the display cases all over the room. You find two Elixirs around the chamber, a Stun Mine, and a Rewire Tool.

Three obvious routes lead out of here. The back-left hallway contains a Wall of Light, so scratch that for now. The other hallway at the back leads directly into Jindosh's lab, but you can't take it yet. Instead, head into the roped-off exit on the lower level.

It says "No Admittance," so you know it's a good choice. The corridor beyond the door contains two Elites, a Guard within hearing range, and a resting Clockwork Soldier. You can wait for the Elites to split up and kill them outside the soldier's detection.

Or you can take them all on at once. It's dangerous, but really exciting. Sneak up lets you kill the Elites almost immediately. The Clockwork Soldier boots up, and the other Guard arrives to check out the noise. Back off to the previous hall and get your Stun Mine ready. Ambush the soldier with your Stun Mine, and switch back to your Pistol after planting it. Shoot and slash repeatedly during the stun period to bring it down almost before it has a chance to attack. The Guard is an afterthought once the machine is down.

The next room features a glass floor. A new machine you've never seen before dominates the center. This is an Arc Pylon. They spew deadly electricity at you if you trigger an alert. The damage is almost directly lethal, so you don't ever want to take a hit (much less two). Never fight in a room when a Pylon is active.

This one is already live because of the fighting you did a moment ago. Blink to get into the lounge on the left. Loot it for food, and then Blink most of the way across the Pylon's room. Reach the far side to find a waiting area with two rich people. Steal from them, and look for a Key not far from there, by a locked door. Open the door to gain easier access to the hallway leading into this entire wing of the building.

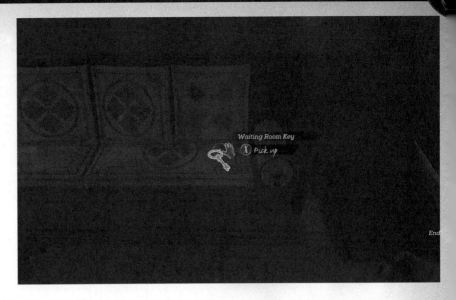

Return to the Pylon room and Blink toward the elevator. Quickly sprint away to avoid getting shot after the Blink. Call the elevator and ride it to the second floor.

Two Elites and a Clockwork Soldier wait above. Rush the Elites as soon as they spot you coming out of the elevator. Kill both before the soldier attacks (a Pistol shot with your rush should make that doable).

If you don't have a Stun Mine this time, the Clockwork Soldier presents more of a threat. Spend your ammo well to augment your Sword's damage, and use your Mana with any attack abilities you have. Elixirs are common around here, so resupplying isn't hard.

Search for various supplies in the area, and then take the hallway back into Jindosh's private quarters. A bedroom lies ahead. Though a soldier is in there too, it's likely in a resting state unless you tick it off.

Grab everything in the bedroom, and use the lever to transform it afterward. Rush into the corner room while this happens. The room descends into a lower level and lets you pick up a **Black Bonecharm** below. Press a red button on the wall to get back up to the bedroom.

This chamber boasts four configurations, two on each side. Visit each—both variations of the bathroom, and both of the study/sitting rooms.

You get a lot of money! You also find a **Painting** in one of the bathroom variants. If you have trouble finding it, stay with the bathtub in the inner circle and rotate it to find the version of the room you want.

When you're done, spin in the bathroom and use a large set of double doors to exit. You enter a red-carpeted hallway that leads quickly into Jindosh's laboratory.

Jindosh walks around the lab. Sneak up on him to break his neck as easily as you would a provincial town Guard's. Splatter this monster without a second thought.

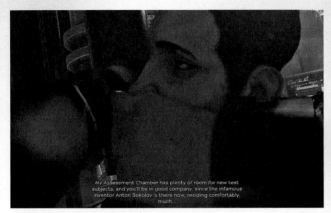

My Assessment Chamber has plenty of room for new test subjects, and you'll be in good company, since the infamous inventor Anton Sokolov is there now, residing comfortably, much...

Find and Rescue Sokolov

Search every single nook in the lab. You can avoid the Clockwork Soldiers if you're really careful, but tons of Stun Mines are hidden here. If you use those, you can win the fights rather easily.

The Stun Mines are in the lower tier of the room; get there by accessing a console on the main floor. Call up a module (such as anatomy) and jump down into the lower tier while the module is coming up. There is a **Rune** on the anatomy module, and the lower tier holds tons of weapons.

A Maintenance Key sits on the side desk of the lower tier. This lets you unlock a door back into the elevator. Otherwise, you have to rise back up on a module to re-enter the main lab. Ride it all the way to the top if you want more loot!

The top tier contains a **Painting** behind the main desk. You also find **Blueprints** (inside the desk), and multiple good regular items.

Finish your fun run through the lab and get into the middle tier again. Use a button by the main exit to create a bridge between the laboratory and the initial greeting chamber you cleared a good while ago.

Backtrack to the original elevator. Instead of going to the second floor this time, descend into the Assessment Chamber.

Kill two Guards at the bottom. They're surprised when the elevator opens, so charge into them for one or even two assassinations. This startles the kitchen staff; either let them go or knock them out if they're bothering you.

Search the kitchen, on the right. There is a piece of Raw Whalebone in there, and another out in a side hallway that connects to the kitchen.

Locate a lever in the back hall. Use it to pull down the waiting room from the guest level. While the room is in transit, get into a small connecting area between the two floors of the waiting room. Use the Configuration Mechanism inside to send the floor up. At the top, exit into another recessed space. A **Bonecharm** is hidden there, on a body. Use a hatch to get back onto the elevator and escape from this place.

Return to the Assessment Chamber. Turn left outside the elevator and walk in that direction. Stock up on Crossbow Bolts on the way, because quite a few are shot into a dummy close by.

Bonecharm (62m)

Lock Bonecharm

You bump into the chamber itself; stairs lead down into it, but wait another moment. Blink up to the walkway beyond and above the chamber. Eliminate a solo Elite, and go past her. The passage leads into a machine room. Search a drawer for a **Bonecharm**.

Take the stairs down into the real Assessment Chamber. A mechanism opens a puzzle area. Each golden square you step onto changes the configuration of the walls. If you don't take the perfect route, you bump into a Clockwork Soldier and are spotted. But that's fine, because it's alone and you're stocked up on weapons. Destroy it if it notices you.

Take the following path:

▶ **Step into the puzzle and get onto the first square**

▶ **Walk forward and right, then step on a square ahead as you continue forward and right**

▶ **Let the walls finish shifting, and then move around the corner ahead and left of your position**

▶ **Break a set of wooden boards on the floor**

▶ **Step on the revealed square**

▶ **Anton Sokolov's cell opens**

SMALL ARMORY

The back-right corner of the Assessment Chamber houses a storage area for weaponry. Make your way back there and stock up if you want to.

Wake up Sokolov. Take the **Painting** inside the cell, and then break another set of boards over a square. Pick up Sokolov and step on the square. This reopens the cell. Blink out of it, and use the square outside to change the walls. Head toward the exit door.

Use a square to the left (if you're facing the exit) to open the tiny entrance area. It's pretty clear from here, so hurry out and get Sokolov back to the elevator.

Get Sokolov Back to the Skiff

Ride the elevator back to the middle level. You've already killed everyone there, so follow the waypoint back through the cleared room and hallway beyond. Use the Configuration Mechanism at the end to open the way out. Carry Sokolov through the front door when it's time to go.

Take Sokolov back to the Lower Aventa District, and then carry him to the skiff. Have Blink ready, because you don't want to get into a fight right now. Blink to avoid being spotted, or to hurry away if someone sees you.

Captain Foster is at the boat, waiting to take you two back to the Dreadful Wale.

ANOTHER STRANGE VISIT IN THE VOID

You rest for a time, but wake feeling strange. You've returned to the Void. Get up and leave your cabin. Walk through the next few scenes and learn as much as you can. There are no fights or challenges to overcome.

The Royal Conservatory

While held captive, Anton Sokolov learned the identity of one of Delilah's chief allies, Breanna Ashworth. An architect of the coup that took the throne in Dunwall, Ashworth is powerful and full of secrets. She is building a mysterious device for Delilah. Breanna Ashworth must be eliminated.

COLLECTIBLES

Runes	6
Shrines	1
Bonecharms	9
Coins	3813
Blueprints	3
Paintings	3

SPECIAL ACTIONS

Shrewd Negotiations	Get the best price for the Roseburrow Prototype
Parley with Delilah	Talk to the statue in Ashworth's office after eliminating Ashworth
Witch No More	Sever Ashworth's connection with the Void
Black Market Heist	Rob the black market
Spying Overseers	Find Vice Overseer Byrne's outpost

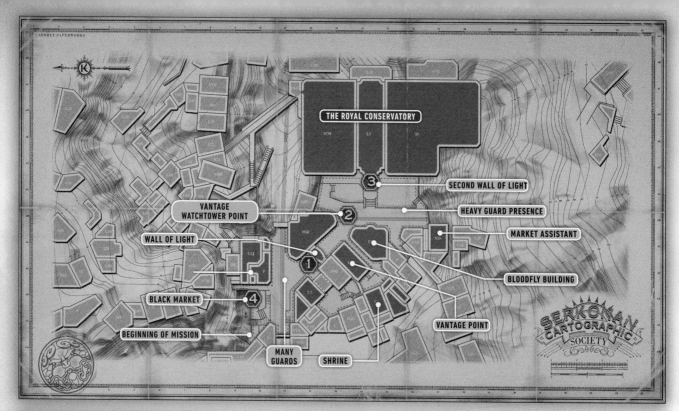

THE ROYAL CONSERVATORY

SECOND WALL OF LIGHT
HEAVY GUARD PRESENCE
MARKET ASSISTANT
VANTAGE WATCHTOWER POINT
WALL OF LIGHT
BLOODFLY BUILDING
BLACK MARKET
VANTAGE POINT
BEGINNING OF MISSION
MANY GUARDS
SHRINE

SERKONAN CARTOGRAPHIC SOCIETY

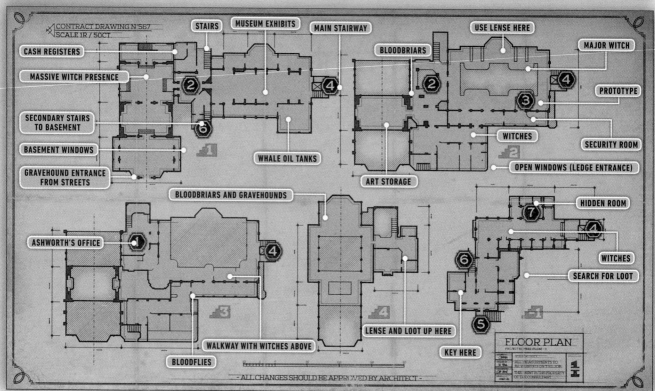

CONTRACT DRAWING N°567
SCALE 1R / 50CT.

STAIRS
MUSEUM EXHIBITS
MAIN STAIRWAY
USE LENSE HERE
CASH REGISTERS
BLOODBRIARS
MAJOR WITCH
MASSIVE WITCH PRESENCE
PROTOTYPE
SECONDARY STAIRS TO BASEMENT
WITCHES
SECURITY ROOM
BASEMENT WINDOWS
WHALE OIL TANKS
OPEN WINDOWS (LEDGE ENTRANCE)
GRAVEHOUND ENTRANCE FROM STREETS
ART STORAGE
BLOODBRIARS AND GRAVEHOUNDS
HIDDEN ROOM
ASHWORTH'S OFFICE
WITCHES
SEARCH FOR LOOT
LENSE AND LOOT UP HERE
WALKWAY WITH WITCHES ABOVE
KEY HERE
BLOODFLIES

FLOOR PLAN

— ALL CHANGES SHOULD BE APPROVED BY ARCHITECT —

ON THE DREADFUL WALE

A Briefing and a Mission

Get up on the real ship and look for your allies in the briefing room. Talk to Captain Foster and Sokolov, then examine the painting in the corner.

Go into the room in back and read a Note on the Bloodfly container. It looks like there's a minor infestation aboard the ship. Walk down into the boiler room, like you did before the earlier mission. This time, kill a small cluster of Bloodflies to keep the ship nice and safe.

Find Captain Foster topside, and talk to her to begin the next mission.

CYRIA GARDENS

Into the Royal Conservatory

Foster takes you into the city. Walk through a small district and then break into the Royal Conservatory to find your target.

After landing, get off of the skiff and walk forward. Minor loot is inside a room to the right as you advance. You quickly reach the end of the docks. Search a ship for an Elixir and some other little goodies, then Blink to the bridge above. Turn left and search for the black market.

Kill a couple of Howlers who harass you in the next alley. They deal disorienting Crossbow attacks and Grenades, but they don't stand up well in direct fights. Use a Grenade of your own to destroy the pair as they approach the bridge, and then lay into them with traditional attacks.

The market is in their territory, on the left. Head inside and see if you can afford any nice upgrades!

BLACK MARKET GOODS

ITEM	COST
Crossbow Bolt	20
Pistol Bullet	30
Sleep Dart	30
Grenade	70
Stun Mine	70
Spring Razor	50
Addermire Solution	150
Health Elixir	75
Rewire Tool	200
Safe Combination	250
Rune	400

After shopping, leave the store and climb a small flight of stairs outside. Look for an open window, and slip into a building. Climb through the structure, noting a locked door on the second floor. Continue to the top, and exit onto the roof.

There are two Guards and an Elite there, but the entire group is distracted. Assassinate the Elite, kill the Guard on the left before he realizes he's done for, and then solo the final target. It's brutal and quick.

Jump down through a skylight into an Overseer's apartment. Weapons are all over the place, but watch out for a trap by the door. Take everything you can, and open a balcony door to escape.

The lower streets are guarded wonderfully. Elites and regular Guards are everywhere, and a fight with one or two of them is likely to balloon into a much nastier battle. If you're nervous, Blink to the balconies and rooftops to explore. This allows you to circumvent the Wall of Light down below without fighting any big groups.

A BIT MORE STEALING!

This store can be robbed just like all the others, but consider waiting until the mission is almost over. This shopkeeper has a side mission for you, and it cannot be completed if you cause too much trouble. So read how to rob the place now, but put it off until later.

Take a valve from the rear of the shop and carry it with you. Buy the upgrades you want, but don't spend anything on items. Look for a window with steel bars on the right side of the shop. A heavy cable is suspended on the other side. Target a red canister on the cable and shoot it with a Crossbow Bolt.

When the red canister pops, leave the store. Put the valve you stole onto a small metal stand back at the canal. Turn the valve to open a gate and allow access to the area underneath the store. A chain hangs there. Climb up and rob the black market.

Or you can do it the best way—kill them all! Start with the Guards on the right. They're closer to the waterway and aren't grouped together as well. You can possibly kill them without being noticed even if you aren't subtle.

Once the big group realizes what's going on, you get rushed. Most of these targets are Elites. Use a Grenade on the initial cluster to wound or kill some of them, then switch to your Sword and keep them off balance with magic (Windblast/Devouring Swarm) or multiple ranged attacks so they don't surround you and deal too much damage.

Rewire the Wall of Light when the battle is done. Its panel is only a few feet from the device.

Before heading through the gap, walk into an apartment building to the right. Climb to the second floor and hunt your targets; there are two Witches in the place, along with a civilian or two. Avoid the civilians while you look for the much more dangerous Witches.

SUFFER NO WITCH

Witches use their teleportation to escape fights going poorly for them, or to jump closer suddenly when they see a way to hurt you. They're hard to predict, and have additional spells depending on the individual.

The best way to kill them is through fast ambushes. Failing that, keep your Pistol or Crossbow ready and hit these enemies right after they finish a teleport. That gives you a moment to catch up to them and score the kill.

Clear the Witches out, and search around. You don't get anything too powerful inside the building, but it's good to be thorough. Leave when you've gotten a bit of money.

Walk through the Wall of Light outside and observe the Guards ahead. Another large battle begins if you rush everyone. That's not the worst of it, though; a Watchtower here is armed with a strong cannon. It blows you apart if you fight underneath it.

For safety, use your Crossbow and pull the Guards over to the Wall of Light. Kill multiple enemies at range, and finish off any survivors who get close. Now that the road is clear, hug the right wall as you advance, and enter another apartment building.

The first floor is clear. Climb to the second and kill two Elites out back. A door takes you outside, where they're patrolling. You start seeing Veterans around this time. They're basically Elites, but they have helmets that mark their station and provide decent protection against headshots. If you have trouble with one, put a Bullet in their torso and assassinate them while they're recovering.

Back inside, find a bar at the front of the building on the second floor. A Bonecharm is on a table, and bodies are everywhere—they're not even your fault for once! A Note suggests the Howlers were making a point.

Eat any leftover food, and climb up the building stairs to the roof after you leave. Kill a solo Elite talking to a civilian, and then knock out the civilian. With the run of the roof, you can reach a couple of important places from here.

Blink across to the balcony of a condemned building. Get out your Pistol or Crossbow, and have it ready while you explore. Kill the Bloodfly nests inside, but don't even think of relaxing until you've discovered and killed a wandering Nestkeeper as well. He's the big threat. You're well-rewarded, because a room at the back contains a large safe and a **Painting**. The safe holds Pistol ammo and loads of money. Buy the combo from the black market to get in.

Retreat to the previous building's roof. Face the old condemned building and turn right. There's another apartment you can reach. Blink twice to get over to it, and carefully advance through the place. It contains multiple Crossbow tripwires to disarm. Blink to the upper floor when you find a damaged ceiling, and use an **Outsider Shrine**.

Retreat to the last rooftop again. From the opposite side, Blink across the street and into a different infested apartment. Clear its nests to grab a Health Elixir, then look for a side balcony. Climb out and Blink onto that nasty Watchtower to disable it.

To get into range, exit onto a white door lying on the balcony. Then jump and Blink to cross the distance successfully. Sabotage the Watchtower and then Blink back to ground level.

The street is yours. From the Watchtower, head to the right side of the street. Assassinate two regular Guards, and enter a normal-looking building. Climb to the second floor, and jump over the banister to get past a barricade.

Watch out for traps as you proceed toward the second floor. Up top, you find a wealth of items—a Bonecharm and a Blueprint on a desk, plus an Elixir, a Rewire Tool, and other lesser goodies. You also find a Document that lets you advance the shopkeeper's side mission (to find their associate). Continue this mission inside the Conservatory.

You're done collecting for the moment. Go to street level and locate the passage that leads underneath the second Wall of Light. A couple more Guards patrol down there, because that's where the Whale Oil Tank for the wall is hidden. Get down there, kill the Guards, and disable the Wall of Light.

You're safe to approach the front gate of the Conservatory now. Do so, and slaughter a Gravehound waiting to appear as you enter. Gravehounds are easy to kill, like Wolfhounds, but they have the same high damage output. In addition, they come back to life after you kill them. Stop them by slashing the skulls of fallen Gravehounds. One shot does the trick.

INSIDE THE CONSERVATORY

Clear the Basement

Turn right and look for two small windows at ground level. They lead into the basement. Crawl in through the one on the left. Inside it you find an Archive Key, a map of the area, a **Bonecharm**, and a Rewire Tool.

Explore the rest of the basement by going through the other window, or by breaking the door that keeps you inside this storage room.

You have to kill another Gravehound, but that's the only protector in this portion of the basement. You discover three pieces of Raw Whalebone as you explore.

Slow down as you get deeper into the level. Two Witches are conversing near a Bloodfly nest. Setting them off prematurely leads to a deadly battle. The safer plan is to alert them but flee into the earlier section of the basement. This forces them to fight you away from the Bloodflies. Ambush them around a corner, and set traps ahead of time for extra help.

Alternatively, you can sneak up on the Witches and assassinate one. Turn, shoot the second, kill her during the stun, and then run away from the Bloodflies before they do too much damage.

Unlock the Archive door in the back. The Archives house a Rune inside a glass case. Break the case and claim the **Rune** as soon as you can. Blink over the bookcase in the rear and jump down into a hidden area. A **Painting** is there.

Leave the Archives and locate the stairs and elevator at the end of the basement. Climb up to the first floor when you find them.

Search the First Floor

Break through boards to access the ground level of the Conservatory. Two Gravehounds are on the floor as skulls, and Witches lurk close by. Use your Crossbow to shoot the skulls from a distance, and then deal with the Witches once they have no extra support. Shoot one of them if they haven't noticed anything amiss, and then retreat to the stairs so the fight doesn't draw more and more targets forward.

Use Bullets or Bolts plentifully to keep the Witches from pouring on their damage. Killing them outright is nice, but it isn't necessary with your ranged attacks. As long as they're taking damage, they can't cast for a short time. So shoot one, kill her, and back off to lure any additional Witches forward.

If you fight them out in the open, they slaughter you. Easily. Their ranged magic does too much damage, and several of them might attack at once. That's why you always pull them back to an area you've cleared. The smaller the location, the better off you are, because they can't teleport to any places that surprise you.

A room to your left contains Whale Oil Tanks, a disabled Wall of Light, and a **Blueprint**. The rest of the level is fairly weak for good items. The cash registers on the other side of the floor hold a little money, but it's not heavily worth your time.

Instead, climb to the second floor.

The Shopkeeper's Request

You hear talking from above. Sure enough, there are two Witches on a chandelier. They're so high up that they couldn't hear the big fight on the first floor. Aim carefully, and nail one of them with a headshot so you can explore without any worries in the future.

The other one teleports down to your level. Fight her among the bookstacks to keep her at close range. It's easier to overwhelm her that way.

It's pretty safe to run around the library now. The other two Witches within notable distance are on the left side of the level, past a door. One is a patroller, and the other is chilling out on a bed on top of a display case. Ambush the patroller, and then snipe the relaxing Witch.

Traverse the halls and track a **Rune** that isn't far away. Grab it from an overgrown room by the corner.

One door in that hallway is locked. Break through it with your Sword; no one hears. You uncover a security room. Rewire the Security Panel inside. Then, with the security disabled, steal the Roseburrow Prototype—marked as your objective—and take it back to the black market at your leisure. Remember to rob the place after you're done!

Return to the main stairs and ascend to the third level.

Kill Curator Ashworth

It's quiet on the third floor, so searching isn't a problem. Your target, Breanna Ashworth, is on the opposite side of the level from the staircase. Turn left and examine that side of the level instead. Steal museum pieces here and there for cash, and track a Bonecharm farther ahead.

The **Bonecharm** is floating in front of a board on the front side of the building. Pass several Bloodfly nests to reach it.

Breanna herself is in a large office that feeds into the library. Have your Crossbow ready when you come into the room, because she has two Gravehounds. If you shoot and eliminate them early in the fight, Breanna can't do much to you. She's just a single Witch, really.

Kill her with ranged attacks while you close on her, and mix in Sword strikes as soon as you can. Her health runs out quickly. Remember to loot her after she's dead for two **Black Bonecharms**.

Talk to the statue inside the office. You get to do a bit of gloating, and it is sweet.

Everyone you love, everything you hold dear, I'll destroy. Want to know why?

Loot everything on the desk and climb the steps at the back of the office. Take a **Painting** off the wall, and continue up toward the fourth floor.

Getting a Few Final Items

A storage area is at the top of the stairs. You gain Raw Whalebone and massive amounts of money with just a few seconds of looting. It's so nice. A set of Lenses is up there too, but you don't need those.

Take a door that leads onto an outer terrace. Two Bloodbriars out there attack if you get close to them. Instead of approaching, pull out your Crossbow and look for two skulls on the right side of the terrace. Shoot those so no Gravehounds spawn, then Blink past the Bloodbriars and search for a **Rune**.

Return to the storage room and look for a door. It opens into an internal room with a **Black Bonecharm**. Leave the room and jump out a small window that gets you onto a walkway. Follow the walkway around the top of the library, and enter a claustrophobic area on the other side. Crawl through to gain yet another **Black Bonecharm**.

With all these items in tow, leave the museum and return to the skiff. Your mission here is finished.

Ashworth won't be a problem anymore.

Dust District

You must travel through the Dust District to Aramis Stilton's Manor, which contains more of Delilah's secrets. Vice Overseer Byrne and his religious followers are at war with Paolo, leader of the Howler gang. Either Byrne or Paolo will aid you, for a favor.

COLLECTIBLES

Runes	5
Shrines	1
Bonecharms	8
Coins	3973
Blueprints	3
Paintings	3

SPECIAL ACTIONS

The Jindosh Lock	Solve the Jindosh Lock on your own
Childhood Home	Explore Corvo Attano's childhood home
Power of the Streets	Side with the Howlers
Theocratic Support	Side with the Overseers
Book of the Fallen	Add Byrne's name to the Book of the Fallen
Another Solution	Eliminate both faction leaders
Black Market Heist	Rob the black market
Uninvolved	Don't take sides with either faction

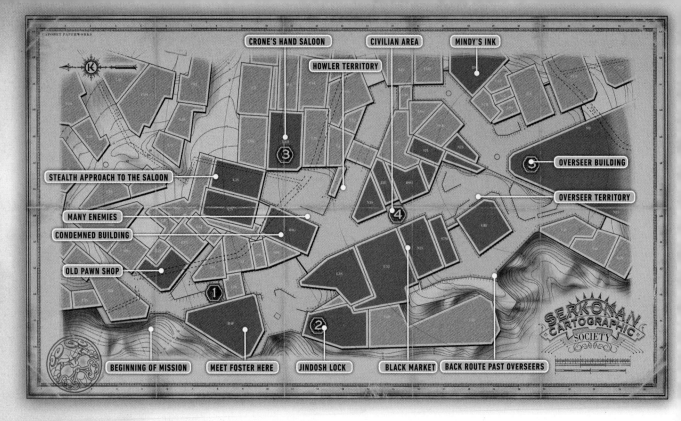

CAPONET PAPERWORKS

CRONE'S HAND SALOON

CIVILIAN AREA

MINDY'S INK

HOWLER TERRITORY

③

OVERSEER BUILDING

STEALTH APPROACH TO THE SALOON

OVERSEER TERRITORY

④

MANY ENEMIES

CONDEMNED BUILDING

OLD PAWN SHOP

①

②

SERKONAN CARTOGRAPHIC SOCIETY

BEGINNING OF MISSION   **MEET FOSTER HERE**   **JINDOSH LOCK**   **BLACK MARKET**   **BACK ROUTE PAST OVERSEERS**

APPROACHING YOUR DESTINATION

You're taken back to the Dreadful Wale. Get up and enter the briefing room. Talk to Sokolov, and search for a few minor pieces of equipment before meeting Sokolov again on deck. Ask him to take you into town when you're ready to start the next mission.

Stilton lived in a bunker, kept secure by a fancy lock, made by Jindosh. Maybe inside you'll learn more about how to stop Delilah.

ENTERING THE DUST DISTRICT

Find Meagan Foster

Sokolov drops you off in some underground docks. There isn't much close by, so make your way out of there. Look for a single piece of Raw Whalebone at a station near the exit.

Leave the dock area to find yourself on a scenic overlook of Karnaca. Climb the stairs up to street level, and watch for Guards. There are four of them ahead; one of them is a Veteran, but the rest are nothing. Blink into their midst for an assassination, and then destroy the others. It's fairly easy to get two before the fight starts, even without stealth.

A Rewire Tool is sitting on a table past the Guards. Take it, and use it on the Security Panel they were protecting. Alternatively, enter a plain building on the left side of the area. Climb to the roof to encounter two more Guards. Kick one off the roof and murder the other. A **Blueprint** sits on a bench up there if you haven't found a version of it in earlier missions. You can turn off the Windmill that's powering the Wall of Light. Either way, pass through the Wall of Light, and Blink into a damaged building on the right. A dust storm is coming soon, and it's best to get inside before it hits. The storm comes and goes repeatedly throughout the day. When it's around, you get a massive boost to your stealth because no one can see anything in that mess. Use that to help infiltrate some of the trickier areas if you run into trouble.

There are Bloodflies all over the old building.

Rune or Bonecharm nearby. Equip the Heart.

Destroy the nests and eat some food if you take damage. It always feels dangerous to eat food from Bloodfly buildings, but somehow it still helps. Blink up to a higher floor to proceed, and follow your waypoint toward Captain Foster.

Talk to the captain and search a side room for more Raw Whalebone. Then leave the building using the exit behind Foster's position..

Immediately turn around after dropping to the street and return inside by breaking a door down. A **Rune** is inside the lower apartment, hidden in a locker. Go back out after grabbing the Rune, and examine the district. Directly ahead of you is the end goal. That building contains the Jindosh Lock you're here to crack. But you don't have the tools to accomplish that yet.

Instead, turn left and take the only route into the main district.

Find and Kill Paolo

To obtain the information you need, one of the big leaders of the area has to fall. Either Paolo (of the Howlers) or Byrne (of the Overseers) suffices. We choose Paolo in this Walkthrough, but you enter the buildings for both factions and loot the heck out of them either way.

Stop at the entrance into the district and search everything before entering restricted Howler territory. To your right are a couple of stores. Steal a Rewire Tool and some money from the safe shop.

Look for steps that lead down toward a soup kitchen and the black market. Climb down the stairs and use your Heart to locate a Bonecharm a few feet away, inside the black market. Search for the green door that grants you access.

Two Howlers threaten you as you enter. Assassinate the first, and lay into the second. Don't use ranged weapons during the fight, because you can't afford to spook the shopkeeper before you've purchased things you need. They're totally cool with you slaughtering the Howlers; those guys are a major hassle.

The fight may cause the shopkeeper to shutter the market for a moment, but it opens very quickly after combat ends.

After buying the upgrades you want, it might be time to steal from the market again.

BLACK MARKET GOODS

ITEM	COST
Crossbow Bolt	20
Pistol Bullet	30
Sleep Dart	30
Grenade	70
Stun Mine	70
Spring Razor	50
Addermire Solution	150
Health Elixir	75
Rewire Tool	200
Map of Stilton's Home	250

Look for a locked door on the same floor as the black market. There is a keypad beside this door. Enter the code after you find it.

The code is located upstairs, in the shopkeeper's private quarters. You can't get in at first because the door is blocked. Break the barricade by going outside and shooting through the barred windows to destroy the wooden planks that are holding the door. Now you can get inside quite easily.

Read the Note up there near a wedding silvergraph. This gives you clues about the shopkeeper's wedding anniversary. Then, look at a calendar on the wall. You see a day circled during the month of rain (the 4th month). That month and day are your code to the market door.

Enter 4xx (with xx being the day marked on the calendar) into the black market back door. It unlocks the door and lets you into the rear of the store. Look for a **Bonecharm** inside a desk, and take everything else.

Return to the front of the district and look for a condemned building on the left. Blink up to the second-floor balcony, and destroy the Bloodflies within. Use your Heart to search for a **Rune** on the second floor.

Use the condemned building to infiltrate the Howlers' territory. Or go back out to the main street if you have something to prove and want the Chaos!

Charge the huge force of Howlers there. Assassinate the first target with a Blink attack, and then toss a couple of Grenades at the reinforcements that approach. Switch to your Pistol and burn down the rest, but be ready to drop a Health Elixir or Blink back to the condemned building if you become overwhelmed. It's a crazy (and wonderful) fight.

HOWLER TERRITORY

Follow your waypoint to sneak toward the Crone's Hand Saloon, and use another Grenade when you find Paolo and his buddies. Cook the Grenade so it explodes soon after you throw it, and race into the midst of the group to destroy them afterward.

Paolo turns into a horde of Rats. Slash at them and finish off any remaining Howlers nearby.

This fight has a slow burn, because some of the Howlers are on upper tiers of the building. Don't relax and start searching while people are still talking or running around.

Paolo isn't dead quite yet. He has to die twice in one day for it to stick! You must find him again.

A Blueprint is on the second floor of the saloon, inside one of the larger apartments (Paolo's). Locate a steel crate in the apartment; open that to claim the **Blueprint**. Then search the rear of the apartment for piles of money.

Climb to the third floor. Paolo reappears up there, so track him down inside another large apartment. A few Sword attacks and a Bullet to the head finish him for the long term.

Loot his body for a **Bonecharm** and a cute cutscene. Also, scour the place for an **Outsider Shrine** and two **Paintings**! Crime paid off for this guy, though not for long.

Leave Paolo's body here for now. Finish searching the building before you start lugging this guy across the world. There isn't much on the fourth floor, so skip it. The other door on the second floor is locked—it's the office of a guy named Durante. Opening it requires a Key from all the way over in the Overseer's area. If you get the Key, return, and unlock the office, you obtain the code to the Jindosh Lock. You also find a Bonecharm on the desk inside the office.

Near the saloon entrance are stairs that lead down into a basement. Take these and look for a **Bonecharm** and a **Blueprint** below. Neither is hidden, nor hard to find.

Take Paolo to the Overseers

Retrieve Paolo's body and hoof it back into neutral territory. The Overseers are marked on your map, so you know roughly where you're heading.

Stop on the way to grab a **Bonecharm**. Your Heart reveals it on the left as you get close to the Overseers' checkpoint. Look for blockaded windows above you. Blink up to them and break through the boards. Get inside and steal the Bonecharm, some Raw Whalebone, and many minor items.

Leave Paolo's body in neutral territory and clear most of the Overseer compound ahead of time. This ensures you get the most loot and have the most fun. Just don't get into a fight with Byrne (we tell you when to stop).

OVERSEER TERRITORY

The front of the compound is guarded by numerous Overseer patrollers and a few Wolfhounds. The safe play is to snipe the Wolfhounds and some of the Overseers with your Crossbow. Let the survivors come out to you so you aren't caught out in the open against too many targets.

Remember to flee quickly whenever a Grenade is tossed your way. Bonecharms that increase Grenade malfunctions (or make people drop them) are very useful.

When the coast is clear, enter the main building. There aren't many people left on the main floor because of your fighting, but kill the couple still standing. Search the ground floor for minor items, then go upstairs to the second floor. A barracks/medical room is near the top of the steps.

Kill the Overseers able to fight, and loot their bodies and the wounded Overseers on the cots as well. You get a Key from one of the men.

A locked door is in the corner of the same level. Unlock it with the new Key and search for Raw Whalebone, money, a Rewire Tool, and a **Rune**!

Return to the stairs and climb to the fourth floor, skipping the third for now. Creep through a window ahead to reach a tiny walkway. Hug the right side of the area, and jump through a broken window farther along. A **Painting** is hidden up there, and it's super easy to miss.

Bring Paolo's body up here with you, and Blink down into the Vice Overseer's room while carrying it. That is a freaking entrance! Byrne, impressed with your abilities, gives you the code you need to open the Jindosh Lock.

For maximum brutality, you can always kill Byrne and the rest of his people on that floor after you finish your conversation. Either way, steal a final **Bonecharm** from a desk along the side wall before you leave.

Return to the Jindosh Lock, near the beginning of the mission. Use the clue you gathered from the Overseers to open it. It's in your Mission menu. Failing that, use the Key from Overseer Byrne's room to unlock Durante's office (in the Crone's Hand Saloon). The answer is also up there.

The correct combo opens the way. It changes each time you play the game, so we can't slip you the answer. You must complete the tasks to solve the lock.

Start the next mission immediately after you open the lock.

A Crack in the Slab

A strange ritual was performed three years ago in Aramis Stilton's Manor, involving Delilah Copperspoon and her followers. Once inside, find out what you can about Delilah's secrets.

COLLECTIBLES

Runes	3
Shrines	N/A
Bonecharms	3
Coins	3334
Blueprints	1
Paintings	2

SPECIAL ACTIONS

Under the Table	Steal the Master Key while hiding under the dining room table
Temporal Investigator	Reach the study without using the door code
A Mind Made Whole	Save Aramis Stilton from going insane
Leaky Basement	Find the Rune in the basement
Collapsed Balcony	Manipulate time to collapse the balcony
A Better Today	Visit Aramis Stilton's office in the altered present

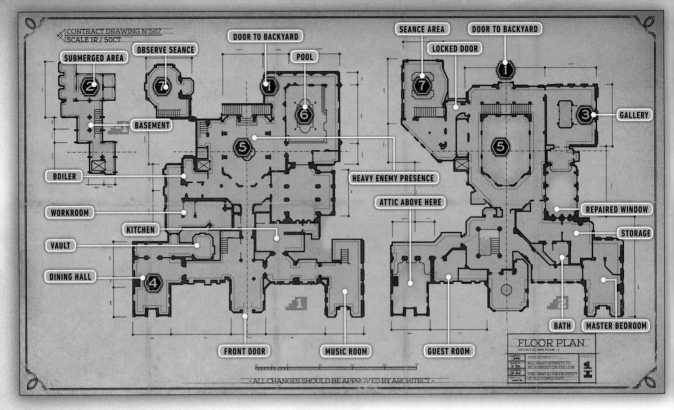

SUBMERGED AREA

OBSERVE SEANCE

DOOR TO BACKYARD

POOL

SEANCE AREA

DOOR TO BACKYARD

LOCKED DOOR

GALLERY

BASEMENT

BOILER

HEAVY ENEMY PRESENCE

REPAIRED WINDOW

WORKROOM

ATTIC ABOVE HERE

STORAGE

KITCHEN

VAULT

DINING HALL

FRONT DOOR

MUSIC ROOM

GUEST ROOM

BATH

MASTER BEDROOM

FLOOR PLAN

1/1

– ALL CHANGES SHOULD BE APPROVED BY ARCHITECT –

ARAMIS STILTON'S MANSION

Find Stilton

Stilton's mansion isn't really guarded at the moment, so you're free to explore. Only a few items show up as collectible when you equip your Heart, but this level has a few tricks up its sleeve, so there are more items than you expect.

Walk upstairs and turn right. Grab a **Rune** lying on the floor, not far from the top of the stairs. Then go toward the noble's private quarters, and drop down through the floor into his music room. Talk to Stilton, and then to the Outsider as well. You receive a new tool: the Timepiece.

THE TIMEPIECE

This new item lets you switch between the mansion as it stands right now, and the mansion as it was three years ago. This allows you to explore, get more collectibles, and proceed through the story. Most of the puzzles and problems in this level revolve around jumping back and forth to avoid various obstacles.

When the cutscene ends, you're left in the music room. Try out the Timepiece, and switch back and forth between time periods. Raising and lowering a lens on the device lets you catch a glimpse of the other timeline without switching, but it obstructs your vision of the current area and should be kept down most of the time.

Exploring and Collecting

Before you leave, consider what should happen to Stilton.

THE FATE OF STILTON

You can kill Stilton, choke him unconscious, or leave him alone. All of these have substantial ramifications on the present. Leaving him alone ensures that Stilton will remain insane and broken. Choke him unconscious to protect him from the things that he's about to see. Or, kill him for maximum Chaos and carnage.

Then walk out of the broken doors and stop at the barricade beyond them. Use the Timepiece to shift into the past. If you're quick, you can assassinate a Guard by the door and down the Elite nearby before she has time to fight.

The doors to the right lead into the kitchen, where two civilians are working. Pass it by for now, unless you need food for health (there is a massive amount in the kitchen).

The left side of the main hallway passes the front door. Wolfhounds and Guards are outside. They're weak targets, but there's no loot to steal, so it's not important to go out there.

Open the doors toward the end of the hallway and get your weapons ready. Multiple Veterans and some Guards are in the next room. They have an alarm set up, and a fight here can chain for a good while. If you hurry across the room, you can kill the Guard by the Alarm to limit the intensity of the engagement a little bit.

Use your reserves of Grenades and other heavy weapons if things aren't going as planned; this is one of the only big fights in the mansion, so splurge a little.

Loot one of the dead Veterans for a Master Key! You can access most of the mansion with this. This isn't required because the Timepiece can get you around the mansion by shifting around the various doors and barricades. But, some people prefer a direct route!

Head around the corner inside this dining room and look for a Vault door. Shift to the present to pass it, and then back again to loot a massive safe. A **Blueprint** is inside. You also get money and a **Painting** from the Vault.

Let's back up for a moment to get more items. Go to the kitchen again, off of the main hallway. Look for the Kitchen Key in the present, inside a cabinet. Use it to unlock the door in back.

Shift to the present and go through a broken window in the next room. You gain access to many side chambers, and it takes a few minutes to explore everything. In the present, you only have to watch out for Bloodflies and a wandering Nestkeeper. It's not too bad. Guards inhabit the past. Use the lens on the Timepiece to see what you're getting into before you jump.

Locate the elevator near the center of the house while you're wandering the ground floor. With your Heart, observe the Bonecharm tucked into the shaft, in the present. Reach it by jumping onto a barrel and then up to the lip over the elevator. Shift timestreams, open the hatch to the elevator, and creep forward as far as you can without falling. Transition back to appear inside the elevator. Grab the **Bonecharm**.

Leave the elevator and look to the right for a set of steps leading down. They take you into the basement. Watch out for Rat swarms, and look for a submerged room. There is a **Rune** inside, but it takes some work to acquire: Go into the past and ambush two Elites working nearby. When they're down, get a valve off the shelves in the corner. Throw it into the room that becomes submerged in the present. A small breach in the wall provides you enough space to do this. Jump forward in time, attach the valve to a pipe in the watery area, and then jump up to grab the Rune.

Return to the ground floor. An iron gate held with a wooden board offers another exit from this major set of rooms. Destroy the board and open the gate. Go around the new bend on the right, and look at a collapsed pile of debris.

Shift to the past and loot a desk in the same spot. Crawl underneath the desk afterward and find a place to transition. This allows you to avoid the barricade and enter the locked boiler room ahead. In the past a **Black Bonecharm** is there, inside a safe. You also get 135 items' worth of money. To claim it, take the body of a dead Wolfhound in the past and put it into the furnace. Press a button to turn on the furnace and wait for it to finish cremating the body. When you return to the present, the safe displays the correct combination on its door. Record it, and go back to the past to open the safe.

There is one more collectible on the left side of the mansion. Above the dining room are three chandeliers. Hop onto the farthest one while in the past, transition, and then leap up to a broken set of joists in the present. The **Bonecharm** is in an attic area above the dining room.

Return to the open yard where the Bloodflies congregate. Climb a hill of dirt to reach the second floor. Walk around the balcony and look for a window with a Document on it. It talks about the repairs to the window. Shift to the past and kill the worker and Guard standing by the same window. Because it didn't get repaired, the window is gone in the present. Climb onto a small set of vines to get over to another broken window. Enter and transition to the past again. Deal with three Guards in the room, and take your **Rune**. Go back out the window and use the same pipes to reach the opposite side of the mansion. Jump over onto a balcony and shift to the past. You find a **Painting** in that room. It's protected by multiple Elites, but you find a Health Elixir and Raw Whalebone to compensate you for your time.

Find the Combination to the Study

That's enough gathering. Return to the kitchen, pass through into the large hallway beyond, and walk into the big yard. Climb to the upper tier of the room again and get right next to the waypoint (it says "Combination").

Switch to the past there. You end up right behind a Veteran, but he doesn't know you're near him. Use the marked door to exit the mansion and enter the backyard.

STILTON'S BACKYARD

The backyard isn't too large an area. Go to the edge of the railing ahead and use your Spyglass to look out over the yard below. A handful of skilled Guards and Elites are protecting Stilton, who is standing in a gazebo.

Kill the only Guard on your level. He's alone and can be assassinated almost instantly. With him down, pull out your Crossbow and snipe targets all over the yard below. You haven't gotten any good Crossbow time in lately, so it's a fun break. Your enemies don't have a long enough range to counter this.

Get the door combination from the gazebo once everyone is down. Turn around and head back into the mansion, using the lower doors.

Get into the Study

The study is your marked waypoint now. Get upstairs and find the locked doors. You get a nice fight on the stairs if you want one. Prepare a Grenade and then charge into the enemies. When they start to gather, toss the Grenade into their midst and continue to the top of the steps to finish off anyone who makes it up there alive.

Use the code from the gazebo to open the séance doors.

Go through the study and the séance room below. You witness a couple of events, and everything you see is important. When it's finished, retreat from the mansion and try to return to the Dust District.

Visit a Very Old Place

When you walk out the mansion's door, you're transported somewhere else. The Outsider explains what you've seen, and he walks you through several places in the Void. There aren't any challenges or tricks here, so just watch and learn.

Look around you, a crumbling island at the very edges of the Void

When he's done, you return to the world.

Return to Your Allies

Run back through the Dust District. Your waypoints are marked, and there are few Guards. It only takes a minute or two to find Sokolov and Captain Foster back by the skiff. Leave this place, and return to the Wale.

Are you ready to leave? The dust is wreaking havoc on my throat.

The Grand Palace

Self-serving and corrupt, Duke Luca Abele rules Serkonos, and orchestrated the Coup against you. Enter the Grand Palace to find and eliminate the Duke, who protects himself from assassins with a body double. You must also locate Delilah's spirit, the only means of counteracting her immortality.

COLLECTIBLES

Runes	5
Shrines	1
Bonecharms	7
Coins	4430
Blueprints	3
Paintings	3

SPECIAL ACTIONS

Through the Pantry	Enter the Vault through the secret pantry passage
Sunken Storage	Swim into the submerged storage room beneath the Palace
Friends in High Places	Place Duke Luca Abele with his body double
Haunted by the Past	Steal the broken gazelle from the Vault
Black Market Heist	Steal yet again from the black market
Addressing Karnaca	Use the speaker in Duke Abele's chambers

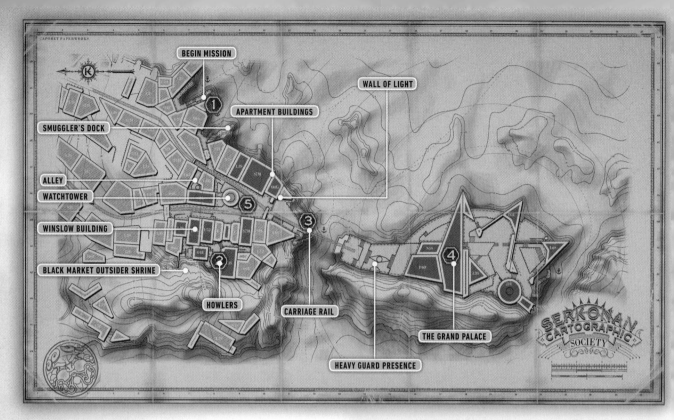

ON THE DREADFUL WALE

You get some rest back on the ship, and then wake up a few hours later. Meet Captain Foster on deck and talk to her. She and Sokolov are figuring out what needs to be done during the assault on the Duke's Palace.

There's a new Audiograph down in the briefing room, if you're interested. After you finish with everyone, head to the skiff and tell Foster you're ready to go!

RAVINA BOULEVARD

Clearing the Right Side of Town

Disembark from the skiff at the docks and follow the only route up toward street level. A small fish stall on the right contains Raw Whalebone, so stop there briefly.

The path takes you up and around a small harbor. Two smugglers are below, talking about their trade with the black market. Ambush them to steal the weapons from their crates nearby.

This is also where you return after getting the Delivery Boat Key from a woman near the black market. The boat holds a code for the back door to the market (for your stealing purposes). It also contains another cache of weapons, and some money too.

Get back up to the street and head into the center of town. You pass a fishmonger out working on a shark. Look behind him for another piece of Raw Whalebone.

When you hit the main part of town, the path splits off to the right or continues straight forward. Explore the right path first, because it's a bit smaller and has multiple items to collect. Also, it leads toward the black market.

Pass by a beggar who doesn't have much of value to say (he divulges a tip about a shrine location). Then cut into a couple of Bloodfly nests ahead.

This route takes you to another road pretty quickly. There are a few patrolling Guards around. Blink over to the Elite on a railing to kill him first, because the other two are chumps.

With them down, Blink to a balcony on your original side of the road. Bloodflies are inside, along with a **Black Bonecharm** locked in a vise. Open the vise to claim your prize.

Loot the Winslow store on the other side of the street. Knock out the civilian who works there, and grab the gate code from the back of the store. Also, locate a cash register that contains a Key. It unlocks an apartment on the other side of town.

Use the gate code to open a locked gate next to the store. Crouch and sneak up on a woman complaining to the black market shopkeeper ahead. Steal the Delivery Boat Key and then return to the boat you passed earlier. The boat has been robbed (although there is an instance where, after getting the boat key, if you're really really fast, you'll find the guards in the process of robbing the boat). To find the missing Audiograph, search the first floor of the building with a windmill on its roof.

Approach the door by the black market and use the password to gain access to the building. Steal the Black Market Key from the shopkeeper, and unlock the front of the store. Go through to buy upgrades from him before robbing the place.

BLACK MARKET GOODS

ITEM	COST
Crossbow Bolt	20
Pistol Bullet	30
Sleep Dart	30
Grenade	70
Stun Mine	70
Spring Razor	50
Addermire Solution	150
Health Elixir	75
Rewire Tool	200
Disable the Carriage Rail	250

EASIEST ROBBERY YET

Since you already have access to the store, steal its items at any time.

Assassinate the Howler inside the market before you leave. Then walk outside and Blink up to the balconies to start dealing with all his aggressive friends. There are only a few of them, but they have ranged weapons and are a real nuisance if you don't use Blink to quickly close the gap against them.

Clear that street and then examine the right side of the path. Jump up some rocks and search for a wooden barricade with a light above it. That's a secret area; break inside and explore to find Raw Whalebone and an **Outsider Shrine**.

Return to the market entrance and search the Howlers' bodies for a Key. Blink onto the balcony above the market. Blink again to get through an open window into a nearby apartment building.

Unlock the first apartment you find with the Key you grabbed. Loot that place for extra cash. Return the market balcony and Blink to another apartment across the street. Loot that as well.

Clearing the Left Side of Town

Hug the right side of the road while you continue. Another apartment building is down that side of the path. The other route takes you into the very center of town, with a Watchtower and all the Guards.

Climb up to the roof and kill a Guard and an Elite. Both are looking away from you, so sneak up on them for melee assassinations.

Blink up and turn off the Windmill, then carefully look over the edge of the roof. Blink down to the balcony beneath the Windmill and enter the blockaded apartment. Bloodfly nests are all over the place, and a Nestkeeper lurks toward the rear of the apartment most of the time. Get your Pistol out and clear the nests and the Nestkeeper. Guards below may hear the noise, but this is your high-Chaos run. Let them freak out!

Search the bathroom of the apartment for a **Rune**. The bedroom contains a **Painting**. Corvo remembers that guy all too well.

Get back onto the balcony and Blink up to the Watchtower. Pull out the Whale Oil Tank, or rewire the system to be really nasty. Either way, Blink off the Watchtower when it no longer threatens to splatter you, and take care of the massive fight below.

Plenty of Elites/Veterans and a few Guards protect the streets. It's a rolling battle that lets you really test your ability to switch between melee, ranged attacks, and defense. It's so much fun.

The Guards try to sound an alert as soon as they see you. Kill the ones who rush for the siren to keep the fight half under control. Or let them sound it, and then stay mobile to prevent the enemies from grouping up well against you.

Think I heard something.

If you set traps in one of the apartment buildings that line the street, it's easy to lure Guards into them.

In any case, defeat the enemies and then search the last two buildings in this district. Both are apartment buildings on the left side of the street.

The first one houses two Guards and a civilian on the second floor. They're not looking at anything too valuable, because the place has been trashed already.

The third floor is more lucrative. Go upstairs and search the bathroom of the apartment above for a **Bonecharm**. There are also a few items of modest value.

The last apartment building contains a locked door on the third floor. Get the Key from the Winslow store and unlock this apartment when you can. You find a **Blueprint** inside, on a desk. Knock a pillow off the bed in the bedroom to grab a **Bonecharm** as well.

A safe in the apartment contains money and Bullets. Search the area by the desk to locate a picture of a man with a safe behind him. The combo is right there in the picture (123).

Now that you have everything you need, use the back door of this apartment or the door behind the Wall of Light to leave Ravina Boulevard and approach the Grand Palace. The door by the Wall of Light is a direct route.

PALACE DISTRICT

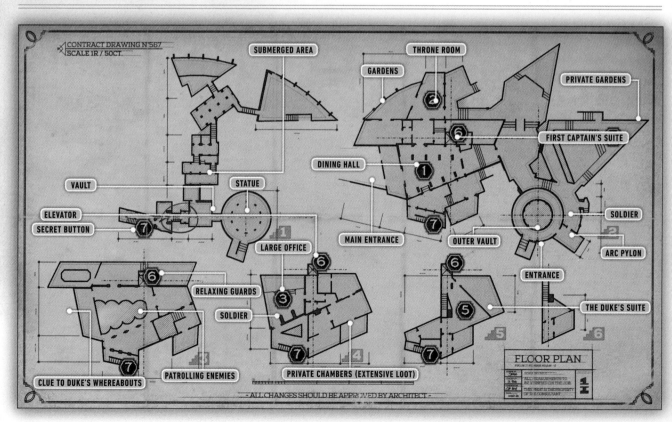

Clear Out the First Floor and the Gardens

Walk forward on the other side of the door and locate two talking Guards. Blink over to them and murder both before they can speak.

Approach the bridge that leads to the Palace, and cross it using Blink and careful walking. If you didn't have the power cut to the bridge, take a carriage across and arrive loud and proud. But stealing from the black market usually includes cutting the power.

It doesn't matter too much either way, because you're about to wake up everyone in front of the place. There are Veterans, Elites, Guards, and a Wolfhound or two. It's entirely possible to sneak in here, using patience, Sleep Darts, and the gardens to the left or some Fish Possession.

But screw that. Get out your Crossbow.

Holy Shit!!

Spend your Bolts liberally as you charge up to the front doors. Make the Wolfhounds and the Elites/Veterans your primary targets. Save Sword attacks for the weak Guards, and watch the resistance melt before you. They have a big weakness: though there are tons of targets, they're spread out and end up coming at you in a trickle. As long as you're tossing out enough ranged damage, you can overwhelm them. It costs 6-10 Bolts or Bullets to do it, but that's what they're there for.

Literally smash through the front doors and stride into the banquet hall. Another major fight breaks out, but somehow you still have the advantage of surprise. Walk up to the first man for one assassination, try it again for the second, and Blink if you're lucky enough to get the drop on yet one more target.

RECEPTION AND DINING

Ignore the civilians in the room, and eat food from the table to restore your Health instead of using Elixirs (unless you get desperate).

When the fighting ends, heal yourself and go out the far end of the room. You are outside again. Veer to the right to approach the private gardens the Duke loves so much. A Clockwork Soldier and at least one Guard intercept you soon after you get out there. Use your Pistol and Sword to cripple the Clockwork Soldier, especially if you've grabbed some Magnetized Bullets. Stun Mines, as always, also work well against these mechanical enemies.

After that fight, hop over a short wall to gain a good view of the gardens. The Duke would be there if the alarms hadn't gone off, but he probably hasn't gone far.

PRIVATE GARDEN

Time to explore. Turn to the left and follow a power line that leads to a Security Panel. Look over the edge of the railing there to find the Whale Oil receptacle that powers everything. This is attached to an Arc Pylon, so it's a good idea to disable the device. Take the Whale Oil Tank out of the receptacle, and then look for a wooden barricade down there.

Destroy the barricade to enter the abandoned storage area.

Trash a few Bloodfly nests and look for a submerged part of this basement. Swim in the water and use your Heart to locate a **Rune** at the bottom.

Break through another barricade to exit the storage room from a different angle. This puts you closer to the throne room. Fight two regular Guards outside the room as you approach. Using your Heart allows you to see a Bonecharm inside. Watch out when you open the doors; the Arc Pylon in the room can rip you in half if you're reckless. Blink to the other side of the room and use the throne for cover. Open a Whale Oil receptacle and remove the tank. This turns off the Arc Pylon.

Take the **Bonecharm** off the throne and clear out any Elites who arrive to check out the noise. For fun, throw your Whale Oil Tank at them when they approach.

Stay inside the Palace. Walk through the main doors that lead into a sitting room, and turn left. You quickly reach the First Captain's Quarters. A side chamber within contains a few weapons and two Guards who are sleeping it off. Murder them and loot the room.

The main part of the suite houses a safe and a few more decent pickups. The safe combination is upstairs, in the Duke's third-floor office. Come back here later to unlock it, and you get a **Rune** and hundreds of coins for your efforts.

On the other side of the banquet hall is another room worth visiting. Use your Heart to track a **Bonecharm** to an unguarded room inhabited by two civilians. Go in and take it.

Go Downstairs

You've gotten pretty much the entire first floor's treasure and enemies out of the way. Return to the banquet hall and look for a side room with a staircase. It leads both up and down throughout the Palace. For now, head down.

Ambush and kill the two Guards in the pantry. There's nowhere else to explore at first, and you don't find loot here either. There's a ton of food to eat, if you need it, but that's it.

Yet, if you search well, you find a button hidden in the pantry. Press it to open a secret door.

You've found the first half of the Duke's Vault. Take everything inside. A **Blueprint** sits on a large table in the main room. You also get a **Black Bonecharm** from a side chamber.

You can't get into the remainder of the Vault until later, but both sides need to be opened either way.

Climbing the Stairs

Retreat to the stairs and ascend to the second floor for more money. There isn't anything important there, but Elites are playing cards in one room, and there is a fair amount of total money if you loot their bodies and the cash that's spread around.

Watch out for a patrolling Clockwork Soldier. If that thing shows up, back off and fight it away from any potential reinforcements.

More important items are on the third floor. Climb up there and open the door on the left first. This one leads into a huge office with another Clockwork Soldier. It's alone, so you're safe(ish). Aim for those white joints and break the machine apart.

A desk in the office holds a **Blueprint**.

The Duke's body double might be in here. He's sometimes in the suite upstairs, but his location varies. Because you're playing high Chaos, you're safe in killing both the body double and the Duke just to be sure you get the guy. If you dislike wanton killing of innocents, then search the second floor for a Document that reveals where the Duke is located. You can also listen in on the servants' conversations to figure it out. It's your call.

Get the combination for the First Captain's safe while you're up here. Return to the first floor, open the safe, and grab your **Rune** and money.

Finish looting the remainder of the third floor. One of the bathrooms contains a **Corrupt Bonecharm**. There aren't many other Guards, so the fighting is minimal and easy. The fourth floor belongs to the Duke's private quarters. Climb up there after you finish looting the rest of the third floor.

Raiding the Duke's Suite

If you haven't already bumped into the Duke in the private garden or the office on the third floor, he's at the top of the Palace. The fourth floor features a suite with multiple rooms. Charge into it and clear out any Veterans; there's usually one if the Duke is present.

The Duke is armed and tries to fight, but you can kill him with a single Pistol shot or an assassination. Loot his body for the Vault Key to take the other half of his treasure before you leave!

If you don't find the Duke here, try to look again in his private gardens outside, or in Delilah's chambers.

Retrieve the Raw Whalebone and coins from his desk, and listen to an intriguing Audiograph from his upper bedroom. The lower tier of the room contains a chest with money and Bullets.

Back to the Vault

Return to the staircase and descend to the basement. Walk into the Vault and use the Key you obtain from the Duke to open the inner Vault Door.

Use a Stun Mine as you ambush a Clockwork Soldier inside the Vault. Once it's destroyed, search the room for a gazelle statue, Raw Whalebone, and minor valuables. Your waypoint takes you to the middle of the room afterward. Trap Delilah's spirit by interacting with the strange statue there.

Leave the Palace

Either backtrack to get outside or use the other Vault door. The latter is much faster, but it requires you to Blink past a Clockwork Soldier and an Arc Pylon. Choose whether to be prudent or expedient, as both routes get you to the lower docks that are your new waypoint.

If you take the quick route, go to the upper tier of the inner Vault. Look for a button on the wall, and press it. This opens the big door to the outer gardens.

Grab a Whale Oil Tank to disable the Arc Pylon ahead, and then make for the docks. If you haven't killed the Clockwork Soldier out here already, have a Stun Mine prepared and go to town once you see the machine.

Reach the waypoint and hold there a minute. Your ride is on its way! When Captain Foster arrives, Blink, swim out to her, and leave the Palace..

LAST TRIP ON THE DREADFUL WALE

Meagan Foster's Cabin Key
(X) Pickpocket

And sooner or later, in ways we can't always fathom, the...

Wake up on the Dreadful Wale and head to the briefing room. Talk to Sokolov and look at his most recent painting. Search the room behind it for a **Blueprint** on the worktable, then meet Captain Foster on deck and talk to her. Pickpocket a Cabin Key when the conversation is over, and return belowdecks. Open Captain Foster's cabin (beside the briefing room), and steal two **Bonecharms** from a desk.

With all that done, use the skiff to go ashore.

Death to the Empress

You must confront Empress Delilah Copperspoon before she changes all the world with her will. Enter Dunwall Tower and find a way to reunite Delilah Copperspoon's spirit with her body to make her mortal again. Only then can you eliminate her and take back the throne.

COLLECTIBLES

Runes	5
Shrines	1
Bonecharms	9
Coins	2562
Blueprints	2
Paintings	1

SPECIAL ACTIONS

Captain's Quarters	Search Meagan Foster's cabin aboard the Dreadful Wale
World As It Should Be	Trap Delilah in her painting
Avenging Jessamine	Take revenge on Billie Lurk for her part in Jessamine's assassination
Heart of the Tower	Reach the Royal Protector's chambers
Saving Your Father	Rescue Corvo Attano
Saving Your Daughter	Rescue Emily Kaldwin
Black Market Heist	Sneak in one more robbery before the end
Your Daughter Is Safe	Take the throne as Corvo Attano, leaving Emily as a statue
Your Father Is Safe	Take back the throne as Emily, leaving Corvo as a statue
In the Coven's Wake	Use the street speakers to address the public

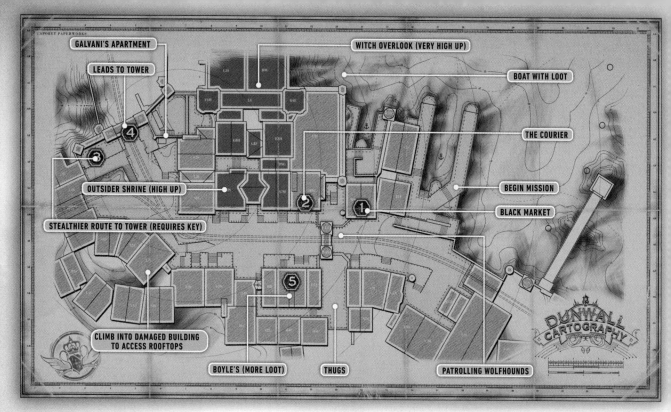

Map labels:
- GALVANI'S APARTMENT
- LEADS TO TOWER
- WITCH OVERLOOK (VERY HIGH UP)
- BOAT WITH LOOT
- THE COURIER
- BEGIN MISSION
- BLACK MARKET
- OUTSIDER SHRINE (HIGH UP)
- STEALTHIER ROUTE TO TOWER (REQUIRES KEY)
- CLIMB INTO DAMAGED BUILDING TO ACCESS ROOFTOPS
- BOYLE'S (MORE LOOT)
- THUGS
- PATROLLING WOLFHOUNDS
- DUNWALL CARTOGRAPHY

DUNWALL STREETS

Looting the City

Corvo lands in almost the same place from which he left after the first mission. The city has gone to ruin, so quite a few things have changed in the meantime.

Jump and Blink to the top of the rocks after you get control of yourself. Several Wolfhounds patrol the street above the harbor. Kill them with assassination attacks, or use Bolts if you don't mind sparing a few.

Clear out the wharf and examine the far side of the harbor. Another boat is out there. Jump into the water and swim out to it. You find minor loot, but the coinage adds up nicely.

Blink back over to the docks and climb up toward the old bar that overlooks the water. It's no longer in service, but the black market has moved in. Buy all the final upgrades you can afford.

ROBBERY

Find the Common Key near the Courier (we explain where soon) and use it to unlock a door at the back side of the black market. It's roughly one floor down from the shop. Once you get into this small warehouse, look for a broken section of ceiling. Blink up there to enter the shop, and steal whatever you like.

Fight through the Wolfhounds all the way down the road as you approach Boyle's and the Courier. Explore the Courier first, because you find many items inside.

Up top, you can also talk to the editor of the paper. Don't miss the Gold Ingots stashed on the upper floor. You could almost buy a whole new upgrade just with that.

When you're done, go to the first floor, but take the building's safe door into a ruined alley. To your right is a metal shelf. Clear away a couple of bottles, and grab the **Common Key**, which is required for you to pull off the black market robbery. A decent man is hiding at the end of the alley beside the Courier building. Talk to him for more background on recent events.

The Hatters are breaking into Boyle's. You've heard of this gang of troublemakers before. Head over to Boyle's place and loot both floors of the store. There are five thugs on the first floor, and another couple are guarding the back-alley entrance.

Use Grenades and bursts of Pistol fire to clear out the heavier group inside. Once they're down, you can get hundreds of coins just by looting the tables throughout the building.

Advance around the bend in the main street and approach the end of the area.

Look for a building on your left. There isn't anything inside, but you hear a Witch talking high above it. Enter the building through the entrance we show here.

Stay quiet and Blink up through the floors of the building. You find the Witch on the fourth floor, talking to herself about a paramour. Assassinate her, and then cross the street from this lofty height; use some fallen beams to accomplish this somewhat safely.

Kill two Hatters in the apartment across the way. They're looking for loot, and they almost found some. There is some stuff still there, but a locked secret room contains a hoard of goodies.

Turn a Barometer in the second room of the apartment to open the door and uncover an **Outsider Shrine**. Grab those easy Runes and talk to your best buddy again.

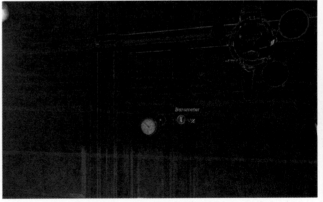

Get back onto the balcony and slip around the corner of the building. Piping leads you deeper across the rooftops. Use your Heart to locate the Black Bonecharm ahead, and guide yourself toward it. Be careful not to fall; it's much safer to Blink than to jump up here.

Take out your Crossbow and snipe the Witch high above before you reach your destination. Search the building behind the Witch when you get up to it. The **Black Bonecharm** is up high, on a mattress. It's easy to get.

Return to the street and keep exploring. Near the end gate, you come across a locked Armory. If you got the City Watch Armory Key from the black market, unlock it and go inside. There is minor loot and a door that grants you a back way up toward the Tower. We don't take that route because it's a stealthier approach.

Galvani's apartment—the building that contained a Painting when you escaped from Dunwall earlier—has new loot. Break through the front doors of the apartment and grab a Blueprint from the lab within.

That's all there is to nab before you leave.

Get into Dunwall Tower

Follow the trail of dead bodies in the main street. The Overseers got royally destroyed trying to retake Dunwall Tower. Walk in their footsteps and head through the door at the end of the street.

OUTSIDE THE TOWER

The next yard has even more dead bodies. Locate a wounded Overseer on the left and talk to him. Let him say his piece, and then check out the right side of the yard. A small building offers Whale Oil Tanks and a refueling station. Use the machine on the left to get an empty Whale Oil Tank. Put it into the receptacle on the right, use the lever to fill it, and then take it to the Gate Control on the opposite end of the room. Press the button once the tank is in place, and watch the gate to the Tower rise.

Blink past the Bloodbriars in the gatehouse and continue up the hill as you approach the Tower. For an easier time, Blink up to a building on the right near the top of the hill. A few Witches are crafting inside. You can ambush and kill them easily. Taking on the group at the top of the hill often brings in all the Witches in the region. Half-a-dozen Witches make life ugly and short for most people.

But if you try it, snipe the Gravehounds' skulls ahead with your Crossbow so it's quiet. Then hit at least one of the Witches from range to start the battle with a minor advantage. One free headshot gives you one fewer Witch to fight!

For the others, blow your Bullets on each target. Keep those Witches wounded and distracted, and use Sword hits only to finish them off. Don't duel, block, or stand still. Use

the few objects in the roadway to block line of sight so the Witches can't use their spells as effectively against you.

Another wave of three Witches waits around the corner, but they're far enough away not to join any attacks here. They have a Gravehound with them. Sneak up on the group to assassinate two Witches and turn that battle into a somewhat easy one.

The building to the right is the Green House. Search it for a Health Elixir and a **Bonecharm** once the Witches are all slain.

Your Heart lets you see a Rune and a Bonecharm outside the Tower. Turn left to go after the Bonecharm. Walk quietly to approach the next group of Witches with an advantage. Another group of three Witches and a Wolfhound are near the Bonecharm's building. It's the waterlock you passed through during the siege on Dunwall Tower all those years ago.

Blink and sneak across the pipes and walkway around the right side of the building. Two Witches are close to the

Bonecharm, but they're unaware of you. Jump over the wall when you hear them talking, and assassinate one of them. Dispatch the other by herself by any means.

Get the **Bonecharm** from a wooden box, and return to the front of the building.

Ascend the stairs ahead and to the left. You find the momentous gazebo where so much of your life changed during the Empress's assassination. Go into the gazebo and pay your respects.

Jump onto the left wall when you're done, and observe several Gravehounds' skulls farther down. Snipe them, and get down there. Take a Painting along the wall.

The algae is all dried out, but that makes it easier to collect. Less messy. You can still smell it.

Head toward the Dunwall Tower entrance, but get one more thing before you go inside. A building to the left of the entrance hides a Rune. Crawl in through a small opening and use a Drop assassination on a Witch. Her companion sees this, but she's isolated and vulnerable.

Kill her and enter a metal walkway above the detected Rune. Hop through a small cubby at the side of the room and crawl over to grab the **Rune**.

Now you can head into the Dunwall Tower front door whenever you want. You have everything here.

DUNWALL TOWER INTERIOR

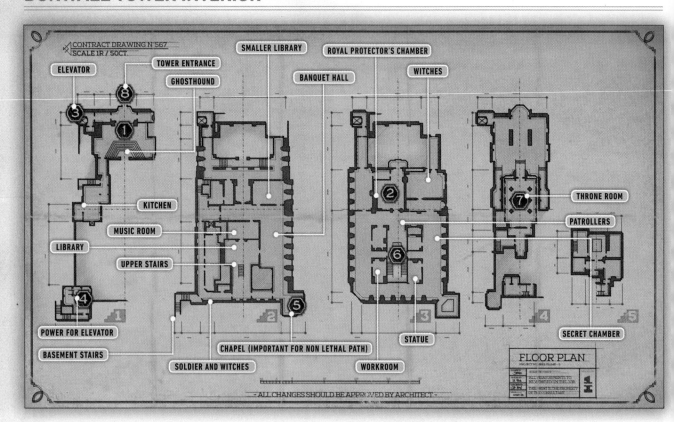

Find Delilah

Turn left when you get inside and Blink over to two Witches. Assassinate one (or both), and switch to swordplay if either survives the initial burst.

Retrieve the map next to the barricade that blocks most of the entryway, and jump over the debris. The High Overseer is in the next room, but he's in no condition to talk. Look ahead for a Gravehound skull that's near the dead Overseer. Destroy that ahead of time so you don't get spotted when approaching. Afterward, get a **Bonecharm** and a **Corrupt Bonecharm** from the Overseer's corpse.

If a battle starts here, Witches come from all over the place. You face many of them in the open room, so speed is your best ally. Either flee into tighter corridors, or rush between the Witches, using gunfire and fast dispatches to keep their numbers low while reinforcements come in.

Use the lower door on the right to leave the room during or after the battle. The next room is quiet, so you have time to recover. Once you regain your bearings, follow this route and climb some stairs on the right until you find two more Witches. Ambush them with a Blink assassination and Pistol shot, and then explore.

Carefully crawl across a board and through a window. If you drop off the board, you end up in the cellar and have to work your way back up here.

The kitchen is on the other side of the window. Eat up, and get ready for a tricky fight. The adjoining corridor contains a Clockwork Soldier and two Witches. Making noise and luring a target to you creates an easier run of the task. Set traps near the kitchen exit for even more help.

Defeat this trio and go to the corner of the building. Stairs lead down into a security room. Use the Heart to scan for a **Rune** on top of several pipes, then get the Tower's elevator working by restoring power to the machinery here.

Use the Whale Oil dispenser's lever to obtain an unfilled tank. Put the tank in the Whale Oil Fueling Station and pull the machine's lever. When the tank is full, place it in the empty red receptacle behind you so everything is happily getting juice.

Two Witches come down to investigate. Hide around the wall and then jump out to cut them apart. Climb back up the stairs and take the hallway directly ahead. You come into the library and find stairs leading up.

Looting the Second Floor (Optional)

To avoid a massive battle, wait for a Clockwork Soldier to look away, and then Blink up the stairs to avoid its attention.

Fighting the soldier gets you into a war with it and about half-a-dozen more Witches.

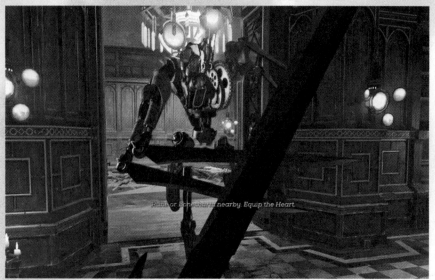

Rune or Bonecharm nearby. Equip the Heart.

If this is the fight you want, trap the preceding hallway ahead of time. Put multiple traps down, with a decent bit of distance between them. Retreat as you fight the Clockwork Soldier, and let the Witches come to you. They teleport behind you and end up eating your traps. Back up more so they hit the second/third layers of your defenses as you get pressed.

The second floor isn't required for completing your mission, but there are two more Bonecharms up there and some optional story aspects as well. Once you're up there, look for the Royal Protector's chambers at the end of the main hallway. Entering gets you credit for a special action.

However, there are patrolling Witches everywhere. Blink assassinations continue to work fairly well against them, and Crossbow sniping is good too.

Rune of Bonecharm nearby. Equip the Heart.

One room, to the left of the main hall, holds a **Bonecharm** defended by a single Witch. Once you clear the hall of Gravehounds and patrollers, you can get it at any time.

The other Bonecharm on the level is weird. There isn't a door leading to it, so look around carefully. Turn right from the main hallway. If you have Dark Vision, locate a man hiding inside the walls. Look up near the ceiling to find a small window leading into this hidden/blockaded chamber.

Retrieve the **Bonecharm** from inside, and talk to the poor fellow.

Confront Delilah

Follow your waypoint to the elevator. You've already restored its power, so getting there is the only issue. Retreat through the areas you've already cleared if you want to save time.

Take the elevator up to the throne room. Nothing but a door is up there, which exits onto the Tower rooftop.

No one else stands in your way except for Delilah. Enter her throne room and use the Heart to take away her immortality.

Follow me, dear Corvo, and see how I will reshape all things.

Delilah retreats into her painting, and you must pursue. Once there, you are confronted by many imposters of Delilah. They all look and fight like her, but they're just fragments of her true self.

To win this encounter, you need to beat more and more of them until you take out the real Delilah. After her replicas are dead, she'll appear in a beam of light in the center of the area. That's when you'll have your chance to destroy her.

Use all of your goodies to kill off the replicas. There isn't anything to worry about once you win, so consider all Health and Mana Elixirs as expandable. Attack with your Pistol and Crossbow in concert with your Sword to wound and then dispatch each imposter very quickly. They won't be able to gang up on you if you take this rapid approach.

Area of effect weapons make a big difference if you start to get overwhelmed. Use Explosive Bullets, Grenades, and Springrazors while backing away from the throng of replicas.

When Delilah falls, the battle stops. Return to the Throne Room and choose whether to free Emily or to leave her as a statue that can never be harmed. If you wish the latter, sit on the throne to end the game. This only works if you have chosen a very high Chaos playthrough, but with all of the bodies that you've piled up, that seems very possible.

COLLECTIBLES

A Long Day in Dunwall

RUNES

No Runes present. However, you do find an Outsider shrine during the sequence ("A Strange Visit") between this mission and the next. This Shrine is not missable.

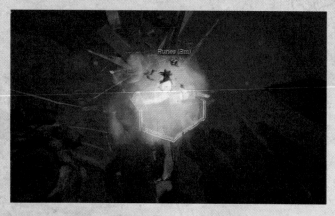

BONECHARMS

There are no Bonecharms present in this mission.

PAINTINGS

The first Painting is in Dunwall Streets, in the escape corridor that you run through before getting outside. It's on the right.

The second Painting is in the Galvani building. Turn left when you get down into the streets and look for a small apartment. It has one Guard inside. The Painting is in the second room of the apartment, and it's hung above a fireplace.

BLUEPRINTS

There are no Blueprints present in this mission.

Edge of the World

RUNES

There is a Rune inside of a whale carcass along the wharf. It's not too far from where you start the mission.

Buy a Rune from the black market in town.

The Overseer building in the canal area has a Rune on a table where someone is speaking to the crowd. Steal that

after defeating the Overseers, or Blink/Far Reach to steal it from the table.

Get into the canal near the Overseer building. Look for a gate where the water comes into the canal and use your Crossbow to break a wooden plank that's partially blocking the flow. This causes a Rune to slide down toward you.

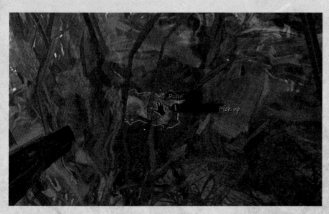

Unlock a safe in the Overseer building, on the third floor. It has 225 coins and a Rune inside of it. The Combination is (516).

A small path stretches to the right before you get to the canal area. This leads to a two-floor apartment building. Kill the two Overseers that are exploring the place, and look for the Outsider Shrine on the second floor.

BONECHARMS

The infested building has a Bonecharm on the second floor. It's inside of a nest, and is visible once you destroy the Nest and kill the Bloodflies around it.

Outside of the Overseer building is a table with a Rune and a Bonecharm. Kill the Overseers to loot these items, or Blink/Far Reach onto the table and carefully steal the goodies before the crowd freaks out and alerts the Overseers to your presence.

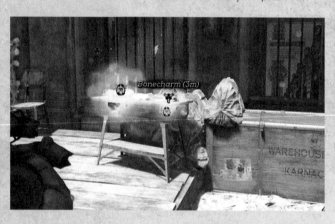

Blink/Far Reach across the rooftops from the Overseer building. Two structures to the side there is a roof with a corpse on it. Kill the Bloodflies that are growing, and take a Bonecharm from the dead person.

An apartment is down a side path before you reach the canal area. Kill two Overseers inside of it, and get a Bonecharm off of the floor, on the second story of the building.

Go to the Winslow Safe Company by the end of the level. On the main floor is a massive safe. Put (**508**) into the lock to open it and get a Bonecharm.

Near the top of the Overseer building you find a locked Interrogation Room. Get the Key from an Overseer in the next room to the right, and unlock the door. Inside is a Corrupt Bonecharm.

PAINTINGS

Before you get into the canal area, there is a side road that leads to a single apartment building. Look in here and defeat two Overseers that are tossing a place. A Painting of the Outsider is on the second floor.

The third floor of the Overseer building has a Painting on the wall. It's near a safe that has a Rune locked inside of it.

Hypatia's apartment has a Painting in the main hallway. She lives above the Winslow Safe Company, in the latter part of the mission.

BLUEPRINTS

Fire Hardening Treatment has a Blueprint inside the Overseer's building. It's up a couple of floors, in an important Overseer's office. Look on the desk for it.

TWO CHANCES FOR YOUR BLUEPRINTS

If you miss a Blueprint the first time it's available, you get another chance to find it. In the next mission, that same Blueprint appears again and is out in the open. Try to get everything the first time the items are available, but don't freak out if you miss one Blueprint.

The Good Doctor

RUNES

Go into the dining hall, on the left side of the institute. Defeat the Guards that are eating there, and look on the wall by the tables. A Rune is hung up.

From the fourth floor, go outside and stop. Look up, and Blink/Far Reach up to the rooftop. Search around for a window back into the building from up there. A Rune is just inside that window.

The Recuperation Room's entrance is on the third floor. Unlock it once you have the Key and go inside. Destroy the first Bloodfly nest ahead, and look in the debris for a Rune.

Break the elevator cables, and Blink/Far Reach from the first floor into the elevator shaft. Hop down into the basement and search it for a Rune on the left wall.

Go out onto fourth floor walkway and follow your Heart to find an Outsider Shrine. It's inside one of the small buildings up there.

BONECHARMS

Start the mission but turn around and look for a pipe underneath the starting walkway. Blink/Far Reach down to that and search underneath the platform for a Bonecharm.

Go into the institute by the main entrance. Use your Heart to find a Bonecharm that is very close, almost on the floor.

As you're going through the Recuperation Room on floor three, look for something that's like an iron lung. Open these human-sized containers when you see them. One lets you crawl through into a damaged room. A Bonecharm is in there.

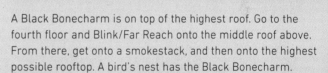

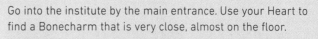

A Black Bonecharm is on top of the highest roof. Go to the fourth floor and Blink/Far Reach onto the middle roof above. From there, get onto a smokestack, and then onto the highest possible rooftop. A bird's nest has the Black Bonecharm.

Dr. Hypatia is in the second floor, but it reached by going through the Recuperation Room on the third floor (it has stairs leading down at the far end). A Corrupt Bonecharm is in a small lab, near Dr. Hypatia's work area.

PAINTINGS

There is a Wall of Light on the first floor. Look right next to it for a Painting.

Break the elevator cables, and Blink/Far Reach from the first floor into the elevator shaft. Hop down into the basement and search it for a Painting on the left wall.

Find Dr. Hypatia's area. Search to her right for a small lab that has a Blueprint. On the wall behind that is a Painting.

BLUEPRINTS

Go to the second floor by Blinking/Far Reaching up and right from the entrance hallway. Search the right side of the building for a Document with a safe combination. Then, look for that safe not far away from where you find the code. Open the safe and get a Blueprint for Combat Sleep Dart Formula.

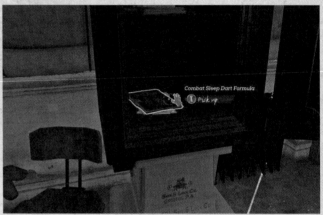

Mercury Vapor Distillation's Blueprint is inside Hamilton's quarters. They're directly in front of you when you enter the room.

Find Dr. Hypatia and look for a Blueprint right next to her. You learn about Dispersed Incendiary Release.

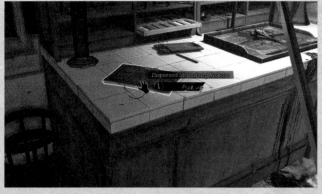

A backup Blueprint for Fire Hardening treatment is inside a small office, on the third floor. It's close to the elevator.

The Clockwork Mansion

RUNES

A gang tries to ambush you in a dark alley, behind the carriage station. Defeat (or avoid) them, and look in a damaged piece of furniture in their yard. A Rune is inside of it.

Buy or steal the Rune from the black market in the first part of the district.

In the Upper Aventa District, you find a Rune. It's in a dilapidated Bloodfly building. Take the side route around the Wall of Light and look for a second story balcony to Blink/Far Reach into. The Rune is in back, inside a desk.

Jindosh's laboratory has many different modules. When you find that room, use a console to bring up the anatomy module and loot that for a Rune.

227

Get into the main part of the district, when you first start seeing Guards. Turn left and look for a building near some civilians. Go inside, kill Bloodlies, and look for an Outsider Shrine on the third floor.

BONECHARMS

From the main street in the district, Blink/Far Reach to get up higher on a short wall of a building. Then, take another jump to get up to a balcony above the road. Go into the office (the mayor's place as it turns out) and break a china cabinet to get a Bonecharm.

A Bonecharm is sitting out on the second floor of the carriage station. It has a Guard and an Elite Guard near it, but is otherwise quite easy to obtain.

In the Upper Aventa District, you find a Bonecharm inside a guard building near the carriage. Look on the second floor, inside the first room.

This is on the Assessment Chamber level. Go back the chamber itself and seek an Elite Guard who patrols that back side of the level. Deal with her, and then search a small machine room behind her route. A small drawer has a Bonecharm for you.

On the Assessment Chamber level, you find a lever that brings the guest waiting area up and down. Pull this lever and rush into an area between the two floors while the machine is working. This recessed spot goes down to the bottom. Press a button to send it back up. Another recess is up there. Search for a dead body and a Bonecharm.

Blink/Far Reach from where the civilians are standing, in the main district, up to some pipes. Blink/Far Reach again to get onto a balcony that overlooks the area. Climb into an apartment and search for a Black Bonecharm.

Find Jindosh's bedroom. Use a lever inside of it and rush into a corner room while it descends into a lower area. A Black Bonecharm is down there.

When you're in the Upper Aventa District, look for this Corrupt Bonecharm. It's in a small Bloodfly building. After you pass the Wall of Light, look for a large awning. Blink into the window above that, and search the room you discover.

Corrupt Bonecharm (4m)

INTRO
STORY
CONTROLS
GAMEPLAY
WEAPONS, GADGETS, & BONECHARMS
THE SUPERNATURAL ARTS
ENEMIES OF THE CROWN
WALKTHROUGH
COLLECTIBLES
TROPHIES & ACHIEVEMENTS

PAINTINGS

Blink/Far Reach from where the civilians are standing, in the main district, up to some pipes. Blink/Far Reach again to get onto a balcony that overlooks the area. Climb into an apartment and immediately grab a Painting that's next to the balcony.

The mayor's office is above the main street in the district. Blink up twice to get to its balcony and head inside. A painting is on the left wall.

Go to the Upper Aventa District. Pass a Wall of Light and look for a brown awning. Blink/Far Reach up to an open window above that awning. The room inside has Bloodflies, but it also has a Painting and a Corrupt Bonecharm.

Sokolov is being held at the bottom of the Assessment Chamber. Find him and loot a Painting from his room.

Jindosh's laboratory has a Painting on the top tier of the room. It's behind a massive desk.

Search for Jindosh's bathroom, on the second floor. Use the lever to spin it and see both configurations of the room. A Painting is in one of them.

BLUEPRINTS

Pyro-Sonic Casing is in the ticket booth of the carriage station. Get the Key from the black market, open up the booth, and search it for the Blueprint.

Alloy Polarization is in the Upper Aventa District. Search the third floor of the guard building for it. Climb the stairs to that floor, turn left, and look in the room at the end of the hallway.

Get Slug Splintering Wedges from the desk in Jindosh's laboratory. It's on the top tier, near a Painting.

Search the desk in the guest's waiting room for a Blueprint. If you've moved the waiting room to another level, use the lever to call it back so that you can search the desk.

The Royal Conservatory
RUNES

Buy a Rune from the black market, on the left side of town.

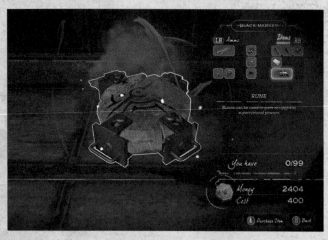

Go to the second floor of the Conservatory. There is a room that's being overtaken by plants near the front of the building. Search there for a Rune.

There is a terrace above Ashworth's office. Go outside and deal with two Gravehounds nearby. With them gone, you can search for the Rune safely.

Go into the basement and find the Archive Key. Then, unlock the Archives (near the stairs and elevator). Break a glass case to get a Rune out of the Archives.

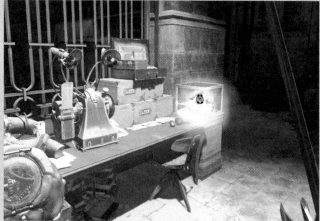

An Outsider Shrine is on the corner of the map. Pass the first Wall of Light and climb to the top of the building on your right. Blink from that roof to an apartment at the edge of the map. Disable multiple traps in the dark room you reach, and then Blink to the upper level of the apartment. That's where the Outsider Shrine is located.

BONECHARMS

After passing the first Wall of Light, go into the apartment building to the right. Inside, a second floor bar has a Bonecharm on a table.

The quest for the shopkeeper's associate takes you to a building that's very close to the Royal Conservatory. Avoid its traps, go to the third floor, and look on a desk. You get a Blueprint and a Bonecharm.

INTRO
STORY
CONTROLS
GAMEPLAY
WEAPONS, GADGETS, & BONECHARMS
THE SUPERNATURAL ARTS
ENEMIES OF THE CROWN
WALKTHROUGH
COLLECTIBLES
TROPHIES & ACHIEVEMENTS

Go to the third floor of the Conservatory. A Bonecharm is tacked to a board, on the front side of the building. It's near several Bloodfly nests.

A small room is on the fourth floor of the Conservatory. It's directly off of the storage room above Ashworth's office. Look inside the room to get a Black Bonecharm.

The Conservatory basement has a locked room with a Bonecharm. To get it, start from the main entrance and turn right. Look for two small windows almost along the floor. Crawl in through the one on the left to access the locked room and loot it.

This one is also on the fourth floor. Start in the storage room and jump out of an open window onto a small walkway. Track a Black Bonecharm with your heart and cross to the far side of that walkway. A tiny area is hidden there, with a body and the Black Bonecharm.

The condemned building, after the first Wall of Light, has a Corrupt Bonecharm in it. Look for the large safe and the area with the Painting. The Corrupt Bonecharm is on the floor close to those.

Loot Breanna Ashworth's body or pickpocket her to get two Black Bonecharms.

Loot Breanna Ashworth's body or pickpocket her to get two Black Bonecharms.

Breanna Ashworth (dead)

Ⓧ Carry

PAINTINGS

After the first Wall of Light, you find a condemned building. Deal with its Nestkeeper and Bloodflies, and then explore. You get a Painting inside a room with a large safe.

Deal with Breanna Ashworth and look in her office for a Painting.

INTRO

STORY

CONTROLS

GAMEPLAY

WEAPONS, GADGETS, & BONECHARMS

THE SUPERNATURAL ARTS

ENEMIES OF THE CROWN

WALKTHROUGH

COLLECTIBLES

TROPHIES & ACHIEVEMENTS

Go into the basement and unlock the Archives. There is a small area behind the Archives that you reach by Blinking/Far Reaching over a bookcase. A Painting is hidden back there.

BLUEPRINTS

The quest for the shopkeeper's associate takes you to a building that's very close to the Royal Conservatory. Avoid its traps, go to the third floor, and look on a desk. You get the Blueprint for Reverberation Tubing.

The Triggered Housing Blueprint is on the first floor of the Conservatory. It's in a room on the right with a disabled Arc Pylon and some Whale Oil Tanks.

Complete the side mission that's given to you by the black market shopkeeper. When you return, you receive a Blueprint as part of your reward.

The Dust District

RUNES

Meet Captain Foster early in the mission. Leave her building and drop to street level. Turn around and break through a door on the ground floor of the same structure. A Rune is inside, hidden in a locker.

Enter the Dust District and look left. There is a condemned building. Blink to the second floor balcony and explore that level to get a Rune.

A locked evidence room is on the second floor of the Overseer building. Look for the Key in a barracks/medical room very close by. The Key is held by one of the Overseers in there. Unlock the room and steal the Rune and a few other goodies.

A Bonecharm is inside Byrne's desk, on the third floor of the Overseer compound.

The third floor of the Crone's Hand Saloon has an office apartment. Search that for an Outsider Shrine and two Paintings.

Get close to Overseer territory and use your Heart to spot a Bonecharm that is close by (but still on neutral turf). This Bonecharm is on the second floor of a damaged building. Blink/Far Reach up to the windows, break the boards that are blocking them, and slip into the structure. The Bonecharm is only a room away.

BONECHARMS

Use code (**428**) to break into the rear of the black market. Steal a Bonecharm from a desk, and take everything else that you want.

Durante has an office on the second floor of the Crone's Hand Saloon. You need to get the Key from the Overseer's building, on the other side of the map. Get the Key, unlock the office, and loot a Bonecharm from the desk.

The basement of the Crone's Hand Saloon has a Bonecharm sitting out in the open.

Kill Paolo, in the Howlers' area, or pickpocket him to get a Bonecharm.

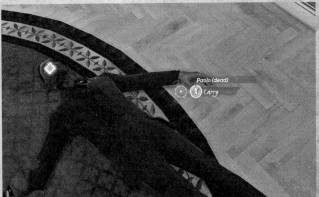

PAINTINGS

The Crone's Hand Saloon has two Paintings in it. Both are on the second floor, in the large apartment where Paolo lives.

The Crone's Hand Saloon has two Paintings in it. Both are on the second floor, in the large apartment where Paolo lives.

There is a fourth floor in the Overseer building. Not much is on it. Climb the stairs, and crawl out of a window onto a tiny internal walkway. Go along the right side and look for a broken window to get onto that side of the level. Do so, and look for a Painting in the destroyed area.

BLUEPRINTS

Conductive Filaments is near the beginning of the mission. Go into a building on the left, before you pass the Wall of Light. Climb to the roof, kill two Guards, and search the lower portion of a workbench to find this.

Spiked Grenade Housing is at the Crone's Hand Saloon, on the second floor. It's inside of a metal crate. Look in an unlocked, large apartment for it.

Secondary Coiling is in the Crone's Hand Saloon basement. It's out in the open.

Crack in the Slab

RUNES

Enter the mansion and climb to the second floor. Use your Heart to locate a Rune that is close by. It's in a room behind you when you get to the top of the steps.

Deal with two Elites in the basement and search for a Valve's wheel. Grab that and throw it through a hole in the brick wall. Transition to the present and jump through the wall to get the wheel. Dive into a submerged room, attach the wheel to its valve, and turn the wheel. This gets rid of the water, revealing a Rune.

The toughest Rune of all is on the right side of the mansion. Get to the second floor and look for a window with a Document on it. They talk about the repairs to the window. Go into the past and kill or knock out the Worker and Guard that are standing by the same window. Because it didn't get repaired, the window will now be gone in the present. Climb onto a small set of vines to get over to another broken window. Go inside and transition to the past again. Deal with three Guards in the room, and take your Rune.

BONECHARMS

Find the elevator on the ground floor, in the center of the house. Approach it from the present. Get onto a barrel and jump up to the small lip above the elevator entrance. Transition between the past and present to get through a hatch and then into the elevator to collect the Bonecharm. It's tricky maneuvering, so creep slowly forward until you're allowed to make the time transition.

Use the stairs to get to the mansion's second floor. Turn left and get to the balcony that overlooks the dining room. In the past, jump onto the farthest chandelier above the room. Transition to the present and leap up to the fallen joists above that chandelier. Climb into the attic and loot a Bonecharm.

Get as close as you can to the Black Bonecharm while you're exploring; use the Heart to locate it. Once you're nearby, look at a collapsed pile of debris in the present. Go into the past and loot a desk in the exact same spot. Crawl underneath the desk afterward and find a place to transition. By doing this, you avoid the barricade and can get into the locked boiler room ahead. In the past, there is a Black Bonecharm in there, inside a safe. You also get 135 coins.

PAINTINGS

There is a vault that's near the dining room. Go into the present to pass through the vault door, and then into the past again to loot the entire room. It has a Painting and a Blueprint.

Go back to the open yard where the Bloodflies congregate. Climb a hill of dirt to get to the second floor. Walk around the balcony and look for a window with a Document on it. It talks about the repairs to the window. Go into the past and kill the Worker and Guard that are standing by the same window. Because it didn't get repaired, the window will now be gone in the present. Climb onto a small set of vines to get over to the left side of the area. Jump over onto a balcony and go into the past. You find a Painting in that room. It's protected by multiple Guards.

BLUEPRINTS

Defeat or avoid the Guards in the dining area (at the end of the first hallway). Go into the room and around a small side area until you hit a vault. Shift into the present to pass through the vault door, and then go into the past against to loot. An unlocked safe has a Blueprint for a Firing Chamber Pivot.

The Grand Palace

RUNES

There is an apartment building with a Windmill that powers the Wall of Light. Explore the roof of it and Blink down to an apartment balcony underneath the Windmill. Clear the nests inside that apartment and get a Rune from the bathroom.

A Rune is locked inside the safe in the First Captain's suite. That's on the first floor of the palace. Get the combination from the Duke's suite several floors up and then unlock the safe later when you come downstairs again.

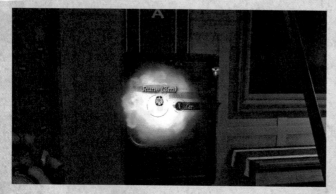

There is an abandoned storage area in the palace. Break through a barricade at the side of the private gardens to get into this area. Descend until you hit the water, and use your Heart to locate a Rune at the bottom.

Leave the black market using the front door. Look right and get up onto a few rocks. Search the grassy area above until you find a set of wooden boards. Break them open and look inside the small cave for an Outsider Shrine.

BONECHARMS

Near the Ravina district's Wall of Light you find two apartment buildings. The first one has a Bonecharm on the third floor. Go into its apartment and search in the bathroom.

Before leaving the Ravina district, search the apartment that's closest to the Wall of Light. Unlock the third floor apartment with a Key from the Winslow store's cashier. Search the bedroom and knock aside a pillow to get a Bonecharm.

In the Palace District you find a Throne Room. Look on the throne for a Bonecharm.

INTRO
STORY
CONTROLS
GAMEPLAY
WEAPONS, GADGETS & BONECHARMS
THE SUPERNATURAL ARTS
ENEMIES OF THE CROWN
WALKTHROUGH
COLLECTIBLES
TROPHIES & ACHIEVEMENTS

The first floor of the palace has a Bonecharm inside of a small room. It's very close to the banquet hall. Track the Bonecharm with your Heart and look for a room with two civilian women. The Bonecharm is in a bed in the small suite.

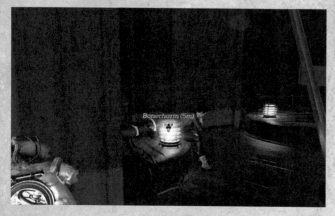

A Corrupt Bonecharm is on the third floor of the palace. Get up there and explore the suite on the right. The charm is inside one of the bathrooms. Open the lower drawers to reveal it.

Blink/Far Reach to a balcony across from the Winslow store. Destroy any Bloodfly nests that might be inside and open a vice against the wall. A Black Bonecharm is inside of it.

Open the Duke's Vault by going into the pantry, in the basement. Search for a recessed button and press that. This opens the Vault and gets you a Blueprint and a Black Bonecharm in the adjoining chambers.

PAINTINGS

Before you reach the Wall of Light in the main district, look for an apartment building with a Windmill. Blink/Far Reach from the Windmill down to a balcony below. Clear the nests inside of it and look in the bedroom for a Painting.

Daud and the Parabola of Lost Seasons

Ⓧ Take

Go into the palace and climb to the third floor. Look on the right side of that level. A Painting is near a piano. It's tucked into a corner and can be hard to see unless you're searching for it.

The other Painting inside the palace is also on the third floor. Go to the other side of the level and open a large office. Deal with the Clockwork Soldier inside, and search on top of the hearth to get your Painting.

BLUEPRINTS

The last apartment building before you reach the district's Wall of Light has a Blueprint on the third floor. Get the apartment's Key from the Winslow store's cashier. Break in and get the Blueprint from a regular desk.

Small-scale Combustion Refinement

Ⓧ Pick up

If you haven't already gotten Firing Chamber Pivot, the Blueprint for that is near the Wall of Light. Look in the stall at street level, to the right of the Wall. It's near a Pistol that's been left out.

Folded Galvani Resin has a Blueprint in the Palace District. Go into the pantry and look for a secret button along the wall. Press that to open the Duke's hidden vault. The first table in the main room of the vault has this Blueprint.

Blade Conversion is on the third floor of the palace. Look in the office suite to the left when you climb the stairs, and defeat a lone Clockwork Soldier. Then, search inside a desk to get the Blueprint.

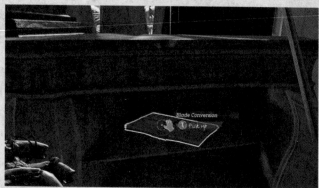

Death to the Empress

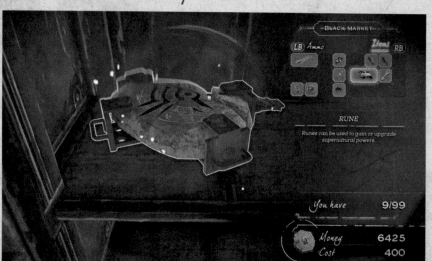

RUNES

Purchase a Rune from the last black market shop in the game. It overlooks the harbor where you land.

Before entering Dunwall Tower, look for a building to the left. It's filled with pipes and there are two Witches guarding it. Slip in through a tiny window and assassinate at least one of the Witches. When both are down, look for a cubby beside a walkway. Drop through the cubby and grab the Rune that's hidden below it.

The security room is in the Dunwall Tower cellar; it's at the back-right side of the building. Get down there and look on top of the pipes for a Rune.

While you're in Dunwall Streets, look for a damaged building on the left (near the end of the road). Blink up through several exposed floors and kill a Witch up top. Cross the street using some beams, and clear out the apartment ahead. Turn a Barometer inside the apartment to open a secret door. An Outsider Shrine is within.

BONECHARMS

Outside Dunwall Tower there is a Green House with three Witches. Deal with them and then look in a basket for a Bonecharm.

The waterlock is a building on the left side of the yards before you enter Dunwall Tower. Go all the way out toward it, using your Heart to detect the Bonecharm ahead. Sneak around the walkways to the right of the building and surprise two Witches when you jump over the wall beside them. Kill that pair and take the Bonecharm from a wooden box.

The High Overseer is in the Dunwall Tower entryway. Get a Bonecharm from him.

One Bonecharm is on the second floor of Dunwall Tower. Turn left from the main hallway and look for a room only a few feet away. Open the doors and kill the only Witch inside, then take the Bonecharm.

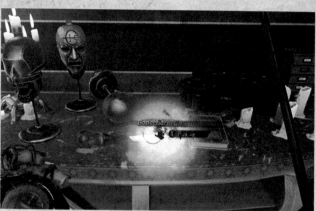

The other Bonecharm on the second floor of Dunwall Tower is harder to find. You see it inside the walls, but there isn't a door leading to it. Instead, look for a small window in the wooden paneling. It's almost at ceiling level. Blink/Far Reach up to that, and get into a secret room with your last Bonecharm.

Get the Outsider Shrine from this area and start from there. Get onto the pipes outside and go around the corner of the building. Use your Heart to spot the Black Bonecharm high above; take the pipes and rooftops to get closer to this target. Snipe or Sleep Dart a watchful Witch above you, and then

Blink/Far Reach up to her level. The Black Bonecharm is inside her building, on a mattress higher up.

Enter Dunwall Tower and look in the entryway for the High Overseer. Take a Corrupt Bonecharm from him.

PAINTINGS

Before entering Dunwall Tower, look for a gazebo. Once you find it, jump onto the wall to the left and snipe three Gravehounds in the yard below the gazebo. A Painting is down there, by the wall.

BLUEPRINTS

Get Counter-Blast Inversion from Galvani's apartment. That's the ground floor place near Dunwall Tower's entrance; you stole a Painting from it during A Long Day in Dunwall. Break open the doors and loot the Blueprint inside the lab.

TROPHIES & ACHIEVEMENTS

TROPHIES AND ACHIEVEMENTS

TROPHY/ACHIEVEMENT NAME	REWARD	ACTION
A Night in 1849	Bronze/10 Points	Went back in time (Story Reward)
Acrobat	Bronze/10 Points	Use 10 Drop Assassinations
Alternative Approach	Bronze/20 Points	Finished an entire mission with zero casualties
Art Collector	Silver/30 Points	Find all collectible Paintings
Black Market Burglar	Bronze/20 Points	Rob a black market shop
Circle of Life	Bronze/30 Points	With one Possession, chain between a Human, Hound, Rat, Fish, and Bloodfly
Clean Hands	Gold/50 Points	Complete the entire game without killing anyone
Clockwork Collector	Silver/30 Points	Obtain all of the numbered plates for the Clockwork Soldiers
Counter-Serum	Bronze/15 Points	Craft and use a Counter-Serum during "The Good Doctor"
Dancer at the Edge of Darkness	N/A	Complete the game with Low Chaos and all difficulty settings maxed out
Dilapidation	Bronze/15 Points	Find the hidden balcony passageway in "Crack in the Slab"
Down With the Duke	Bronze/10 Points	Defeated Duke Luca Abele (Reward)
Empire in Chaos	Silver/30 Points	Completed the game in High Chaos
Eureka	Bronze/15 Points	Cracked the Jindosh Lock
Faithful to the Abbey	Bronze/15 Points	Sides with the Overseers during "Dust District"
Familiarity Breeds Contempt	Bronze/15 Points	Steal items from the Galvani building during "A Long Day in Dunwall" and "Death to the Empress"
Fatal Redirect	Bronze/10 Points	Kill an enemy with their own Bullet
Fearless Fall	Bronze/15 Points	During "The Good Doctor" you have to leap off of the highest point on the roof and do a successful Drop Assassination
Flesh and Steel	Silver/50 Points	Complete the game without using supernatural abilities
Flooded Basement	Bronze/15 Points	During "Crack in the Slab" you have to use a wheel to drain the water in the basement
Freedom of Speech	Bronze/15 Points	In "A Long Day in Dunwall" you have to save the editor of the Courier from an attacking Guard
Gazebo	Bronze/15 Points	Go to the Gazebo when you reach Dunwall Tower
Ghostly	Silver/30 Points	Finish an entire mission without being spotted
Greatest Assassin	N/A	Complete the game with High Chaos and all difficulty settings maxed out
Heart Whispers	Bronze/10 Points	Use the Heart and listen to 40 people's secrets
Heartbeat Reaper	Bronze/30 Points	Eliminate 6 enemies in less than 1.5 seconds
Howlers 'Til the End	Bronze/15 Points	Sides with the Howlers during "Dust District"
Imperial Seal	Bronze/10 Points	Recover your Signet Ring (Story Reward)

TROPHY/ACHIEVEMENT NAME	REWARD	ACTION
In Good Conscience	Silver/50 Points	Complete the game with Low Chaos
Jewel of the South	Bronze/10 Points	Arrive in Karnaca (Story Reward)
Labyrinthine Mind	Bronze/10 Points	Find Anton Sokolov (Story Reward)
Morbid Theft	Bronze/15 Points	During "Edge of the World" you need to steal a corpse from the Overseer building and deliver it to Mindy
Occult Carver	Bronze/10 Points	Craft 10 Bonecharms
Oracular Echoes	Bronze/15 Points	Listen to the voices of the Oracular Order during "The Royal Conservatory"
Platinum	Platinum	Complete all other Trophies
Rogue	Bronze/10 Points	Eliminate 20 unaware enemies
Royal Spymaster	Bronze/10 Points	Find all Journals and Audiographs for Captain Foster and Anton Sokolov aboard the Dreadful Wale
Shadow	Gold/50 Points	Finish the entire game without ever being spotted
Silence	Bronze/15 Points	Deal with Jindosh without him ever realizing that you were there
Sliding Marksman	Bronze/10 Points	Use your Pistol to score a headshot while sliding
Songs of Serkonos	Bronze/10 Points	Find all 3 musical duos across Karnaca (must hear entire song each time)
Souvenirs	Silver/30 Points	Collect all of the decorative objects for the Dreadful Wale
Spirit Thief	Bronze/10 Points	Take Delilah's soul (Story Reward)
Stay of Execution	Bronze/15 Points	During "Edge of the World" you need to defeat two Guards that are about to push a civilian through their Wall of Light
The Beast Within	Bronze/10 Points	Deal with the Crown Killer (Story Reward)
The Empress	Silver/50 Points	Finish the game using Emily Kaldwin
The Greatest Gift	Bronze/10 Points	Saved your family member (Story Reward)
The Lovers	Bronze/10 Points	Use Domino to link two characters just before one kills the other
The Royal Protector	Silver/50 Points	Finish the game using Corvo Attano
Three Deaths	Bronze/15 Points	Kill Paolo three times (once during "The Clockwork Mansion" and twice during "Dust District")
Under the Table	Bronze/15 Points	Stole the Master Key during "Crack in the Slab" without killing the Guards in the dining hall
Well Funded	Silver/30 Points	Find at least 60% of the available loot in the entire game
Well Informed	N/A	Read 20 Newspapers
Years Ago, Another Time	Bronze/10 Points	Talk to Meagan Foster near the end of the game, or steal her Key and listen to the Audiograph in her cabin

Additional Trophy Information

Let's go into greater detail for some of the trickier Trophies.

ACROBAT

Use Blink/Far Reach to get above people as often as possible until you get your notification for this Trophy. Bend Time + Blink is a super powerful combo to snag Acrobat quickly.

ALTERNATIVE APPROACH

Use Sleep Darts, stealth, and routes that take you above most of the action to complete missions without having to kill anyone. If you are attacked by someone, parry their strikes, grab them, and choke the person out to avoid killing them.

DILAPIDATION

During "A Crack in the Slab" you need to track down a hidden balcony passage. This is explained in our walkthroughs. You go toward the rear of the building in the modern time. Climb a hill of debris to get to the upper floor, and switch to the past. Take out or knock out a workman so that a window doesn't get repaired. Return to the present and go through the open window. Go around the ledges on the other side, and stop on a balcony to the left. In the past, you find an art gallery there! You also get credit for the Trophy.

FAMILIARITY BREEDS CONTEMPT

Go into the Galvani building during A Long Day in Dunwall. It's the place on the left when you first reach the streets. Loot the Painting and the safe inside that area. Then, in the final mission of the game, go back there. Break through the door or find the Key from the housemaid to unlock the building. Loot it again so that you get your achievement.

FEARLESS FALL

During The Good Doctor, you can Blink or Far Reach onto the rooftops once you climb upstairs and go outside onto the terrace. There is a tower with some good items inside. If you Blink or Far Reach onto the top of that building, you find a bird's nest. This is now the location you need for getting the Trophy. Jump off of here and go a massive drop attack onto one of the Guard's below.

FLESH AND STEEL

To survive without using supernatural abilities, you have to rely on superior skill and equipment. Practice both stealth and swordplay so that you don't get into as many fights, and can defeat everyone safely when things go wrong. Search thoroughly so that you get tons of money, and use that to upgrade your gear as early as possible.

Take more time to set traps before fights that you can't avoid, and lure people into them so that you're often thinning groups of enemies before attacking them directly.

FLOODED BASEMENT

Search for the steps to the basement during A Crack in the Slab. Watch out for rat swarms, and look for a submerged room. There is a **Rune** inside of it, but it takes some work to acquire it. You have to go into the past and ambush two Elites that are working nearby. When they're down, get a wheel off of shelves in the corner. Throw it into the room that gets submerged in the present. Jump forward in time, attach the wheel to a pipe in the watery area, and then jump up to get the Rune.

FREEDOM OF SPEECH

During A Long Day in Dunwall, you can save the editor of the Courier. Go into the paper's building; it's on the left side of the main road. Climb to the top of the building and crouch while you enter the main room up there. Listen while a Guard threatens the editor. Knock out the Guard before he murders the editor, and then you're good to go.

GAZEBO

This one is unlocked during Death to the Empress. Search around before you enter Dunwall Tower. There are many Witches patrolling the outside, but you run into a gazebo on the left portion of that map. That's the spot where the former empress was killed. Enter the Gazebo to pay your respects.

GHOSTLY

Use abilities like Blink or Far Reach to find the alternative routes through each area. When you're up high, you can observe your enemies carefully and figure out the best time to proceed. Unless you're trying for Merciful play as well, you can assassinate targets to keep your path safe and clear. Shadow Kill is a very useful addition to this style of play.

HEARTBEAT REAPER

Find an area that already has a decent number of people. The streets in the early portion of The Grand Palace works decently. To further enhance the quantity of Guards, disable defenses in the area (like the Watchtower that overlooks the streets during that part of The Grand Palace). Then, make enough noise to disturb the Guards. Let them use the Alarm there to summon everyone nearby.

Equip area of effect weapons. Throw a Grenade down toward this group of enemies, and switch to a Pistol with Explosive Bullets while it's in the air. Fire immediately as the Grenade lands so that you have the best chance to clear everyone out within the tight time limit. If you fail, immediately reload so that you can set up the attack again without taking much time.

MORBID THEFT

As explained in the walkthrough, you have to steal a body for Mindy during Edge of the World. Sneak into the Overseer's building, by the canal. Go up a few floors and deal with the two Overseers that are close to a locked room. One of them has the Key to the room. Unlock it and get the body. Carry it to the window and use Far Reach or Blink to go toward the waypoint that appears. Drop the body where you meet Mindy to get credit.

ROYA

The Jou
find ab
up on
search
you're
one a
next t

SONGS OF SERKONOS

This Trophy can be tough if you are used to causing too many panic. The three duos that you need to find are in Edge of the World, the Dust District, and the streets of the Grand Palace. They're always playing their sets if you approach safely and quietly. Avoid trouble and get close to them so that you get credit for finding them. If you start any fights, they'll run off.

Edge of the World: Before you reach the carriage station, stay down in the main street and don't cause any chaos. Look for two musicians who are playing on the right side of the path. If you see the Winslow safe company, you've gone too far.

During the Dust District, you find the duo again in the Howlers' area. Go to the Crone's Hand Saloon. They'll be playing on the ground floor, near the entrance.

Finally, you spot them during the Grand Palace mission, when you're still in the streets. They'll be very close to the black market, by the front entrance of that building.

SOUVENIRS

There are several collectible items that aren't worth anything to your character directly. These are just fun things to collect while you go through the game. Here is a list of the souvenirs:

AN ELITE'S HELMET: During Edge of the World, kill one of the Elite Guards to get their helmet.

Syringe: In The Good Doctor, you receive this for doing the non-lethal route against the Crown Killer. Our stealth walkthrough describes this at length.

Clockwork Head: Destroy one of the Clockwork Soldiers during The Clockwork Mansion, The Grand Palace, or Death to the Empress.

WITCH'S SWORD: Look for this during The Royal Conservatory; the Sword is inside a display case.

SILVERGRAPH: This is in the Dust District. It's a small picture on the wall.

CORVO'S TROPHY: You also get this one in the Dust District, in a dilapidated building.

CALENDAR: During Crack in the Slab, look for the Calendar in the past. It's resting on a desk, beside a set of double doors.

GAZELLE: Look the vault during the Grand Palace; the Gazelle is in the circular room near the outer exit of the vault. It's not far from the effigy that you need to interact with.

SAMUEL'S BOAT: This is found during Death to the Empress, in the streets of the area. It's on a small shelf above a striped bed.

EMILY'S DOLL: You get this last one in Death to the Empress, in the actual tower. It's inside a trashed old bathroom.

STAY OF EXECUTION

There is a Trophy you get at the Wall of Light in Edge of the World. Two Guards are going to shove a civilian through the Wall of Light. Knock them out or kill them before they're able to do this so that the civilian survives.

THREE DEATHS

Find the black market in The Clockwork Mansion street area. Paolo arrives soon after. Ambush and kill him with his group. Then, find him at the saloon in the Dust District. Kill him again. Look upstairs for a shrine. He'll appear there a final time. Kill him to get your Trophy.

UNDER THE TABLE

During Crack in the Slab, crouch in the dining hall when you're in the present and shift back into the past. You appear underneath the dining room table. Steal the Master Key from an Elite, and then go back into the present to avoid conflict.

DISHONORED 2

Written by Michael Lummis

DK/Prima Games, a division of Penguin Random House LLC
6081 East 82nd Street, Suite #400
Indianapolis, IN 46250

Collector's Edition
ISBN: 978-0-7440-1745-8

Standard Edition
ISBN: 978-0-7440-1778-6

Printing Code: The rightmost double-digit number is the year of the book's printing; the rightmost single-digit number is the number of the book's printing. For example, 16-1 shows that the first printing of the book occurred in 2016.

19 18 17 16   4 3 2 1
001-300403-Nov/2016
Printed in the USA.

CREDITS

Development Editor
Matt Buchanan

Book Designer
Tim Amrhein

Production Designer
Julie Clark

Production
Tom Leddy

Copy Editor
Serena Stokes

PRIMA GAMES STAFF

VP & Publisher
Mike Degler

Editorial Manager
Tim Fitzpatrick

Design and Layout Manager
Tracy Wehmeyer

Licensing
Christian Sumner
Paul Giacomotto

Marketing
Katie Hemlock

Digital Publishing
Julie Asbury
Tim Cox
Shaida Boroumand

Operations Manager
Stacey Ginther

Acknowledgments

Prima Games would like to thank Mike Kochis and everyone at Bethesda and Arkane Studios. The help and support we received on this guide was truly excellent.

Thank you to Julien Authelet, David Cros, Laurent Gapaillard, Vincent Gros, Piotr Jablonski, Aimé Jalon, Sergei Kolesov, Elodie Marze, Lucie Minne, Jean-Luc Monnet, Nicolas Petrimaux, Cédric Peyravernay, Mathieu Reydellet, Thomas Scholes, Sebastien Chaudet, Dan Todd, Danny Becker, Maxime Maroukian, Steve Lee, Raphael Gilot, Johan Lalanne, Thomas Boucher, Yoann Saquet, Christophe Carrier, Jérôme Braune, Jonathan Foudral, Alex Leboucher, Anthony Gomez, Dinga Bakaba, Harvey Smith, Sandra Duval, Guillaume Curt, Matthew Dickenson, Jennifer Tonon, Denis Foulie, Carlos Guice, Paris Nourmohammadi, and Lisa Cole.

Michael Lummis and Kathleen Pleet would like to thank Christine Dickens for helping to bring so much into their lives. They will always be in your debt.